Postmodern Welfare

Postmodern Welfare

Reconstructing an Emancipatory Project

Peter Leonard

SAGE Publications
London • Thousand Oaks • New Delhi

© Peter Leonard 1997

First published 1997

 SAGE Publications Ltd
6 Bonhill Street
London EC2A 4PU

SAGE Publications Inc.
2455 Teller Road
Thousand Oaks, California 91320

SAGE Publications India Pvt Ltd
32, M-Block Market
Greater Kailash – I
New Delhi 110 048

British Library Cataloguing in Publication data

A catalogue record for this book is available from the British
Library

ISBN 0 8039 7609 7
ISBN 0 8039 7610 0 (pbk)

Library of Congress catalog record available

Typeset by Photoprint, Torquay, Devon
Printed in Great Britain by Redwood Books, Trowbridge, Wiltshire

For my children:
Jane, Katharine, David, Nick, Polly

Contents

Acknowledgements

Two generations have been powerfully affected by Michel Foucault's transformative archaeologies of knowledge and practice, and I certainly number among them. I am also indebted, of course, to the many contemporary authors who are frequently cited in the text, and among those who have been most influential in my thinking I must mention Zygmunt Bauman, Judith Butler, Nicholas Fox, David Harvey and bell hooks. At a personal level, my thanks go to Glenn Drover, Robert Fisher and Robert Mullaly, whose critical comments on my earlier attempts to confront the implications of postmodernism directly informed the writing of this book, though only I am responsible for any strangulation of their ideas which may have occurred in the process. To Liesel Urtnowski and to many of my graduate students at McGill University I owe my greatest debt. Their commitment to both political practice and theorization and their willingness to engage in an educational dialogue provided me with a form of learning from which I have benefited immensely. I am also grateful to Janet Meldrum for the remarkably careful and accurate way she transformed my often inchoate manuscript, chapter by chapter, into a printed script; and to Chris Rojek, of Sage Publications, who responded enthusiastically to my ideas for this book as well as providing subsequent editorial guidance, many thanks.

Finally, I want to express my special appreciation to Lynne Leonard. Apart from providing me with emotional support, including at times a much-needed optimism, she has enabled me to gain some understanding of feminism as an everyday practice of resistance.

Peter Leonard
Montreal and Ottawa

Introduction

In the contemporary political discourse taking place amongst those who assume a critical, oppositional stance to the now triumphal world capitalist order – feminists, socialists, anti-racists, defenders of minority cultural rights and others – a critical question is being posed. Is the emancipatory potential of the project of modernity, which expressed its resistance to domination in the universal terms of justice, reason and progress, now at an end?

Many issues enter into this discussion. The recent history of the collapse of state socialist regimes and the reckless scramble to institute market economies, together with the swing to the Right of many social democratic parties and governments, combine to produce a profound questioning and uncertainty on the Left and, more widely, a discrediting of socialist ideas and policies. Feminists, in particular, have been able to demonstrate the existence of deeply embedded impulses to domination and gender inequality often lurking beneath the surface socialist rhetoric of equality and liberation. Into the debates between different critical perspectives enters that complex of unsettling ideas manifested in the practice of postmodern deconstruction. Postmodernism challenges the modern idea of a universal, essential subject, common to all humanity, which has been at the core of a socialist belief in the possibility of a world-wide political struggle, and as well as under-pinning the Western drive to colonizing the Other in the name of a single notion of 'Civilization'. But postmodernism also challenges all the meta-narratives of emancipation as espousing a singular idea of Truth which leads invariably to domination, thus fixing feminism and anti-racism with its beady, critical eye.

So the questioning of the problematics of modernity becomes increasingly urgent. Does the postmodern insistence on the recognition of difference and of cultural relativity rather than universal reason, which might initially appear to validate the perspectives of those confronting gender domination and racism, in fact spell an end to the chances of reconstituting a mass politics of liberation? The overriding question in critical political discourse is this: what are the possibilities of a politics which is based upon a full recognition of the reality of socio-cultural diversity but which nevertheless achieves solidarity in the interests of populations which now experience, in this post-Cold War period, the unmitigated onslaught of the global market economy of late capitalism?

The idea and practice of welfare occupies a central position in this questioning and debate. Welfare as a function of the state under capitalism, postmodern critique argues, epitomizes that contradiction between domination and emancipation which has been historically the invariable feature of modernity. As the political agenda of the Right comes to dominate the discourse on welfare, its empowering and caring side loses ground to a brutal individualism intent on the further degradation of the poor. Even where the radical Right has not directly taken control, state welfare continues to be characterized by surveillance, control and repression, its critics maintain.

Here, the question is what to *do* about welfare as well as how to theorize about it. The postmodern emphasis on difference and its accompanying disillusionment with 'big state' solutions to social problems leads to a focus on the liberatory potential for local, small-scale forms of welfare – community-based advocacy and consumer-controlled projects and agencies. These organizations of welfare, close to the people they serve, are able, it is argued, to relate to the diverse needs and social identities of specific populations with their particular configurations of gender, class, culture, ethnicity and other social characteristics. It is a compelling argument, especially to those who are active in the identity politics of the new social movements. But such postmodern political solutions – micro-political resistance rather than the tired old mass politics of confronting and attempting to win state power – pose serious problems. In relinquishing the universalistic ideas of welfare embodied, in however partial a form, in the Keynesian welfare sate (now deceased), credence is given to the political discourse embraced by neo-conservatism and by parties traditionally of the Centre, or Left-of-Centre, which have now adopted a similar political agenda. This new discourse on welfare aims to reduce drastically state social expenditures, establish residual lower cost forms of welfare, fragment opposition and divide sites of resistance, all in the name of local diversity and control. The 'Higher Good' espoused by this right-wing discourse is that leaner models of welfare using minimal state resources serve ultimately to improve a country's competitiveness in the global market through reducing corporate taxation, increasing the rate of return on capital, reducing labour costs and returning to the traditional virtues of family cohesiveness and hard work.

How do I propose to address the questions and issues I have raised? Having a political and intellectual history rooted in Marxism, and subsequently strongly influenced by feminism, I approach postmodern critique with many doubts and reservations. At the same time, I acknowledge its profound impact and importance, especially in its challenge to Eurocentric assumptions about knowledge, science and culture, and its deep questioning of the narrative of emancipation. My perspective, therefore, must be seen, first, as one which attempts a critical engagement with and within the Marxist tradition. It is not, therefore 'postmodern Marxist' in the sense that the work of Laclau and Mouffe (1985) might be so described (if it is not called 'post-Marxist'), a perspective which appears to give priority to postmodern critique over the potential which, I believe, remains powerful in the Marxist tradition. I do not see postmodernism, in other words, as taking over the critical role of Marxism (or feminism, for that matter) but as providing a now essential ingredient in a revitalized Marxism. My view of the relationship between Marxism and postmodernism involves a deeply felt critique of some of the 'old Marxisms' which reflected the side of the project of modernity which was rooted in domination. It is a perspective which engages with postmodernism alongside feminism and anti-racism, and demands the acknowledgement and celebration of diversity in cultures, sexualities, abilities, ages and other human characteristics which, within an unreconstructed modernity were excluded, suppressed or discriminated against. My view, unlike that of Laclau and Mouffe, is that we are not at the end of emancipation. The project continues, but under changed histor-ical conditions – economic, cultural, social – and with a newly reflective ability (always existing at least as a potential in Marxism) to understand the contradictions of the emancipatory projects of the past as well as that of the present. A reconstructed project of emancipation, in this book seen as central to the future of human welfare, builds upon the liberatory potential of the whole *idea* of emancipation still expressed, sometimes in muted form, within socialist, feminist, anti-racist and other struggles against domination.

This book begins, in Chapter 1, with an overview of the *argument* between modernity and its postmodern critics. The old, liberal and social democratic welfare state is under attack, not only by the radical Right but as part of the overall challenge to modernity and its knowledge claims. What are the grounds for this attack and in what sense might we see the postmodern not only as critique, but also as the cultural condition of the present period of capitalism? After examining the contention that welfare is rooted in modern domination, I begin to answer the question of whether, following postmodern deconstruction, it is possible to envisage a form of welfare which reflects the emancipatory side of modernity. Chapter 2 concerns itself with the construction of the individual *subject*, a starting point which marks the dramatic shift in political discourse resulting from the potent combined intervention of postmodernism and feminism. Central to this discussion is the question of the relation between the self as socially constituted, including through the surveillance and control of state welfare, and the self as a relatively autonomous moral agent, capable of resistance. The discourses on dependency and on the mutual interdependence of subjects are discussed in the context of the individual and the collective as actors in the field of welfare.

Following through the implications of a conception of the subject as culturally constructed rather than as reflecting a basic, universal human essence, Chapter 3 turns to a discussion of *culture*. First, we examine the postmodern deconstruction of culture in the anthropological sense of 'a way of life'. We explore its implications for an emphasis on the validity of difference in the provision of welfare and the issues of moral judgement to which debate about cross-cultural communication and the existence of embedded racism gives rise. Next we examine the impact of culture as representation and in particular the effect of the mass media in the constitution of subjects and the possibilities of resistance to dominant media discourses on welfare. Chapter 4 focuses on the *organization* of welfare as a manifestation *par excellence* of modernity as a state system of surveillance, monitoring and control. The knowledge/power of the expert and the ever-present threat of individual resistance to professional power are a prime focus of attention. This is followed by discussion of whether the notion of postmodern organization is valid or oxymoronic and leads on to an account of another alternative to modern bureaucracy: the collectivist organization.

The changes which have taken place in the world-wide *economy* in the past twenty years is the subject of Chapter 5. Drawing primarily on Marxist analysis of the dynamics of capital accumulation and social regulation, discussion covers the implications for welfare of economic restructuring and its impact in terms of unemployment, job security and poverty. The conceptualization of this new economy as post-Fordism and its connection to the culture of postmodernity is examined in relation to shifts in the discourse on welfare in the context of the crisis tendencies of late capitalism. The micro-resistance of subjects in everyday life, a common theme in the book, gives way in Chapter 6 to an exploration of the *politics* of collective resistance. Beginning with a discussion of the continuing importance of Marxism as a narrative of political struggle, we turn to the particular problems of a collective politics of resistance under the cultural conditions of postmodern scepticism. I argue, however, that postmodernism has some-thing to offer in terms of an ethics which might underpin a new collective politics of human welfare despite its reluctance to envisage a mass struggle for emancipation. Commentary on the political potential and limitations of the new social movements and politics of identity, and their relationship to struggles over welfare, leads to a preliminary discussion of the possibilities of an organized solidarity emerging from a politics of difference. I argue that, on its own, postmodernism is unable to provide an intellectual or practical basis for the kind of politics necessary to a new welfare project: only as linked to feminism and Marxism does it realize a capacity to move from deconstruction to reconstruction.

The final chapter of the book gives attention to the possibilities of *reconstruction*. I argue that these possibilities already exist in prefigurative form, but need to be widened and built upon, and I suggest an underpinning ethics of reconstruction which draws upon both postmodern emphasis on the Other, and feminist and Marxist concern with interdependence. I sketch, in outline, a welfare project whose objectives are to meet both common and particular, culturally specific human needs as the preconditions necessary to the exercise of moral agency. The political means of achieving these objectives – strategies of collective resistance and the building of prefigurat-ive forms of welfare – are suggested. In the end, we come to the question of the crucial role of state power in achieving welfare and how it might be won. In responding to the unassailable critique of political parties, especially as

now constituted, as predominantly instruments of domination and homogenization, I introduce the possibility of constructing a party as a confederation
of diversities. Such a party would be based upon an organized alliance
between a range of social movements, each pursuing its own vision and
interests, but with the potential for solidarity rooted in a commitment to the
struggle to meet certain common human needs and a realization that some
form of mass politics is necessary if the struggle is to be pushed forward.

This is a book which, though reflecting, I hope, a commitment to political
struggle in the field of welfare, to *action*, is heavy with theory. This
theorization derives mainly from postmodernism and its critics, and especially from the mutual interrogation of Marxism and feminism with postmodernism. Much of postmodern writing is inaccessible, using an esoteric
and arcane language which then infects those who must debate its conceptualizations in order either to affirm or contest them. Authors of texts
such as this one are continuously in danger, therefore, of reproducing a
distanced, privileged and academically élitist kind of writing which fails to
communicate effectively with a politically relevant readership, thus rendering the possibility of dialogue difficult, remote or, in the worst scenario,
non-existent. There is, however, another side to the question of language.
The argument in favour of simplicity and immediate accessibility of
language in the interests of effortless communication is usually based upon
the assumption that language is a neutral vehicle of expression, that it
represents an objective empirical world which ideally can be rendered in the
language of 'common sense'. But 'common sense', the taken-for-granted
assumptions which are embedded in the individual's effortless belonging to
a culture, is highly suspect. Common sense and plain language tend to mask
the reproduction of a specific kind of discourse – that which supports
the existing economic and social order. The invention of new kinds
of language which challenge the common sense assumptions contained in
the language of everyday are, it is argued, a necessary part of a challenge to
dominant social forces: a critical politics requires a critical theory and a
critical language. Giroux (1992) writes that 'every new paradigm has to
create its own language because the old paradigms often produce, through
their use of language, particular forms of knowledge and social relations that
serve to legitimate specific relations of power'.

Throughout the writing of this book I have been acutely aware of both
sides of this argument. The consequence is that I have attempted to avoid the
use of the kind of language which I associate most closely with academic
gamesmanship (the masculine form is intentional) where the discourse is so
restricted that it is accessible only to a very small minority of academic
specialists. In following this side of the argument, I have attempted to avoid
some complexities of postmodernist language wherever possible in order to
communicate with a wider readership. Perhaps I have, at times, fallen into
the trap of over-simplifying a complex set of ideas. But I have also tried to
use the core concepts and language of the various theories I have discussed

in order to connect with a set of political discourses which I believe to be indispensable to thinking about the present and future of welfare. The reader, in any case, will supply her or his own interpretations, regardless of my intentions. As the postmodern author is dead, readers are free to be their own authority.

1

Argument

Throughout Western countries, it seems now self-evident that the role of the state as the provider of a wide range of public services rooted in the promise of dramatically evening up the life chances of individuals and populations is coming to an end. In education, housing, social services and social security support, the state is rapidly drawing back from previous levels of commitment, and even in the field of health care, the most supposedly inviolable part of the 'welfare state', the same story can be told. How are we to understand this particular historic moment of retreat? We may be aware, almost viscerally, of being immersed in a process of change over which we have no control and of experiencing the vertigo which comes with profound uncertainty. Marx and Engels in 1848 saw such experience as an inevitable element in the process of transformation which accompanies capitalist development. They speak of the 'uninterrupted disturbance of all social conditions' and of the production of 'everlasting uncertainty and agitation' (Marx and Engels, 1848/1948). In their famous phrase, used as the title of Berman's (1982) book, 'All that is solid melts into air . . .'. Are we to see the state's retreat from welfare in primarily economic terms, then; another stage of capitalism producing another transformative social shift? Certainly, we are surrounded by voices which declare that the party is over, that the economic constraints and opportunities produced by the growth of the global market require, in the interests of maintaining a competitive edge, a dramatic withdrawal of welfare provision, that we must learn to live with 'social policy in real time' (Mendelson, 1993).

My argument is that in explanations of the state's retreat, or, more neutrally, of the changes in the idea of welfare that accompany the closing years of this century, the critical role of the global economy is a necessary element, but that it is not sufficient to provide us with the depth of understanding that we need if we are to begin to comprehend what is happening to us now. I shall maintain in this book that rather than place the economic as the prior and contextualizing element in a convincing explanation of the present, with the social as its *consequence*, that we should reverse the starting point of our analysis. We should begin by attempting to throw some light on the profound changes in culture, in social organization and in conceptions of the person, that appear to be emerging within a period which we may call 'late capitalism', the capitalism of mass consumption within global markets. A precondition of understanding the economic present, in other words, demands attention to the production of mass culture as a commodity and to the manufacture of individual identities in a context of apparently increasing value diversity and the recognition of cultural and moral relativity. The assumption lying beneath this ordering of analysis is not that the socio-cultural determines the economic, nor indeed the reverse, but that they are mutually determining and that we cannot attempt to understand the one without equally attempting to understand the others. We can go further, however, and say that the very notion that the economic and the socio-cultural are separate, even though interconnected, is to fall into the conceptual trap of assuming that exclusive binary categories, reflecting, in this case perhaps, the disciplinary divisions imposed by the academic ordering of knowledge, represent in some way the *real* world. What these categories reflect are, however, better understood as discourses, as linguistic systems of statements through which we speak of ourselves and our social world. When I suggested that understanding the 'economic' demanded attention to the 'socio-cultural', and then went on to use the economic terms *production* and *manufacture* to illustrate the socio-cultural, I was pointing to the indissoluble enmeshing of these linguistically separated spheres. Of course, using the linguistic conventions of one's own culture is an unavoidable constraint, not least because of the obvious need for communication with relevant others in the culture. But though we are bound to draw upon the categories embedded in the different discourses of, for example, economics, sociology or political science, we should approach them sceptically, aware of their historical and cultural contingency. Furthermore, we must recognize that in the attempt to understand what is happening to the idea and practices of welfare at this historical juncture, I am writing predominantly within the discourses of Marxism and postmodernism. Indeed, in referring to discourse and the linguistic ordering of knowledge, I have already begun to speak in the language of postmodernism, although as the analysis proceeds I shall hope to show that the writing reflects a particular strand of postmodern reflection to which the term *critical* might be prefixed, indicating the strength of its connection with the emancipatory aspirations associated with Marxism and feminism. I return to these points later in this chapter.

Although the rest of the book proceeds from the discourse on the individual subject, then through consideration of culture and organization to an examination of the economic and the political, I shall in this chapter begin with the economic and political debates which have raged around the welfare state in recent years. I do this in order to start on the familiar ground of the conventional politics of Left and Right before digging beneath this politics in order to begin to unearth the social and cultural transformation of late capitalism which make the idea of emancipatory struggle in the West so problematic, but still, I shall argue, possible.

The Welfare State Under Attack

We can begin to see what happened to the idea of welfare within the political discourses which formed Western thinking at a particular historical point by noting that envisaging the state as the major provider of welfare emerged in its most powerful form during and after the Second World War. Western countries embraced the idea of substantial intervention in the economic and social lives of their populations. The political and economic justification for what amounted to a profound strengthening of the state was founded in some countries, such as the United States, on an essentially liberal conception of intervention as a way of maintaining strong capitalist economies and social structures. In other countries, such as Britain and Sweden, a more clearly social democratic set of ideas ruled, involving the proposed social and economic reform of the structures aimed at creating a 'mixed economy' or a 'post-capitalist society' (Crosland, 1967), or on the further but still social democratic Left, a non-Marxist socialist state. In the thirty years following the Second World War these ideas of progress through social intervention, an intervention which could, it was supposed, improve the life chances and freedoms of individuals and communities, were the basis of a broad consensus amongst the ruling classes and élites of the West. The critics of these welfarist ideas, both on the Left and on the Right, were rendered relatively ineffective in the face of the dominant discourse, though we might claim that the Left was able to mount a substantial critique of social democratic ideas of welfare in the form of various 'radical', socialist, and ultimately feminist proposals for policy and practice in the welfare field.

What came to break this ruling social consensus was, as we can now see, the result of a combination of profound economic, political and cultural changes. The 1970s mark the end of the long boom in Western economies and their radical transformation into a new stage of development (Mandel, 1975). The growth of a world economy and the accompanying development of new forces of production, signalled by the rapid growth of computer-based technologies and means of communication, led to a massive restructuring of capital and labour, a restructuring which we continue to experience in our daily lives. The negative consequences of this transformation process – unemployment, new populations in poverty, the crises experienced in state expenditures and income – all led to or were associated with a fundamental change in the material conditions under which welfare states functioned. This economic transformation provided one element in a context within which a number of distinct but related political and ideological trends emerged which challenged and eventually defeated both the broad social consensus on welfare and the 'radical', socialist critique to which it had been subjected.

The first, and most obvious of these trends was the break between the reluctant conservative welfarists who believed that state social intervention was necessary to the reproduction of capital and labour, and a neo-liberal radical Right which rejected all such ideas. This New Right took command of the conservative discourse on welfare by reasserting what were after all fundamental Western bourgeois values: the rationality of market forces compared to the bureaucratic irrationality of state intervention; the moral superiority of individual choice compared to the tyranny of collective decision making; the necessity for a strong state apparatus in terms of law and order compared to the weakness exhibited by welfare models of justice. In due course this radical Right approach to welfare came to determine the dominant questions addressed in the discourse within a wide political spectrum from conservative to social democratic. The triumph of the Right was undoubtedly aided by the ultimate collapse of 'actual, existing' social-ism in its various forms. In the West this *second* trend was experienced as a ideological collapse stemming from widespread disillusionment with the bureaucratic and centralized state forms beloved by social democrats. Within the state socialist camp, of course, this collapse took the form of a dramatic disintegration of the state apparatuses themselves and a wholesale renunci-ation of socialism and communism as ideologies, practices and structures. The effect of these profound historic ruptures was to call into question the socialist enterprise as a whole. Is socialism desirable or feasible – including socialism as a set of ideas and practices underlying the political programme of attempting to enhance people's welfare through state and other forms of collective intervention?

As if attacks from the Right, coupled with a collapse in widespread beliefs about the moral and practical superiority of various forms of socialism were not enough, dominant welfare ideas came under attack from a *third* source, namely feminism. The various forms of feminism, whatever their particular and different political orientations, were united in providing a radical critique of liberal, social democratic and socialist conceptions of welfare: they were products of patriarchy. The dominant welfare ideas of the post-Second World War era were seen as serving the material and ideological interests of the ruling male gender. The very notion of 'human needs' to which the services of a welfare state claimed to be a response, was seen as an ideological means by which an oppressing class of white males sets out to legislate for and control a population which includes women and cultural/ethnic minorities, using ideas set in its own image and serving its own interests.

The dissenting voice of the socialist Left, of the feminists and of those committed to cultural diversity and anti-racism, all eventually found them-selves faced with a political paradox: as the welfare state, which they had previously attacked, was dismantled by the Right, they were forced to defend it. Even the monolithic, centralized welfare state might be preferable to no welfare state at all. We might take the example of Marxist discourse on the welfare state in order to illustrate that within a specific critical political perspective, discordant voices could be heard which weakened commitment to a welfare state. All Marxist critics of the social democratic welfare state would point to the domination of the state apparatuses and to the inequity and inadequacy of services. Some, however, saw the idea of welfare simply as an illusion perpetrated by bourgeois class politics to mask its role in the exploitation of the working class and therefore not worth defending (Holloway and Picciotti, 1978), while others saw the welfare state apparatus as containing contradictions which enabled its use as an arena of class struggle (Gough, 1979; Leonard, 1979).

In contrast, the attack on the welfare state from the Right was unambiguous: the provision of universal public services directed to the well-being of citizens was simply incompatible with the moral virtues embedded in the operation of market forces. A combination of a Hobbesian minimalist view of the state as holding the ring while competitive individuals struggle each against each, and a sociobiological and social Darwinist belief in the innate aggressive territoriality encoded in human nature as a necessary condition of species survival, provided some of the intellectual foundations of the New Right's rejection of the welfare state.

Since the international economic recession of the mid-1970s introduced the restructuring of capital and labour together with the development of new forms of capital accumulation and production, mainstream political debate has perhaps understandably continued to focus on the economics of welfare and has often failed to understand or acknowledge fully the underlying social and cultural dynamics of the transformative processes currently taking place. I shall draw upon postmodern critique in attempting to throw some light on this current transformation as the context within which we must understand the discourse on welfare. We begin with the notion of *modernity* in order to locate welfare as a product of modernity, but in understanding this concept, turn to the *postmodern* in two senses: *postmodernity* as the period in which we are now living, the most recent stage in the development of late capitalism, and *postmodernism* as the critical challenge to the universalistic knowledge claims of modernity and its belief in reason and progress.

The Challenge to Modernity

To refer to modernity as a historical period and then to subject this period to a critique from the present standpoint, *looking back* as it were, is immediately to plunge into a debate which is complex and encompasses a whole range of disciplines in the social sciences and humanities. It is not my intention here to explore the many avenues to which this debate leads, but to focus on certain major issues central to the discourse on welfare, leaving to others the task of more wide-ranging exploration of modernity and postmodernism, to be found for example in the work of Bauman (1992), Rosenau (1992), Seidman and Wagner (1992) and many others.

Modernity as a historical period in Western culture may be seen as having its origins in the 'Age of Enlightenment' which began towards the end of the eighteenth century. The historical trajectory from these origins to the present (or possibly recent past) may be understood as having been founded intellectually on a belief in the power of reason over ignorance, order over disorder and science over superstition as universal values with which to defeat the old orders, the old ruling classes, the *anciens régimes* with their outmoded ideas. Modernity was revolutionary, indeed it was personified in the French Revolution itself, and was the founding complex of beliefs upon which capitalism as a new mode of production and a transformed social order was established. These sets of beliefs were to provide the basis upon which humanity was to be able to achieve *progress*. Instead of forever looking backwards to the past as a 'Golden Age', enlightenment was now seen as possible in the present through the application of reason. It was through reason that enlightenment, the conceiving of infinite possibilities, would enable the emancipation of humanity to take place: emancipation from ignorance, poverty, insecurity and violence. If modernity is conceived of as an ongoing project of enlightenment, then clearly it is incomplete because humanity has yet to be emancipated. Can the project be completed? Capitalism and socialism as rival versions of modernity have both promised emancipation: one, socialism as a political and economic system, has collapsed, and the other, now transformed into a global project, has yet to show the commitment or capacity to fulfil this promise.

The revolutionary rupture which enlightenment reason was to bring to *anciens regimes* can be glimpsed in Kant's philosophical work, which inaugurates the discourse on modernity. Osborne (1992) refers to Kant's 1784 essay 'An Answer to the Question: What is Enlightenment' in distinguishing between two aspects of his work. First, instead of looking backwards to ancient Greece and Rome for his philosophical foundations, or to the future as a place of decline and doom, Kant sees the historical *present* as the ground upon which a philosophy of knowledge can be established. Secondly, a consciousness of the present as a source of knowledge is the basis upon which is founded the conception of *autonomous reason*, able to establish its own laws without reference to the past, to tradition. Thus reason creates its own independent norms and in principle the use of this autonomous rationality is available to all of humanity. Thus 'Enlightenment Reason' becomes universal in its claims to be the means by which knowledge is created as well as the standard against which knowledge is validated. Looking back from the present, we can see that the knowledge claims of intellectual élites living in Europe and North America at the end of the eighteenth century were not formulated as culturally and historically specific, as the philosophical basis, for example, of early Western capitalism, but were inaugurated as essential to the dawning of a New Age for all of humanity. Cultural relativity did not enter into these claims, they were universal, certain and objective; they came to represent Truth.

The subsequent history of modernity as an enlightenment and emancipatory project is of course subject to intense debate. Those who support the continuing validity of the project of modernity include neo-liberals such as Hayek (1973), Friedman and Friedman (1980) and Huyssen (1986), Marxists such as Geras (1987) and Ryan (1982) and feminists like Lovibond (1989), although in every case the support is not without a critique of the aspects of modernity which impose obstacles on the various and contradictory emancipatory aims – capitalist, socialist and feminist – which are demanded of it. But is modernity any longer a convincing vehicle for emancipation in the name of those universal values which have in the past legitimated revolutionary struggles: reason, justice and individual rights? Do the specifically Western cultural and historical origins of modernity invalidate it, and especially its claims to universality? Postmodernists argue that modernity has represented in practice, a Eurocentric, patriarchal and destructive triumphalism over populations and over nature itself. Modernity, it is maintained, represents the 'triumph of the west' reflected in colonialism and post-colonial domination in which the interests of Western capitalism lead to the attempted homogenization of a world of diverse cultures, beliefs and histories. In part to counteract these assertions, Habermas (1985, 1987) maintains that flawed and defective as it is, the modern project of emancipation retains its possibilities if we separate the universal claim to reason from the repression and domination which have historically accompanied it. The traditional modernist idea of autonomous rational individuality must be reworked, Habermas suggests, to emphasize a concept of reason based on egalitarian communication and the development of consensus amongst pluralities.

If Habermas attempts to salvage something from the critical ruins of the modernity of late capitalism, Foucault (1965, 1973, 1975, 1980) is intent in excavating the origins of Enlightenment ideas embedded in the social practices surrounding madness, delinquency and sexuality, to reveal the immersion of modernity in processes of domination legitimated in the language of science, order and truth. Foucault's approach to modernity is through the analysis of the discourses of scientific disciplines and their utilization by the emergent nation state of the eighteenth and early nineteenth century. He studied the administrative and professional control of populations undertaken in the name of a single concept of truth and its categorical separation from the false. These scientific and professional discourses, like all others, are subject, Foucault argues, to rules of exclusion which ensure the invisibility of subordinate claims to truth. It is through such rules that the enlightenment project of modernity excluded from consideration the voices of the subordinate populations of the poor, of women and of the oppressed and subjected masses of non-Europeans.

It is, perhaps, the writings of Lyotard which most clearly and unambiguously represent the political case against modernity. Whereas Marxists will tend to analyse modernity in the same way as Marx understood capitalism, namely as containing contradictions between emancipation from the past and domination in the present, Lyotard is overwhelmingly hostile to modernity:

> One can note a sort of decay in the confidence placed by the last two centuries in the idea of progress. This idea of progress as possible, probable or necessary was rooted in the certainty that the development of the arts, technology, knowledge and liberty would be profitable to mankind as a whole . . . After two centuries, we are more sensitive to signs that signify the contrary. Neither economic nor political liberalism, nor the various Marxisms, emerge from the sanguinary last two centuries free from the suspicion of crimes against humanity . . . I use the name of Auschwitz to point out the irrelevance of empirical matter, the stuff of

recent past history, in terms of the modern claim to help mankind to emancipate itself. What kind of thought is able to sublate Auschwitz in a general (either empirical or speculative) process towards universal emancipation? (Lyotard, 1989: 9)

Against the progress which has been supposedly achieved under the emancipatory banner of modernity – democratic institutions, improved material existence for some populations – Lyotard argues that the crimes against humanity must be weighed. Other names signifying recent history – Dresden, Hiroshima, the Gulag, Cambodia – all refer to crimes, like Auschwitz, justified in the name of ideologies committed to the pursuit of progress and order: fascism, liberal democracy and Marxism. Modernity appears to Lyotard so malignant in its effects that political justifications issued with reference to the ambitious social theories which have grown in the nineteenth and twentieth centuries should be treated with incredulity. Indeed, for Lyotard such incredulity is the essential feature of postmodernism. 'The grand narratives of legitimization are no longer credible,' Lyotard (p. 9) argues, and so they have lost their power to provide a foundation for social criticism. Thus the attempt by Habermas to salvage what is left in Marxism as critique, in order to reconstitute modernity as an emancipatory project (Roderick, 1986; Rorty, 1989) is seen by Lyotard as doomed to failure.

Drawing on Lyotard's work, we can identify one of the central strands of the postmodern critique of modernity, namely modernity's construction of human subjects as *objects*, as the bearers of ideologies by which individuals can embody a certain form of racial purity, or a biological destiny, or a revolutionary commitment. Furthermore, it can be argued that basing its appeals on reason and science enables the projects of modernity to legitimate the power of those who *know*, the administrative and professional functionaries of the state, while denying such power to those *who do not know* what reason and science has discovered. Thus the voices of the masses of the oppressed and dispossessed, especially those confronted with 'the terrible ancient task of survival' (Lyotard, 1989: 10) are excluded from the discourse on human well-being, a discourse which, after all, modernity claims as its central rationale. This strand of postmodern critique is not only incredulous when faced with the claims of Philosophy in the Kantian tradition of universalism and the self-validation of transcendental guarantees of knowledge (Rorty, 1989), but is equally sceptical of the claims of History. Belief in an impersonal force called History as the objective embodiment of progress, a force which unfolds through the specific concrete histories of particular peoples (Bennington, 1989), objectifies historical subjects in a narrative which elevates the role of political élites and in practice subordinates all others. Although one can read this postmodern critique as an especially powerful attack on Marxism, and by many it is certainly intended to be, some Marxists, such as Bennett (1989), maintain that rethinking forms of Marxism in the light of the problematic of modernity is entirely necessary even if Marxist concepts have to be 'so thorough-goingly revised theoretically that they bear scarcely any recognizable relationship to their classical antecedents' (1989: 63). Bennett expresses forcibly the need to face critique as a necessary way forward:

> Obviously, acceptance of such criticisms entails that Marxists should critically review all those economistic, scientistic and historicist conceptions by means of which Marxism has traditionally sought to supply itself with such warrants . . . It's singularly odd to expect that Marxists should feel placed on the defensive by the 'discovery' that there neither are nor can be transcendental guarantees, any absolute certainties, or any essential truths since, in recent years, they have devoted some considerable effort to expunging from Marxist thought precisely such residues of nineteenth century theologies, philosophies of history or ideologies of science. (p. 65)

The Postmodern

Bennett's description of what is happening within Marxist theory points to a general critical upheaval taking place in social and political theory as well as in the social sciences generally, an upheaval which Rosenau (1992) documents in concise detail. Although we have already identified the postmodern as a critique of modernity, we need to explore fully the *basis* of this critique. The attack on modernity is rooted in part, as we have seen, in a rejection of its self-validating knowledge claims and, in Foucault's case, an identification of this knowledge – signified as universal truth – as crucial to the administrative and professional power of the modern state. But on what theories of knowledge is postmodernism itself based? We must now take note of postmodernism's epistemological challenge to modernity before we examine the different, but related idea that we are living in a postmodern historical period.

Briefly, we can begin by referring to what has been called the crisis of Western knowledge, a crisis implicit in what we have already discussed, namely critiques 'which challenge Western civilization's stories about itself' (Hennessy, 1993). More precisely, this crisis may be called 'a crisis of representation'. Modernity's knowledge claims, from Kant onwards, are based upon the idea that language performs the function of *representation*. Language, in this philosophical tradition, consists of symbols which are created by human subjects and which stand for or represent the things which humans want to talk about. Things are named as a way of grasping hold of reality. The aim of social or economic theory within this perspective, for example, is to provide accurate representation of an objective social world. Rival theories can be judged by criteria constructed to enable us to evaluate how well a theory provides a convincing representation of the real – the more accurate theory survives and the others perish or certainly deserve to. Within this perspective, discourses, as regulated systems of statements, are determined by the *real*, by the objective world. Furthermore, we can discover the truth of this objective world through theories and methods which create bodies of knowledge that approximate ever more closely to the reality that they represent. Representation theory is the epistemological

theory of modernity *par excellence* which, though now profoundly challenged, is still intellectually pervasive, in part because to contest representation theory is to lead one into a crisis of authority, the authority of Western
knowledge. Woodiwiss (1990: 2) suggests that 'most social theorists today
continue to assume that the aim of social theory is to provide verifiably
accurate, if supposedly abstract, representations of social reality. What they
appear not to realize is that, in maintaining this assumption, they impose
serious constraints upon their sociological imaginations – they can only hope
to picture whatever the received wisdom tells them is present . . .' This idea
that we can *know* reality through language might be said to underpin the
assumption that there can be *certainty*, an assumption which Woodiwiss
(p. 7) dismisses as a 'humanly fabricated object of desire'.

If representation theory may be an example of *reality determinism*, its
opposite, *significatory theory*, may be seen as a manifestation of the
assumption of *discourse determinism*. This approach proposes that language
does not represent things outside of language at all, but rather that language
is based on arbitrary graphic and mental images, respectively signifier and
signified, which are the result of elements of language itself reflecting the
characteristics of a social formation or culture. In other words, human
intention does not enter into language, and the arbitrary combinations of
images of which discourses consist determine what we might assume to be
our knowledge of 'objective reality'. So how do we know whether a
statement is true or not? The answer, within this perspective, is that we
cannot know 'the truth', because on the 'outside' of the particular discourse
with which we try to understand something, is only another discourse. So the
criterion of 'truth' is entirely internal to discourses within cultures and the
'real' only exists insofar as there is a discourse which describes it.

But if language is based on arbitrary images and 'truth' is internal to
discourses, then how are we to understand the meaning of the concepts we
use to describe the social world we inhabit, in our case the concepts of need,
health, illness, well-being, and other ideas which we might consider central
to the discourse of welfare? One most challenging answer is to be found in
the work of Derrida (1978) who uses the notion of *différance* (the French
word for deferral) to indicate that meaning in language is never stable, never
able to be decisively pinned down; meaning is always deferred, slippage
continuously takes place. This implies that meaning can always be contested
on the basis of *différence* (the French word denoting unlikeness or dissimi-
larity). Derrida uses the play on the similarity between the two words to
suggest a politics of deferral and difference which challenges the modernist
belief in the truths of history. As Lemert (1992: 38) points out, 'if there is an
essential truth, of any kind, then there is only one truth – and virtually
certainly that is the controlling truth of the dominant class'. Because
meaning is continually slipping away from us, there can be no essential,
certain meanings, only different meanings emerging from different experiences, especially the experiences of those who have been excluded from
discourses, whose voices and whose writing have been silenced. In the

Western culture of modernity this has meant especially the excluded voices of women, non-white populations, gays and lesbians, and the working classes in general. In a detailed account of the relevance of Derrida's work for a critical politics of the excluded, Lemert (1992) points to the fact that the two words *différance* and *différence* sound the same when spoken and are only dissimilar when written:

> Recall that the written form 'différance', with the 'a', reveals the missing, lacking, element in speech. Writing, the politics of *différance*, is the politics of those who, on a daily basis, experience the pain of social exclusion, of lack, of loss. This is why the concept has been taken up by representatives of social groups most acutely aware of social pain ... *Différence* in its most recent form, is a radically ironic concept. (1992: 39, 40)

To refer to a *politics* of difference, a politics of those excluded from dominant discourses, suggests a need to elaborate one further element in the debate between representation and signification as alternative epistemologies. The fundamental assumption of modernity is that knowledge can be based upon primary processes in the 'real world' that are beyond and independent of the effects of discourses about them. The attempt to demonstrate convincingly that knowledge refers to truths which can ultimately be verified independently of discourses, takes place, typically, in the context of struggles about authority (academic or professional) and legitimacy (by reference to 'scientific principles'). Are these struggles essentially non-political, simply debates about method and evidence, as positivists would claim, or are they political struggles over meaning, as postmodernists, alongside feminists and Marxists, would argue? The recent history of debates about the concepts of needs, health, well-being, dependency, and so forth, and the connected arguments about evidence, show us, I believe, that these are *ideological* debates. The excluded challenge the included, and in so doing reveal that politics is, in fact, embedded deeply within knowledge-producing activities.

In the discourse on welfare, developing knowledge about individual and social problems requires an exploration which goes beyond the boundaries of scientific and professional disciplines and encompasses the various kinds of knowledge found in everyday practices in a variety of social institutions such as family households, community organizations, the experiences of employment and unemployment, the activities of officials in state agencies, and many other social practices. The articulation of discourses about 'problems' takes the form of a political arena in which sets of activities, discursive and material, have mutual effects. So, a discourse on a problem within the field of welfare (for example, 'dependency on state financial benefits') is not constituted simply as a system of statements or a set of questions, a discourse about the 'real world', but is immediately caught up in a set of material practices (the activities of social security claimants and officials, for example) which are historical products. My argument then, following Henriques et al. (1984), is that rather than be forced to choose between the extremes of 'reality determinism' and 'discourse determinism', we can construct an approach to discourses on welfare which suggests that understanding is not simply a matter of the reality of particular experiences of the world, nor only a questions of the internal rules of scientific and professional discourses, but that what we consider to be 'the truth' is implicated in a set of political arguments which includes 'what is to be done'. Discourses, in other words, are constructed through linguistic rules and social practices which direct our attention to the politics of knowledge-producing activities.

Postmodernity?

As we have sought to understand on what basis the knowledge claims of modernity are being challenged and taking the form of what might be described as a postmodern politics of difference, when we acknowledge the transformations wrought by the development of global markets, new infor-mation technologies, and the growth of mass cultural consumption, are we speaking now of new times, of a 'brave new world'? Has late capitalism reached a new historic moment? Hall (1991) describes the 'new times' as a period in which the subject is changed as well as the wider structures:

> The wider changes remind us that 'new times' are both 'out there', changing our conditions of life, and 'in here' working on us. In part, it is *us* who are being 'remade'. A recent writer on the subject, Marshall Berman (1982), notes that 'modern environments and experiences cut across all boundaries of geography and ethnicity, of class and nationality, of religion and ideology' – not destroying them entirely, but weakening and subverting them, eroding the lines of continuity which hitherto stabilized our social identities. (1991: 58; emphasis in original)

How might we describe this complex set of changes involving the economic, the political, the cultural and the subjective? Within orthodox classical Marxism it was argued that everything could be reduced to the economic base, that the characteristics of the mode of production, here late capitalism as a global market, determined the 'superstructures' of politics, culture and subjectivity. That such a simple reductionism and economic determinism is no longer convincing is the result, in part at least, of the growth of a cultural politics, fuelled substantially by feminist and post-modern critique, which argues for the, at least, relative autonomy of the cultural and its role in constituting the subject.

The work of Jameson (1984) is a useful starting point for a discussion of the characteristics of these new times, whether we want to call it 'post-modernity', 'post-Fordism' or as Giddens (1994) proposes, 'post-scarcity society'. In this new period of late capitalism, cultural production assumes a centrality and significance never previously attained. Image, appearance and surface effect dominate forms of cultural production in which the distinction between original and simulacra dissolves, nostalgia and kitsch supersede realism and naturalism in art, and cultural aesthetics penetrate everyday life and obliterate the division between 'high culture' and the popular culture of the masses. For Jameson, still maintaining a Marxist perspective on the crucial significance of the economic, this period constitutes 'the cultural logic of late capitalism' whereby the production of culture has become fully integrated into commodity production – culture, in other words, has become commodified. This commodification process may be seen as the reason why political struggle becomes increasingly expressed in the arena of cultural production – in literature, film, art, theatre, music, and in the work of cultural critics. These locations for conflict have largely replaced those traditional areas of commodity production where previously labour and capital waged a high-profile political battle.

In order to maintain its markets and, in so doing, manage its characteristic and fundamental crisis tendencies, capitalism has entered into the business of producing desires which can only be satisfied by an increasing reliance on commodity consumption. Culture, through the mass media, plays the central role in this creation of desire by generating new cultural needs and producing new kinds of individual identity which rest upon new wants that can be, fleetingly, satisfied by the fashion industry, by the attendance at public cultural performances, by the projection of a certain self-image chosen from a number of gender and sexual alternatives. These cultural developments and forms, Jameson argues, have become hegemonic since the early 1970s.

The attempt to designate the present as a particular period of history is fraught with obvious problems, not least the difficulty of attaining sufficient critical distance from the period one is living in. If we are writing within discourses that reflect the connection between knowledge, power and the constitution of the subject, as Foucault maintains, then perhaps we can only hope to understand the dominant discourses of the past. This is precisely why Foucault focused his investigations on the early histories of madness, punishment and sexuality, on the origins of present discourses rather than their current manifestations. Another problem which faces those trying to *periodize* either modernity or indeed postmodernity is expressed in the title of Osborne's (1992) paper, 'Modernity is a Qualitative, Not a Chronological, Category'. In discussing the uses of the term modernity, Osborne points to

the main problem with the concept and the source of its enduring strength – namely, its homogenization through abstraction of a form of historical conscious-ness associated with a variety of socially, politically and culturally heterogeneous processes of change. The key to the matter will be seen to lie in the relation between the meaning of 'modernity' as a category of historical periodization and its meaning as a distinctive form or quality of social experience – that is to say, in the dialectics of a certain *'temporalization of history'*. (1992: 65; emphasis in original)

By the end of his argument, Osborne appears to accept both historical and qualitative uses of the term 'modernity', a form of social consciousness embedded in a historical period which gives priority to 'the present' and which is theorized in a somewhat different way to the Marxist conception of modes of production. He points out, indeed, that 'born, like capitalism, out of colonialism and the world market, "modernity" as a structure of historical consciousness predates the development of capitalism proper' (p. 84).

If the concept of modernity is both useful but also complex and difficult, then the periodization of *postmodernity* is, if anything, more problematic. We can speak of postmodernism as a cultural and political critique of the present, we might even speak of a postmodern consciousness – incredulity, transience, fatigue, perhaps – but can we talk about 'postmodern times', a present which appears to be *beyond* the present, namely *after* modernity? Perhaps postmodernity is best understood as simply the latest stage of modernity in which we look *back*, from the present, and are critical in a new way about the trajectory by which we arrived in the present. We look back at the historical period of the Enlightenment and at the subsequent contradictions which flowed from the imperative of a universalizing Reason – the dialectic of emancipation and domination – and what we see sobers us, forces us to rethink the narrative of human progress through a modernizing scientific knowledge. But looking back in this way is only possible, perhaps, under the particular conditions of the present, which are a product not only of cultural challenges but also of economic transformations and political shifts and which lead us to say, 'the present is different'.

A postmodern incredulity in the face of metanarratives might make us hesitate to grasp hold of the present and designate it as postmodernity, because to do so requires a metanarrative which describes and analyses at a high level of abstraction a social formation and its articulation at economic, cultural and ideological levels. If, however, we are looking at the possibility remaining in the notion of emancipation, then, however tentatively, we must be prepared to erect our own metanarrative. Their protestations notwithstanding, postmodern critics are, in any case, unable to avoid producing their particular metanarratives – in the case of Foucault and Lyotard, for example, narratives of the history of modernity as domination.

Can we grasp hold of this contemporary stage in the history of modernity and try to name it as a way of pinning it down, making it accessible to our understanding in a way which enables us to envisage new emancipatory projects, in our case, the project of welfare? Jameson (1984) is prepared to make sufficient concessions to postmodern theory, whilst maintaining a Marxist concept of late capitalism, to construct a depressing metanarrative of a monolithic *postmodern late capitalism* in which active political struggle becomes virtually impossible in the face of hegemonic cultural discourses. This is because the global system of late capitalism is so large and complex that we are forced only to think in fragments rather than social totalities. Here Jameson demonstrates a characteristic paradox in postmodern neo-Marxist thinking – despite the 'impossibility' of conceptually grasping the whole system, he nevertheless attempts to do so, using a complex theoretical mechanism by which to achieve it.

If Jameson (together with other cultural critics such as Eagleton, 1984, 1986) sees postmodernity as an economic and cultural formation inimical, at least in the short run, to the emancipatory projects of socialism, others see postmodernity in a more positive light. We can take the work of Bauman as an example of a commitment to embrace postmodernity precisely because of its 'all-deriding, all-eroding, all dissolving *destructiveness*' (1992: vii, viii; emphasis in original). It is an approach which finds the new uncertainty invigorating after the experience of the absolutist Truths of modernity. Although at one time sympathetic to a humanist Western Marxism, Bauman now sees socialism as one version of the failed project of modernity. Capitalism and socialism, Bauman maintains in an interview conducted in 1990, were 'a family quarrel inside modernity', a quarrel about 'how best to implement it, this progress, which everybody agreed about. I think that now we are past this moment, and it is the very value of this [modernity's] vision of the world which is in question' (p. 222). So, postmodernity's iconoclastic stance is to be welcomed, Bauman assures us, because it gets rid of the assumptions of an old, now discredited, order: a ground-clearing operation which, as the title of his essay collection *Intimations of Postmodernity* implies, only hints at or suggests the possibilities which might emerge, the new ethical choices that become available with the collapse of the legislated ethical rules of once-dominant moral authority.

> Postmodernity (and in this it differs from modernist culture of which it is the rightful issue and legatee) does not seek to substitute one truth for another, one life ideal for another. Instead, it splits the truth, the standards and the ideal into already deconstructed and about to be deconstructed. It denies in advance the right of all and any revelation to slip into the place vacated by the deconstructed/discredited rules. It braces itself for a life without truths, standards and ideals. (p. ix)

Whether such a view of a world without universals, without ethical rules and standards, is experienced as courageous, as nihilistic or as the product of romantic illusions of individual autonomy, will depend upon many factors: the preferred social analysis of the present, what future social structures can be *imagined*, and ultimately whether modernity has come to an end or whether its contradictions between emancipation and domination continue to provide opportunities for the kinds of large-scale transformative change which Marxists and socialist feminists, for example, still hope for without, any more, being able to imagine how they might be achieved. Certainly, we might question whether the various kinds of moral authority which thrived under the conditions of modernity, especially the nation state and religion, are now so eroded that individuals must face the 'loneliness of moral choice'. The growth of the New Right, or 'born-again' Christianity in the United States, of the widespread return to religious fundamentalism and extreme intolerance of diversity, are trends which suggest that the impulses to order, certainty and transcendental moral rules retain a vigorous hold over populations in many parts of the world, including the West. Perhaps, for intellectuals writing about postmodernity, the reference group which fuels their awareness of a decay of authority – epistemological and moral – consists primarily of other members of a cultural élite experiencing the elation mixed with fear which comes from living with uncertainty. This is

not intended to suggest that uncertainty and vertigo in the face of transformative changes are not widely experienced characteristics of the present
period, but to point to the alternative routes which people might take under
these circumstances, including a return to fundamentalist religious and
political beliefs (Giddens, 1994; Smart, 1993). We might add, also, that the
various forms of authority characteristic of modernity are unlikely to relinquish their ideological controls without many battles and, at least, rearguard
actions, if it is considered by them to be in their interests to do so.

The Subject of Modernity and Postmodernity

Bauman's argument is that the erosion of modernity's vision of the world
leaves the individual without the authority which shows us what is True and
Good and thus releases the subject to be an autonomous moral agent.
Whether this argument is convincing or not, debate about it brings us,
finally, to one of the most crucial issues raised by the critics of modernity –
how the individual subject is actually formed within the dominant discourses
of modernity. The constitution of the individual subject will be the exclusive
focus of the next chapter, but at this point we need to locate subjectivity
within the wider debate about modernity and the postmodern.

What is clear when we look at these debates is that something has
changed in the political terrain as a result of postmodern critique. On the
Left there has developed, sometimes reluctantly and with reservations, a
cultural politics of subjectivity. There are many reasons for this shift,
including the impact of feminism's focus on the politics of gender identity
and the failure of orthodox socialist thinking to address, adequately, feminist
political concerns. We can turn to Foucault for what has become the classic
commentary on how the subject is formed within modernity, a commentary
which resonates with and has contributed to feminist theorization on the
woman as subject (Deveaux, 1994). In brief, Foucault (1983) maintains that
the dominant discourses of modernity transform human beings into subjects
through 'modes of objectification'. Foucault's studies have been concerned
with three of these objectification processes. *First*, Foucault notes the effect
of forms of knowledge, enquiry or research which give themselves the status
of sciences, such as linguistics, economics or biology. The 'human sciences'
create the individual as a subject who is the object of study and intervention.
The state utilizes 'scientific advances' to monitor, supervise and control
populations of subjects 'in their own interests', for their, and the state's,
well-being. *Secondly*, Foucault identifies 'dividing practices' by which the
subject is divided within the self or from others by various binary inclusions
and exclusions. Foucault identifies such absolute divisions as mad/sane or
sick/healthy, and we might add a number of other categorical divisions upon
which the discourses of modernity have been established, including
heterosexual/homosexual, male/female, true/false. The significance of these
binary opposites is that they not only objectify, regulate and aim to unify the
different identities within the individual subject, but that they do so by

dividing the subject from others, or more crucially from 'the Other'. These dividing categorizations are essentially forms of the division between 'us' and 'them', between normative and deviant, between order and disorder, and ultimately between what is valued as superior, and what is devalued as inferior. *Thirdly*, Foucault identifies the ways in which individuals, through seeing themselves as objects, are able to become subjects, for example, sexual subjects.

All of these modes of objectification are, of course, interdependent, and reinforce each other in confronting the individual with discursive practices within which he or she constructs themselves as a subjects. Foucault's perspective on the constitution of the subject reveals to us that the identity of the individual is a site of domination, but also an actual or possible site of resistance, of political struggle. That a new turn to a (postmodern) politics of the subject has proved difficult for the more orthodox Left, a Left which, after all, was committed to modernity and the singular identity of the emancipating proletarian, is not difficult to understand, as Hall points out:

> The conventional culture of the left, with its stress on 'objective contradictions', 'impersonal structures' and processes that work 'behind men's (sic) backs', has disabled us from confronting the subjective in politics in any very coherent way . . . In part, the difficulty is in the fact that men, who so often provide the categories within which *everybody* experiences things, even on the left, have always found the spectacle of the return of the subjective dimension so deeply unnerving. (1991: 59; emphasis in original)

The political critique of modernity, and the return of the subjective in mounting this critique, is the context in which a cultural politics, connected to individual lives, becomes possible. We can illustrate this politics of the subjective by taking the example of racism and anti-racist struggles. In the older, orthodox socialist tradition, racism was seen as a part of class struggle within capitalism and Marxist analysis focused on the objective economic conditions of exploitation in order to explain it – racism, with colonialism, was functional to capitalism. Although classical Marxism gave substantial attention to ideology as superstructure, the economic base was seen as the determinant of racism in the last instance and so little attention was given to how racism, and differences in skin colour and culture, were constructed ideologically, and what effects the discourse of racism has on individual identity.

How might we attempt to understand the social practices of racism and its impact on the subject? If we return to my earlier discussion on representation and signification, and on how we are to understand the relation between discourses and 'reality', we can recall the emphasis on the politics of knowledge production which this discussion led to. Here, we might endorse Venn's (1992) argument that we cannot know the 'reality' of the history of racism and colonialism when the discourses, the 'texts', of this history are those of the European conquerors and exploiters. Foucault's analysis of binary categorizations as a means of objectifying the Other contributes to

our understanding of the colonial racist discourse. Western cultural discourse attempts both to distance itself from the Other (non-Western cultures)
by fixing its subordinate place and the identities of its populations, and at the
same time 'strives to capture an otherness it conceptualizes as wild,
chimeric, excessive and unknowable. Such an ambivalence allows colonial
discourse to claim for itself always already to know its object, precisely in
its recalcitrant inscrutability.' writes Venn (pp. 48, 49), commenting on
Bhabha (1983). In this dominant colonial discourse, the Other, the 'native'
of subordinated cultures, is domesticated by exclusion, internalizes herself as
Other and can only achieve 'progress' by becoming 'white' through accul-
turation, through renouncing the culture of the Other. The process of
'passing' for white, either physically or symbolically, is a recurrent feature
of white societies, illustrated most powerfully, perhaps, in the late stages of
the colonization of North America. It is within recent memory and experience for example that Aboriginal children were removed from their families
and communities and sent to residential schools so that they could be
separated from the 'backwardness' of native cultures and educated into a
new identity, that of 'Canadians'.

The history of the discourse of colonialism and racism points unambiguously to the negative, exclusionary side of the project of modernity which
was, in principle and through the notion of autonomous reason, available for
the whole of humanity. But the dominant discourses of modernity were
fearful of any influence, internal or external, which might destabilize the
supremacy of autonomous reason, introducing uncertainty and forms of
difference which might undermine modernity's order and progress. The
subject, within this discourse, had to possess a fixed identity, able to be
located in an appropriate place in the social order either as one of 'us' or one
of 'them'. The subjects constituted as 'them', as Other, were excluded from
dominant discourse on the grounds of culture, race, gender or sexuality,
their voices silenced, their very existence as active subjects erased from
'history'.

Modernity and the Discourse of Welfare

If modernity, as an emancipatory project of progress and order, became the
foundation upon which a belief in human betterment was constructed, then
we can trace the ways in which its domain assumptions constituted the
discourses on welfare and, more widely, the welfare state. At the most
general level, we can see that the modern state was concerned to form
certain 'progressive' kinds of subjectivity. As we will see in the next
chapter, this involved addressing individuals in the dominant language of
work, family, consumption and sexuality, and social policies of many kinds
contributed significantly to these discourses. Giddens (1994: 75) sees the
welfare state as tied to a model of 'traditional family and gender systems'
most evident in the fact that 'welfare programmes have been aimed mainly
at supporting male participation in the paid labour force, with a ''second

tier'' of household programmes oriented towards families without a male breadwinner'. Although he refers to the treatment of the 'masculine' sectors of the welfare state in terms of rights and purchases of services compared with the treatment of the 'feminine' sectors in terms of client dependency, Giddens's conceptualization of this division only begins to scratch the surface. To unearth the ideologies which lie beneath that surface requires us to critique the welfare state in a manner more clearly focused on its ideological discourses.

In what follows I shall illustrate the embeddedness of the welfare state within the assumptions of modernity by drawing upon two examples. The first refers to the history of financial support provided for single parent mothers in the United States. The second explores some characteristics of the social democratic discourse on the British welfare state, a discourse profoundly influential in the 1960s. By looking at these examples of discourses which occupy places on the political spectrum from Right to Left-of-Centre, we will be able to see how all-pervasive the assumptions of modernity are in the constitution of welfare discourses and practices.

If we want to go below the surface in attempting to understand the historic gender division within the welfare state, then we must see these divisions in terms of exclusion and moral regulation. In studying the development of programmes directed to poor female-headed households in the United States, Handler and Hasenfeld (1991) show that taking account of the process of *inclusion* and *exclusion* is essential to understanding the aid to dependent children (ADC) programmes. They argue that the establishment of these programmes did not represent a 'progressive' change in attitudes to poor single mothers, because the great majority of poor single mothers were, in fact, excluded from them. Upon what rule of exclusion were this majority of a putative target population denied admission? Handler and Hasenfeld write of what was called, in the early years of the programme, 'mother's pensions', in terms of 'myth and ceremony'.

> The myth was that now worthy single mothers would be excused from the paid labour force and their homes would not be broken. The ceremony consisted of granting small amounts of relief to a select group of white widows. White widows were defined in terms of the Other – the *excluded* single mothers. The myths and ceremonies of the mothers' pension movement thus spoke to *both* the non-poor and the poor. The values of patriarchy and the 'proper' female role were rewarded; and the nonconforming poor, those who were morally degraded to begin with (people of colour, never married, and those who were divorced, separated or deserted) need not apply. (1991: 21, 22; emphasis in original)

The successor of ADC, renamed in 1962 AFDC (Aid to Families with Dependent Children), continues to carry similar symbolic functions addressed both to welfare recipients and to the poor in general: the importance of the work ethic, the moral obligations of mothers, the exclusion of categories of undeserving. Most recently, the New Right attack on welfare has targeted AFDC in pushing to recreate historic categories of exclusion. The symbolic Other in the US welfare system – young, poor mothers on the dole – are subject to a moral discourse in which they

represent the disorders, irrationality and source of ethical decay which is
believed to infect American society. As in the colonial discourse of
modernity, there is in the dominant American politics of welfare a solid
basis in racism: the stereotype of the welfare recipient is the young African-
American unmarried mother, a population from which the majority white
society must be protected. We shall return in the next chapter to the
stereotypes involved in the notion of 'welfare dependency' as they construct
the subjectivities of those who live on state benefits.

It is not difficult to see that the dominant discourse of welfare has been
laden with the assumptions and problematics of modernity. We can point to
the belief in the necessity for binary classifications: good mothers and bad
mothers, workers and shirkers, productive consumers and unproductive
dependents, deserving and undeserving. We can identify rules of exclusion
operating within health, education and welfare support systems, rules
determined by the social relations of class, gender and 'race', rules which
legislate against difference. How could the welfare state of the post-Second
World War era and of late capitalism fail to reflect its genesis as a project of
modernity, committed as it was, and still is, to the administrative and
professional surveillance, control and 'progress' of populations in the
interests of their well-being as defined by the state itself? However, to speak
of the welfare state as if it were simply a creature of right-wing intentions to
exclude, punish and protect, whilst understandable in a period when conservative and neo-liberal agendas appear to dominate all political discussion,
is surely to fail to render a full account of the *contradictions* of the discourse
of welfare. If we were to see the idea of the welfare state as an expression of
the humanist dialectic of enlightenment, then we would expect to find not
simple repression, but rather a contradiction between the discourses and
practices of domination and those of emancipation. In the European,
Canadian and Australian welfare states, for example, the principle of the
universality of entitlement, at least in health, education and social insurance
provision, reflected a social democratic politics of modernity which appears
to stand in stark contrast to the practices of the exclusion of the Other. In
order to examine whether this is the case, I turn now to my second
illustration of the ways in which welfare is embedded in modernity by
giving attention to the once hegemonic social democratic discourse on the
British welfare state.

The British social democratic approach to the welfare state, profoundly
influential from the early 1950s to the mid-1970s, had its roots within the
Fabian tradition of social reform and was expressed most clearly in the work
of a group of academics researching and teaching in the field of *social
administration*. Many of these writers were closely involved in the political
structures of the Labour Party and of Labour governments, acting as
advisers, recommending policies, sometimes directing parts of the state
welfare apparatus, but also acting as critics of its practices. This social
democratic discourse powerfully advocated an ever-expanding universalistic
welfare state which would, it was believed, improve the life chances of the

whole population, but especially the working class: the market and welfare were to coexist.

The principle of universalism lay at the root of this social democratic politics of welfare and it underpinned the view that welfare provision should be seen as a moral transaction based upon altruism rather than self-interest. Richard Titmuss was foremost in advocating this moral foundation for the welfare state, clearly seen as providing no space for the processes of domination and exclusion to which I have pointed as characteristics of the welfare state of modernity. Titmuss develops the moral distinction between social policy and the market as a defining characteristic:

> Social administration is thus concerned, for instance, with different types of moral transactions, embodying notions of gift exchange, of reciprocal obligation, which have developed in modern societies in institutional forms to bring about and maintain social and community relations . . . The grant, or the gift or unilateral transfer – whether it takes the form of cash, time, energy, satisfaction, blood or even life itself – is the distinguishing mark of the social (in policy and administration) just as exchange or bilateral transfer is the mark of the economic. (1968: 21–2)

The altruistic moral transactions of welfare, *The Gift Relationship* expressed in the title of Titmuss's (1970) comparative study of blood donor systems in the USA and Britain, signify the high ethical ground claimed by the notion of the welfare state as embodying *moral progress*. It is difficult to deny the attraction of such an idea – it seems now perhaps one of those socialist aspirations long since submerged beneath a flood of neo-Darwinist competitiveness and brutality. We need to ask ourselves, however, whether the rhetoric of the universalism carried within it a certain assumption about homogeneity and an apprehension when faced with difference. We might enquire also whether the moral transactions of welfare required so much administrative and professional regulation, and the attendant forms of classification upon which the judgements of eligibility were founded, that *exclusion* of the Other remained fundamental to the system. We can trace a contradiction here, moreover, not only to some distinction we might make between theory and practice, or principle and operation, but more fundamentally to some of the very foundations of the British social democratic discourse on welfare.

The Fabian approach to social reform, through advocating gradual change by means of legislation supported and carried out by administrative and professional expertise, was profoundly influential in the construction of the social democratic welfare discourse. In its turn, the historic roots of Fabianism lie in its links to early twentieth century 'social imperialism' and colonialism (Jacobs, 1985). Social imperialism was a liberal political movement which reflected growing ruling class concern about the health and welfare of the working class population of the 'mother country' of the British Empire. It expressed deep anxieties about the threat of the Other in the form of a focus on 'racial purity' and the supposed superiority of the British racial stock. Fabian reformism was deeply implicated in this racist discourse on welfare, expressed most clearly in their justifications for health insurance and child welfare programmes in terms of the claims of the developing 'science' of eugenics, a science which reached its triumphal apogee in Nazi Germany where it provided a similar rationale for services directed to promoting the Aryan race. In the case of Britain in the early twentieth century, the Fabians argued that health and welfare programmes were necessary to help preserve white superiority and ensure imperial survival. Thus fear of contamination by the Other lay in the origins of the idea of a British welfare state, a fear which continued to influence the social democratic colonial and welfare policies of Labour governments since 1945, especially in relation to immigration, employment regulation and the access of non-white populations to health and social services (Jacobs, 1985; Joshi and Carter, 1985).

What Follows Deconstruction?

The central argument of this chapter has been, thus far, that the retreat from welfare and the disintegration of some of the ideological foundations which once sustained it, need to be understood not only in terms of the impact of economic changes flowing from the growth of a global economy, but also as the result of profound social and cultural changes. These changes may be summarized as challenges to modernity, in which the erosion of belief in the authority of a universal autonomous reason, and in the politics which has accompanied the different forms of modernity – capitalist and state socialist – leads to increased questioning, doubt and uncertainty. Whether the outcome of these elements of what we may call postmodern scepticism will be positive or negative remains, of course, to be seen: it is certainly a central issue in the argument and debate between the optimists and the pessimists. Should we look to the *benefits* of this contemporary shift in the culture of late capitalism: the new emphasis on difference, the challenge to authority, the increased choice in individual identity, the disapproval of ethnic arrogance? Or should we focus, rather, on the detriments of the way we live now: the mind-deadening impact of mass-produced culture, the manufacture of desire, the increase in poverty and uncertainty, the collapse of mass class politics? We must try, I believe, to understand and, as far as possible, face up to the contradictory consequences of living in 'New Times'.

Out of all the confusion and disagreement, the hope and despair, one thing stands out clearly: something has now passed away. The old welfare state, that once-seeming jewel in the crown of moral progress in democratic societies, is finished, though it has taken nearly twenty years for the gradual erosion to reach the present point of collapse. So, where do we go from here?

The question I ask myself and share with the reader is this: how could a new, reconstructed conception of welfare, a new discursive project, be developed to replace the old, dead version? It was a version which, in the end, over-represented the features of modernity which are locked into institutions and practices of domination. Can the enlightenment project of modernity be shifted towards the fulfilment of its emancipatory claims? Achieving some reconstruction of the discourses and practices of welfare would be a key test of the emancipatory potential which may still remain in modernity. Upon what ideas, social practices, institutions and cultural politics would a reconstruction of welfare as an emancipatory project be based? This is the question which underpins this book and which, at its conclusion, it attempts to begin to answer.

But to begin to circle around this question, even in a most preliminary and tentative way, requires us, I believe, first to undergo a process of reflection which touches upon the most cherished notions of those who have, in the past, through a political commitment to an ideal of universal well-being, embraced the project of emancipation. It is a reflective process whereby we come to recognize what is *past*, what it is that is 'over', realize what the *present* now enables us to think, and what we might, despite everything, conceive of as a *future* for the idea of welfare. In other words, we need now and will need throughout the argument of the book as a whole, to engage in the act of deconstruction, the unearthing, prising apart and facing-up-to of perhaps our most cherished and taken-for-granted assumptions about individual identity and culture and about the possibilities of economic, political and organizational change in the interests of human well-being. Through deconstruction we are able to see our knowledge and beliefs as historically and culturally specific products no longer able to be legitimated by reference to the universal authority of Reason, the transcendental guarantor. Although Bauman (1992: ix) writes, as we have seen, of postmodernity as that critique which 'splits the truth, the standards and the ideal into already deconstructed and about to be deconstructed', I take a different track. Bauman maintains that postmodern critique denies the claims of any ideal to take the place of that which has been deconstructed, while I believe; in – it might be suggested – a most *un*postmodern way, that deconstruction may be followed by reconstruction in the *light* of the critique, but not necessarily through following its every turn.

The Past as Another Country

If postmodernity represents a condition of cultural uncertainty, the erosion of transcendental guarantees, the loss of moral authority, the end of convincing political metanarratives, then it is hardly surprising that we might look to the past as a blessed time of *certainty*. In searching around to reconstruct a narrative of emancipation, we are tempted to sift through the shattered pieces of defunct ideas because in a present without foundations only the past can speak to us. The past offers us a possible security; we are, after all, the products of history. But we are not the products of History, the objective sweep of events determined by the 'laws' of economic and social development. That kind of history is also dead, and history now becomes a cultural narrative, a discourse governed by its characteristic rules of exclusion and inclusion. We must look at our own past sternly, eschewing a romantic nostalgia for an earlier politics of struggles against domination even while we can understand the impulse which might drive us to the imagined comforts of the past.

The past may seem to us now as a place, 'another country' in L.P. Hartley's often quoted phrase, a place where they 'do things differently', and where dreams of the future were possible. Socialism was an alternative future where the contradictions of that rival form of modernity, capitalism, would finally be overcome, resolved and put to rest. This vision of a different and better future could not be specified in detail for fear of succumbing to utopia-building in the manner of William Morris or the French Utopian Socialists. It was the dynamic of struggle which would produce a socialist future, and this was the focus of Marxist narrative: a metanarrative primarily of *process* rather that of end result. One of the outcomes of this emphasis on the process by which transformation would take place was that it largely prevented us from closely examining the contradiction embedded in the socialist emancipatory project itself, namely its impulse to domination 'in the interest of emancipation': the world was to be shifted in the name of progress, science, reason and Truth. Whilst it was founded on an analysis of the contradictions of capitalism, an analysis central to the dialectic of historical materialism, socialist theorization and politics was largely unable to acknowledge its own contradictions, except to see them as merely remnants of that other form of modernity, capitalism. As a practice, socialism appears, theoretical protestations to the contrary notwithstanding, to have been bound up in modernity's *principle of non-contradiction* (McGowan, 1991) in which a synthesis would result from the dialectic of thesis and antithesis. This aspiration to a Unity which would overcome contradictions required that the Other could not remain Other, different in all its diverse forms, but had to be incorporated into the One, the proletarian revolution which was the antithesis which would lead, with the eventual establishment of communism, to the resolving synthesis.

Within the idea of socialism, welfare was therefore the welfare of the One, the homogeneous mass whose future life chances would be ensured through the antithesis to bourgeois exploitation provided by socialist social policy. The state was the instrument of this antithesis. In the state socialist form established, for example, in Eastern Europe, we are speaking here of a post-revolutionary state which will retain many of the contradictions of pre-revolutionary times, but nevertheless be in a position to meet the basic human needs of its population as an admittedly imperfect stage towards ultimate emancipation from the material, social and cultural deprivations which it suffered under previous domination. The 'dictatorship of the proletariat' was the necessary interim form of politics required to ensure the well-being of the One and the assimilation or exclusion of the Other.

Within the social democratic form, the road to socialist emancipation and well-being was less clear, not least because in the 'foreseeable future' the contradictions of capitalism would remain firmly embedded within existing social relations, contradictions captured in the phrase 'Welfare and the Market'. At its most ambitious, social democratic welfare could be envisaged as creating those morally superior prefigurative forms and relationships which would be the precursors of the social arrangements of a future where human need could be more fully met. Welfare was to be built on the One through the provision of universal services, services directed to individuals but designed to encourage a community 'oneness'. In the West, these socialist ideals of the state-planned well-being of its citizens received their *coup de grace* when the long international economic boom came to an end. The vision of a wide range of human needs being met through universal state services could not compete, as we have seen, with the brute reality of economic recession and the restructuring of capital and labour. The notion of the warm community of Oneness collapsed before the ever-deepening dichotomies of rich/poor, employed/unemployed, male/female, white/black. At the same time, the perceptions of these dichotomies also underwent a change some twenty years ago. The previous exclusions, the silencing of voices, which were a hallmark of capitalist modernity, now began to create new shifts in consciousness not only about the exclusions of capitalism, but also about those of socialism, both 'actual, existing' forms, and those aspirational ones, manifested in social democracy and Western Marxism. The disillusionment of the excluded ones, the Other, with the homogenizing impulse of a socialism of Oneness, acted as a chorus accompanying the final Act of that particular form of modernity as idea and practice which had lasted for a century and a half.

The Present as an Uncertain Place

In spite of the widespread disillusionment of the Other in state-managed plans for their state-defined well-being, and the support they receive from reflexive intellectuals committed to deconstruction, the impulse of modernity to Oneness and the subordination of the Other do not appear to have lost their strength. The form of Oneness now dominant is not manifested in the Nation State, which was the midwife of modernity, but takes the form of the Market, specifically the single global capitalist market.

The global market is a Oneness which is truly universal: it touches, through technology, cultural production and increasing market dependency, virtually all of humanity. Fewer and fewer can escape it. Although its origins lie in Western culture, in the logic of Enlightenment rationality, its universal principle of exploitation through the operation of market forces, now takes many non-Western forms. Japanese capitalism, for example, has developed and prospered without that once-thought essential underpinning of an ideology of autonomous individualism (Abercrombie et al., 1986).

Although it reflects some cultural diversity, especially concerning conceptions of the subject, the Oneness of the global market is united in its commitment to the pursuit of the ideals of modernity: progress through scientific rationality and order. It is a commitment constructed in the interests of national and international élites: a class project of universal dimensions. The multitudinous Other (workers, the poor, subordinate women, subjects of racism, oppressed cultural groups) confront this hegemonic Oneness with uncertainty and ambivalence. The ambivalence arises from a crucial contradiction: on the one hand the desire, even if at least partially manufactured through market seduction, for the material benefits which the market brings, and on the other, the alienation, cultural losses and subordinacy which market domination also involves. The uncertainty flows from profound doubts about what kinds of resistance to the negative effects of global market forces are possible.

We might begin the exploration of this uncertainty by asking whether resistance to a global Oneness might require the establishment of a global Other, a newly minted version of the universal proletariat as humanity's revolutionary instrument. The problem, of course, is that in the assumptions, organization and strategies of this unified (though diverse) emancipatory Other, a politics may once again emerge which results in a drive to homogenization and domination in the name of critique, struggle and solidarity. But if the idea of solidarity amongst the diverse Other is either an impossible aspiration, or especially *not to be trusted*, then perhaps certain kinds of accommodation to global market forces would be possible? It would be an accommodation designed to gain maximum benefit from the products of the global market – material and social needs, including those manufactured through cultural production – at the same time as holding on to difference, to positive manifestations of the diversity of the Other, as long as possible. Thus maximizing human welfare would be achieved through a politics of securing continuous strategic balances between production, consumption and diversity. The difficulty which confronts such a politics of accommodation is that the Oneness of the global market, its dynamic of continuous innovation and change, drives it to obliterate, as far as possible, all cultural differences except in so far as they support the proliferation of market goods and services. The notion of welfare as including the meeting of heterogeneous human needs confronts the economic logic of maximizing homogeneity. It may be argued that developments in flexible production and new forms of communication, to which we will turn later in a chapter on the economy, provide at the same time increased opportunity of meeting more diverse needs; however, it must be acknowledged that such consumption diversity is also market-driven within the context of a mass culture which determines the extent which diversity can be responded to, the 'bottom line' criterion being the maximization of capital accumulation.

The present uncertainty of oppositional politics, especially those that focus on identity and difference, lies also in the realization that while the new 'postmodern' politics addresses and even, to some degree, rectifies the old discredited socialist politics, it cannot satisfactorily confront the domination of the global market Oneness in the interest of the Other. The Other is, by definition, diverse, fragmented, excluded and so its multifarious component populations cannot separately empower themselves sufficiently to oppose the massive power of the new market forces of subordination, exploitation and homogenization. The politics of difference, of the diverse Other, remains paradoxically locked into the past through continuing to do battle with the features of exclusion and domination which characterized a socialist politics which is now already dead, or at least on its death-bed. At the same time, this postmodern critical politics has not yet been able to envisage a strategy which builds upon difference through a new conception of a universal emancipatory struggle. In this, as in many other ways, the past haunts the present: it speaks to us of a lost hope, of disillusionment, but also of the comfort once gained from a certainty which we shall never again experience.

The Future as Illusion or Possibility

Can we any longer speak of the future, of the prospects for human welfare, in other than cataclysmic terms, because 'the party is over'? Especially when associated with emancipatory claims, all talk of *plans* for the future must now be greeted with profound scepticism, or more likely, cynicism. Within modernity, political talk of the future has always been articulated in terms of progress, of human betterment: the postmodern condition makes such metanarratives appear hollow or dishonest. Modernity, in both its capitalist and socialist forms has been, in practice, unable to deliver on its promises of universal freedom, material abundance, security and increased equality, so its metanarratives no longer hold water. Postmodernism, on the other hand, offers its own metanarrative, though its protagonists often deny that this is the case. It offers, of course, a metanarrative on modernity, on the contradictions and false hopes of the Enlightenment, a powerful and persuasive critique. But this critique, if it remains distant from the project of modernity, cannot become a metanarrative of 'the way forward', because ways forward are seen as an illusion of modernity.

Is it not possible, then, to envisage an emancipatory politics of welfare, one which takes the risk of looking to the future, rather than only continuously adapting to the present and having a love/hate relationship to the past?

To start to answer this question in a tentative, preliminary way appropriate to the opening chapter of this book, we must begin to suggest what an emancipatory politics *cannot*, any longer, strive to achieve. It cannot *predict* the future because its metanarrative cannot be constructed on the basis of a unilinear perspective on history, the unfolding of inevitable laws of development which, within certain boundaries, are proposed as determining the overall trajectory of human societies. If it is to be convincing, to work politically and theoretically, a metanarrative of emancipation can, with respect to the future, only engage in the imagining of diverse 'ways forward', only suggest the possibilities which are open to human beings in the act of furthering their own welfare. Uncertainty about the future, then, is the only thing we can be certain about: that there are many possibilities, most of which are hidden from us, because each moment is a time already past as soon as we mark it. There can be no transcendental guarantees of what the future will bring, no principles of Reason, Truth or History upon which we can depend, and, in Arnold's words from 'Dover Beach',

> And we are here as on a darkling plain
> Swept with confused alarms of struggle and flight,
> Where ignorant armies clash by night.

Of course, Matthew Arnold was a Victorian who was trying to reconcile capitalism, science and religion and understand the relation between culture and the imperatives of a modern life. We need not share the pessimism of this passage but we must, I believe, none the less accept that the narrative of emancipation must be one of uncertainty, a story without guarantees as to the outcome. If we accept this uncertainty, must we also renounce the universalizing discourses of justice and equality within which the historic emancipatory struggles against domination have been conducted *inside* the project of modernity itself?

An answer to this question begins, perhaps, from recognizing that the universals of the discourse of emancipation are what they have always been, socially constructed. Nothing about these 'universal' narratives has changed except our acknowledgment that the Western notions of justice and certain kinds of equality have been culturally produced within a specific historical period of short duration. They are, therefore, culturally relative and are not necessarily shared, even as ideals, by other cultures. Other notions of human well-being, long rendered silent by Western colonialism, begin to take their place alongside those of the Eurocentred West – African, Aboriginal, Asian, and other culturally produced conceptions of welfare – and we slowly start to learn that it is possible to think differently than we have previously thought, perceive the world differently, even feel differently. But the fact that the narrative of emancipation is a ship which sails in a sea of different cultures and diverse social conditions enables us, at least, to envisage a process of arriving at some agreed values, which we can call *universal by consent*, and which are established as a result of political struggle which resolves itself in a consensus amongst those striving for emancipation. What might be agreed?

We have already noted that contemporary anthropology maintains that what is unique about the human species is not a set of social characteristics which members of the species have in common, their '*essential humanness*', but rather their immense diversity (Geertz, 1973). If we take cultural diversity as a central feature of human existence, then the first universal, constructed on this foundation must be *the value of diversity*. This might be seen as a universal in which humans take pride: the cultural achievement of human evolution unmatched by any other species.

The universal of diversity immediately provides a critique of social forces whose objective or function is to attain Oneness, disregarding the fact of the difference of the Other and the dissent of the Other in the process of losing elements of diversity. It may be that in future stages of human evolution the diversity of the human species will become less pronounced. If this is so, then the universal of diversity implies the need to attempt to achieve the maximum possible consent for this change in the direction of greater homogeneity. The universal of defending or celebrating diversity does not imply that no change can take place, that tradition rules over choice, or that people cannot search for commonalities with others which they decide are in their interests, but rather that valuing diversity becomes the basis upon which emancipatory challenges can be made both to global institutions – corporate and inter-government – and to national and local political and social systems. However, acknowledging the fact and the value of diversity is insufficient to provide a basis for an emancipatory struggle. The idea of gaining agreement on certain 'universal values' requires the establishment of a degree of solidarity amongst those struggling for emancipation; it suggests something which carries with it a certain risk, namely that the politics of specific social and cultural identities has to be transcended in the name of emancipation itself. A politics of solidarity has to be built alongside a politics of difference, but not dominate it. The risk is obvious: we have been here before. The danger of solidarity *appropriating* diversity in the supposed interests of a 'higher good' is an ever-present problem. We might acknowledge that at this point in history white bourgeois males, even as disaffected intellectuals, have as a population disqualified themselves from the leadership of emancipatory movements: the narrative of resistance against oppression indicts them. But the risks of solidarity must be accepted even as it is necessarily approached with great caution and a healthy scepticism about its objectives. Ultimately, the actual interdependence of individual identities and cultures means that emancipation from the late capitalism of global exploitation must be on a broad front and that nothing less can provide the degree of critique and political challenge which is necessary in order to have any impact at all.

It is at this point in my argument for the construction of emancipatory universals around which solidarity might be formed, that the issue of defining human needs and human welfare becomes especially important. Acknowledging that human needs are cultural, and therefore relative, in their expression or manifestation, can we nevertheless identify some universal preconditions for the expression and satisfaction of culturally produced needs (Doyal and Gough, 1991). We can attempt to answer this question by pointing to the conditions of material existence of the Other. We can argue that discourses on difference and exclusion must be related to concrete practices which play their part in the constitution of the Other: racism, sexism, material exploitation and other forms of domination, usually closely interconnected with each other. A precondition for the expression of diverse needs may be seen as the establishment of a level of material existence which allows the subject to participate in, and if necessary struggle against, cultural discourses on needs and well-being, and thus be able to act as a moral agent in the making of choices.

What is considered 'adequate' or 'necessary' in terms of material levels of existence will, of course, be subject to cultural variation. These variations are rooted in the political and economic characteristics of different social orders and must take into account a range of forms of social regulation and exploitation, both national and global, including, in late capitalist societies, the manufacture of desire. Nevertheless, I believe it is possible to use the *discourse on poverty* as a starting point in constituting a second universal upon which solidarity might be built. In Western countries, especially as the welfare state disintegrates and is restructured on minimal residual lines, there lies beneath the politics of difference, of identity, amongst those embattled in issues of gender, racism, age or disability, a common concern with poverty. The question is whether this common concern can be built upon as a basis of solidarity. Does an emancipatory struggle over poverty, national and world-wide, imply a return to Marx's contention that 'all history is the history of class struggle'? By placing difference and material exploitation *together* as a focus of struggle, we are acknowledging that there are many ways in which oppression can be experienced by the Other, but that there are many populations whose conditions of material existence prevent their full expression as diverse moral agents. It is true, however, that when we speak of poverty, we are speaking predominantly of class; in the present conditions of late capitalism we are pointing to the class project of exploitation through the economic and political forces of the global market. In other words, considerations of class enter into the preconditions for the defence and celebration of diversity, an understanding of forms of exploitation and their impact on material and social existence.

Although class exploitation re-enters emancipatory discourse as an obstacle to the positive experience of diversity – a key element in the domination of the Other – this does not mean that the collective bearer of this exploitation, and the vanguard in the struggle against it, takes once again the form of a Universal Proletariat. As we have already argued, the redemptive figure of the proletariat is obviously too limited, too mythical, too unitary, to serve this purpose. The struggle against class exploitation is the struggle by diverse emancipatory forces reflecting different identities and interests within a range of social orders against a common obstacle to their liberation to express more fully their difference. If it were possible to build an emancipatory welfare project on a common understanding, reached through inter-cultural dialogue, of the centrality of difference and exploitation in the constitution of subordinacy, then we may find that a common signifier emerged which, for now, we might call the Universal Other.

Already, the reader might protest, an unguarded note of optimism enters my argument, an optimism as yet unsupported by analysis. How can this argument about a future emancipatory politics of welfare be substantiated, or even elaborated sufficiently to give it any credence? At this point, what I have written contains only the merest hints about possible ways forward.

Substantiation necessitates a commentary on those discourses, institutions and practices which have characterized welfare as a project of modernity, accompanied by both critique and ultimately by a speculation on the reconstruction of the project which enables new forms of emancipatory welfare to emerge. These are the tasks for the remainder of this book.

2

Subject

In the attempt to re-think the idea of welfare in the postmodern world, and especially to reconstitute it as an emancipatory project, we must ask what might constitute emancipation for an individual subject, and from what constraints. To what extent, if at all, is the individual relatively autonomous, a moral agent able to act upon the surrounding world in his or her own interests? What external forces might affect such potential and actual autonomy? Some might answer that class and gender oppression or racism constrain individual autonomy while others would suggest that systems of state welfare tend to remove autonomy from individuals to induce dependence on the state. Or perhaps the question should be posed another way: is the very idea of a relatively autonomous individual simply an illusion, a cultural creation of a particular period of Western history? Is the individual person's sense of self, of identity, of the ability to act as a free agent, the product of cultural conditioning, of dominant discourses or ideologies? Perhaps, as some would suggest, state welfare is a product of late capitalism's need to constitute, through health, education, unemployment assistance and other services, individual identities as productive workers, insatiable consumers and the reproducers of family life.

The two ways of posing the question – from the perspective of constraints on individual autonomy, on the one hand, and from the idea of autonomy as an illusion, on the other, signal the core issue which we must address in this stage in the discussion. We will also need to ask ourselves whether the binary form of the question – either autonomy or determinism, either individual freedom or life in the monolith – is the only form of interrogation possible. Certainly, if we want to speak of emancipation, of the possibility of new ways being invented of advancing human well-being, then it might be argued that it will be necessary to show how individual and collective human intentions, especially of those most subordinated within a social system, can have their effect. Alternatively, we might take the view that because of present historical conditions – the transformations involved in the development of a world market economy – active struggle is futile, indeed impossible, and we must await more propitious historical moments to emerge before emancipatory projects are taken up again. It is clear, in any case, that the answers we give to these questions about individual autonomy crucially affect how we view the present condition of state welfare, and how we might envisage the future of the idea of welfare and its articulation in practices and institutions.

I focus here on the concept of the *subject* because the term contains within it meanings which reflect to some degree both sides of the debate about individual autonomy and structural determinism. The first meaning of the term 'subject' is often referred to as the 'humanist subject' or the subject of modernity, because it rests upon an assumption of the existence of an essential, self-directing individual person, able to act in modern, 'advanced' societies with relative freedom of choice. This subject carries, therefore, substantial individual moral and social responsibility for her or his conditions of existence. The second meaning of the term 'subject' is that which refers primarily to subjection, in the sense of being subject to another's power or authority. Here, we might speak of being subjects of the monarch, or subject to the law of the land, or the constitution. This is the subject as socially constituted, personal identity being the product of membership of specific cultures during particular historical periods. Individuals, it is suggested, occupy 'subject positions'. The humanist notion of an essential self, a central core around which culture is agglutinated, is, within this social constructionist perspective, either viewed with scepticism or as an idea to be rejected entirely. Whereas the first meaning of subject directs our attention to human agency and intention, to the individual claimed to be sovereign and the central actor in history, the second meaning, to varying degrees, decentres the subject and gives attention to economic and social forces which constitute the individual's identity.

The term 'subject', then, may be used to explore the theorization behind the different meanings attached to the term in contemporary debate, and whether individual agency is possible within the context of dominant discourses or ideologies and their attendant social practices. The centrality of these questions to current discourses on welfare will need to be given specific attention. In particular, we will need to explore the possibility of reconciling agency and determinism, whether we can avoid binary opposition in favour of a more dialectical understanding of the relationship between individual and society. Between the ideas of the 'sovereign individuals of capitalism' (Abercrombie, et al., 1986) and 'the death of the subject' (Jameson, 1984), is there some space for the notion of resistance and critique of and within welfare systems even while acknowledging their role in constituting subjectivity?

The Subject as Socially Constituted

We can begin to approach these questions by examining the idea that our subjectivity is constructed by the social order in which we live. No contemporary social or political theorist would argue that the individual is free from social constraints, from the effects of the social, economic and wider cultural context: the question is how we are to understand this context, how significant it is in forming subjectivity and what effect it has on individual agency.

I shall begin by outlining the thrust of the argument put forward by the social constructionist perspective which identifies the major contextual elements that constitute subjectivity in terms of modes of production and social reproduction which may be signified as capitalism, patriarchy and/or neo-colonialism. This theoretical perspective begins by acknowledging the biological and genetic differences between people, and forms of domination, ascription and ranking which legitimate themselves by reference to these differences. Later (in Chapter 3) we will examine in detail the issue of whether there are also common social characteristics, beyond biology, which are to be found, though culturally mediated, in all human beings, or whether this common characteristic is better identified as *difference* itself. At this point, we can see that the social constructionist views subjectivity as a product of the social relations characteristic of a specific social formation at a particular point in history. As subjects with a sense of identity, a view of self and others, and a set of understandings of the social world, we are, in short, culturally and historically specific. In the particular condition of late capitalism, it is argued that the subject is subordinated to the imperatives of a developing world market economy, and the consequent means by which class, gender and ethnic domination is maintained.

How does this subject connect to the world of late capitalism and the social relations it reproduces? One view, within this general perspective, is that the connection is maintained through discursive practices, that it is through discourse that subjectivity is established. The subject's sense of herself is achieved by her identification with the discursive formation which dominates her, assigning her to a subject position 'appropriate' to her class, gender, ethnic and other characteristics. The result of this identification is that traces of dominant discourses which determined her subject position are 'reinscribed' in her own discourse, and so she experiences this subjection not as oppression, but as autonomy (Althusser, 1971; Pêcheux, 1982). We shall return to this possibly over-determinist and certainly pessimistic scenario later, but at this point ask what is the connection between these dominant discourses and the material relations which, it is argued, such discourses maintain and reproduce? If it is possible, as I suggested in the previous chapter, to speak of social practices *outside* of discourses, then in this instance we may speak of the individual subject's material activities and exchanges, such as occur, for example, when engaged in various kinds of labour, in personal relationships, in ingesting the commodities manufactured by cultural production and in interaction with agents of the state. It is through these various activities that the subject's sense of self, of coherence as a person, of 'place', is produced through the meanings, definitions and common sense assumptions sedimented in the activities themselves. Marx maintained that ideology is a material force and in a similar vein we might argue that discourses are manifested in social practices.

Without discounting the idea of discursive struggle, of the existence of competing and alternative discourses, such as those of welfare, or poverty, or racism, and to which we shall give attention later, what might at this point be identified as the determinants of subjectivity in late capitalist societies? Without necessarily endorsing a monolithic picture of Western capitalist societies, we can still speak, I believe, of how subjectivity is constituted within hegemonic discursive formations characteristic of these societies. Out of the many dominant discourses which exist we can identify four which appear critical in the formation of contemporary subjects of late capitalism and are especially relevant to the current debates on welfare: the discourses of work, consumption, family and sexuality. These discourses are the means by which, on a daily basis, the social relations of class, gender, ethnicity, age, disability and sexuality are maintained and reproduced as elements in the subject positions of individuals.

The Virtue of Work

The central dynamic of capitalist societies involves activities directed towards the accumulation of capital and the reproduction and social regulation of the labour power upon which it rests and for which it requires the performance of various kinds of labour, both waged and unwaged. The dominant discourse of work is concerned mainly with waged work, for it functions primarily to reinforce commitment to abstract labour, that which, Marxists and feminists would tend to argue, subordinates individual needs and capacities to the imperatives of accumulation, profitability and social regulation. Because engaging in waged labour not only provides, for most people, a primary means of material subsistence, but also a source of social solidarity – membership of 'the world of work', the dominant discourse of work focuses substantially on these latter benefits and is framed within a notion of work as a *moral* obligation.

The ethical basis of the discourse of work may be seen historically as a prerequisite of the development of modernity in its capitalist form – workers are free from the social obligations of their feudal ancestors, and may, in theory, sell their labour to the highest bidder. We will explore later how profoundly important to capitalism has been the idea of a free individual worker. But to be such a worker, to be hardworking, is also an ethical responsibility, arguably reinforced by a religious movement in early and middle capitalism which placed emphasis on 'work' as much as 'faith', for as Weber maintained in *The Protestant Ethic and the Spirit of Capitalism*, religious discourse, individualism and capitalist development were closely interrelated (Weber, 1930). That maintaining the subject position of worker implies an ethical obligation is shown in a study of American welfare policy and its symbolic function in the 'moral construction of poverty' (Handler and Hasenfeld, 1991). The authors show that the work ethic assumes that productive work is an individual responsibility and that, with rare exceptions, it is the individual who is blamed for failure to find an adequate job, thus being morally culpable:

> Those who fail to find work, without a socially approved excuse, at a socially approved job are condemned. They are defined as deviant. The chronically

unemployed, able-bodied malingerers, paupers, bums, tramps and those who work in socially disapproved jobs are considered threats to the ideology of labour discipline – hard work, thrift and reward through individual effort. (1991: 18)

What is socially approved, then, is productive work and the discourse on work as productive labour is a distinctive characteristic of modernity, as Weber demonstrated. 'Productivism' is the term which Giddens (1994) uses to denote this particular discourse in which work, as paid employment, has been separated from other domains of life. Giddens sees work as becoming 'a standard bearer of moral meaning – it defines whether or not individuals feel worthwhile or socially valued; and the motivation to work is autonomous' (p. 175). The extent to which the subject position of worker involves identification with the hegemonic discursive formation and reinscription in the worker's own discourse can be judged by Giddens's comment that 'why one wishes, or feels compelled, to work is defined in terms of what work itself is – the need to work has its own inner dynamic' (p. 175).

Weber showed that the uniquely compulsive pressure to work is characteristic of modernity, an inner compulsion which the worker experiences not usually as oppression but rather as autonomy. On the compulsive and segregated nature of the work ethic of modernity, Giddens remarks that most premodern societies seem to have had no word for 'work', presumably because working was not readily distinguishable from other activities. Moreover, insofar as it was recognized as a distinctive type of activity, work was not something which defined a specifically male role (p. 176). By the nineteenth century, the process whereby work was defined primarily as men's productive labour and the work of women in physical and social reproduction was relegated to a subordinate status, came to fruition. The project of emancipation itself became associated with the revolutionary destiny of the working man – the symbolic figure of the industrial proletarian was always male, standing erect and defiant with the support of women whom he would also protect and provide for. The consequences of this association of work with male productive labour for the foundational ideologies of the welfare state will be explored later in this chapter. At this point we can make note of the contradictions which emerge when the dominant discourse of work no longer, because of economic and political changes, fits the gender division of labour. At the same time, productive labour as a moral imperative becomes problematic under conditions of rapid economic transformation when unemployment, under-employment and part-time employment become a widespread experience. The discursive formation which requires subjects to internalize an ethical compulsion to engage in productive work begins, perhaps, to weaken under postmodern conditions.

Consumption and Desire

In the early and middle stages of capitalism, the work ethic reigned supreme and was critical to the formation of the working class. In the earlier stages of capitalism, the entrepreneurial drive for accumulation was fuelled by the gospel of thrift, an exhortation to calculation, caution and abstinence which, at least for the middle classes, could not be squared ideologically with any inner compulsion to personal consumption. Conspicuous consumption took place of course, and is documented in Veblen's classic work (Veblen, 1931), but the activity itself was not raised to the status of a moral imperative, or necessary condition of capitalist development. In late capitalism, however, the discourse of consumption takes the central ideological position in capital accumulation and social regulation. As computer-based technology replaces the mass of physical labour once required for production, the critical requirement to continuously expand commodity consumption in order to maintain demand world-wide takes on a new urgency. At the same time, the kinds of commodities that are consumed also undergo change. At an earlier stage, mass consumption meant primarily the consumption of the material requirements of a life to be spent within a particular set of cultural/class expectations – food, housing, transportation – but under contemporary conditions consumption includes an ever-expanding demand for the commodities of cultural production. The consumption of television, film, music, pulp fiction, fashion and other cultural products expands at a rate which will require us, in a later chapter on the economy, to give special attention to this burgeoning economic sector and especially its relationship to the more traditional sectors of manufacturing.

Under the conditions of late capitalism, how is the subject position of consumer constituted? Bauman (1992: 97, 98) refers to the *weapon of seduction to the market* as a major mechanism whereby subjects are integrated into a consumer society. His argument is worth following in some detail. Seduction, together with *repression*, is seen by Bauman as replacing, under postmodern conditions, the political legitimation of 'universal' values which modernity once demanded. Instead, seduction becomes the paramount tool of domination, a possibility once the market is able to make consumers dependent on it. Market dependency, an essential characteristic of the consuming subject, requires in turn destruction of the kinds of social, psychological and technical skills which previously enabled individuals to meet a substantial number of their needs within the domestic economy and social relations of the family and on the exchanges within a local community, such as story telling and other forms of entertainment, food production, even domestic furniture making. Such skills do not sufficiently require the use of marketable commodities, so their elimination is a necessary prerequisite for the creation of new skills such as 'computer literacy' which require market-produced commodities in order to be exercised. 'Market dependency is guaranteed and self-perpetuating once men and women, now consumers, cannot proceed with the business of life without tuning themselves to the logic of the market' (p. 98). Furthermore, those values which were central to the development of modernity, namely rationality and certainty, become, in late capitalism, transmuted into valued aspects of the good consumer: 'rationality comes to mean the ability to make the right purchasing decision, while the craving for certainty is gratified by conviction that the decisions made have been, indeed, right' (p. 98).

What emerges from this analysis of the manufacture of desire is that the need for the market is one of the most crucial needs which are socially created as a component of the subjectivity of individuals in late capitalism. These socially constituted needs may be referred to as a 'thick' description of needs (Drover and Kerans, 1992) – those needs which people name in a specific cultural context and which require interpretation because such needs are particular and not self-evident. The manufactured needs of market dependency are amongst those needs which most demand perhaps a 'politics of need interpretation' (1992: 71). Such an interpretative politics includes a focus on the discursive practices whereby market dependency is reinforced through forms of cultural production – media advertising, especially as reflected in film and television, popular fashion, music – which appear to directly manufacture a desire for commodities. These 'thick' needs may be contrasted with an attempt at a 'thin' description of needs, where a few 'objective', 'universal' and abstract needs are named as a necessary basis for emancipatory critiques of those features of social formations which fail to provide the personal and social conditions which human beings need in order to live 'a fully human life as a moral agent' (Doyal and Gough, 1991). Such an attempt is, of course, situated within the notion of a continued possibility of universal values, a reconstituting of modernity in the interests of a discourse of universal human rights. We shall turn to this possibility and its problems later.

Family

Whilst it may be perceived as self-evident that growing up in a family has a powerful, if not determining, influence on the constitution of subjectivity, what requires clarification is how the dominant *discourse* on the family contributes to the construction of a subject position. Like the experience of work and of consumption, living in a family household is a material thing; it involves engaging in various social practices in a group alongside other subjects. These practices, however, may be conceptualized as the material manifestations of discourse, and it is on this basis that we examine *the family as discourse*: subjectivity may be seen as constructed, in part, by the actual material and discursive location, the family household, within which most people experience their childhoods and in turn become parents. Under the conditions of late capitalism this location provides a site for the continuing promulgation, though weakening and contested, of the *'ideology of familialism*, a celebration of the virtues of the nuclear family, the nurturing roles of women, the subordination of children and other requirements of the social order' (Leonard, 1984: 111; emphasis in original). It is also, of course, the location where the discourses of work, consumption and sexuality play a significant part in the construction of subject positions and interact with the imperatives of family discourse.

The fact that the traditional nuclear family form is a minority phenomenon in many Western countries, declining against the growth of single parented families, 'blended' families, partners without children, and same gender partners with or without children, has not yet fatally weakened the power of the 'traditional family' in dominant discourse. The strength of familialism as a discourse is evidenced especially in its role in debates about welfare: do state provided services weaken family values?

We may identify the major elements and functions of dominant familial discourse, whilst at the same time recognizing the existence of struggle and resistance to this domination in both nuclear and non-nuclear households. Most important, we might argue, is the role of dominant familial discourse in the establishment and reproduction of gender and age *hierarchies* involving continuous struggle over subordinacy and control in a situation where sexual difference and the physical and social dependency of young children on adults is used to legitimate gender oppression and parental control. But the discursive support for familial hierarchies, and the opportunities such hierarchies provide for the abuse of women and children, takes place in a wider context in which family members, especially adults and older children, not only occupy subject positions within households but, at the same time, act as the *bearers of dominant discourses*. If we consider the discourses on work and consumption, for example, we can see immediately that a range of family practices act as carriers of such discourses. These discourses aim to construct and reinforce the subject's commitment to 'productive' labour, or to domestic labour and child care, according to gender, though always under conditions of struggle and resistance, and within the differing circumstances and imperatives of specific cultures and class positions. The manufacture of desire and the inculcation of market dependency are processes which take place within the very heart of the household. Through the consumption of television programmes and advertising and, as a result, the opening up of an ever-widening range of commodities, the market enters directly into family discourses and practices. As bearers of the discourse of consumption, older family members present each other and younger members with the possibilities, or otherwise, of fulfilling the desire for commodities generated through cultural production. They provide models of behaviour considered appropriate to the 'good consumer' just as they might do for 'the hard worker', 'the caring mother' or 'the dutiful daughter'.

Sexuality

The theoretical perspective which emphasizes the social and cultural construction of subjectivity through discourses and practices, while it acknowledges the biological constitution of human beings, attempts to distinguish carefully between what is biological and might often therefore be considered 'natural', 'normal' or even universal, and that which is the clear result of the social construction of subject positions. While it has been possible to gain increasing recognition of gender as socially constructed and distinguishable from the sexual differences between women and men, when we turn to sexuality itself we face powerful dominant discourses which place great emphasis on what is 'natural'. It is in the discourses of sexuality and how they construct subjectivity that we meet in a strong form the traditional commitment of modernity to the logic of binary opposites and its connection to the belief in fixed subject identities. Dominant discourse, that which constructs sexual subjects, is founded on a categorical distinction between what are considered to be two sexualities: heterosexuality and homosexuality. Furthermore, these two sexualities are seen as constituted into two separate and fixed sexual identities: the majority as heterosexual, 'straight', and the minority as homosexual, 'lesbian, gay'. The discourse of fixed sexual identities is internalized not only by the heterosexual majority but also, to a considerable degree, by the homosexual minority. When, later in this chapter, we come to consider the possibilities of subjects being able to resist dominant discourses, to act upon their own intentions, we will see that the discursive notion of fixed identities presents us with a number of contradictions.

We can turn to Foucault's *The History of Sexuality* (1980) in order to point to some of the issues relevant to our discussion. Foucault argues that sexuality is socially constituted through discourses and practices, through a *machinery of sexuality* which acts upon sexual partners, reproducing acts of relations traditionally through a family form which has defined and controlled both the female body and infantile sexuality. This machinery of sexuality is not only, for the subject, repressive, but also generative, producing new sexualities. For example, the discourse on homosexuality is a relatively recent development. Whilst certain biological capacities are required for human sexuality – a body with genitalia, and a brain with a capacity for language – these biological capacities, Foucault maintains, do not *determine* the sexuality of human subjects. Sexual desires, in other words, are not biological things but are constituted as social practices and are therefore historically and culturally relative. Foucault writes:

> Sexuality is the name that may be given to a set of interlocking historical mechanisms; not some reality below the surface on which it is difficult to get a hold, but a great surface network on which the stimulation of bodies, the intensifications of pleasures, the incitement to discourse, the formation of sciences, the strengthening of controls and resistances are linked together in accordance with a few great strategies of knowledge and power. (1980: 105–6)

When Foucault is describing sexuality as discourse, as social practice, he is describing an understanding of sexuality which is directly opposite to the sexual essentialism of dominant discourses. Psychoanalysis, for example, was founded on a conception of the unruly power of human instincts, instincts which are biological in nature and which have to be restrained or repressed in the interests of adaptation to the demands of living in a society. Thus, sexual instincts were given theoretical priority and resistance to sexual oppression was conceived in terms of the liberation of an essential biological sex from the restraints – political, cultural, religious – imposed by the social order. Rubin (1993: 11) maintains, however, that resistance to dominant sexual discourse must be founded on a different set of assumptions: 'It is often easier to fall back on the notion of a natural libido subjected to inhumane repression than to reformulate concepts of sexual injustice within a more constructivist framework.'

It is this essentialism of the dominant discourses of sexuality which produces fixed dichotomous sexual categories and the fixed subject positions within which sexuality is generally experienced. The dominant discourse of sexuality as biology, anatomy, instinct, has had the effect of masking the heterogeneous nature of sexuality under the single notion of sex as a basic human drive which required social regulation. Foucault writes:

> A history of sexuality should not, therefore, be referred to sex as if to a higher authority. Rather, we must show how 'sex' is historically dependent on sexuality. We must not place sex on the side of reality and sexuality on the side of confused ideas and illusions. Sexuality is a real historical figure; it is what gave rise to the notion of sex . . . (1980: 157)

If the dominant discourse of sexuality constructs subject identities, what is the effect of this construction? We have already referred to the discursive imperative to assume a fixed sexual identity, that of heterosexual or homosexual. Butler (1991: 14), writing of her own position under 'the sign of lesbian', states that she 'would like to have it permanently unclear what precisely that sign signifies'. This is because assuming the identity of lesbian is risky, in that although it might be seen as a form of resistance – challenging dominant discourses on sexuality – at the same time, it can be seen as an extension of homophobic discourse, an acceptance of, or an identification with, a fixed notion of sexuality. Instead of this notion of stable sexual identities, Butler's critical Foucauldian stance leads her to embrace the idea of unstable sexual categories.

> I'm permanently troubled by identity categories, consider them to be invariable stumbling blocks, and understand them, even promote them, as sites of necessary trouble. In fact, if the category [lesbian] were to offer no trouble, it would cease to interest me: it is precisely the *pleasure* produced by the instability of those categories which sustains the various erotic practices that make me a candidate for the category to begin with. (p. 14; emphasis in original)

Identities and Bodies

This discussion about the contradictions experienced in assuming a fixed identity – both adaptation and resistance – is relevant, by extension, to all fixed identities whereby the subject assumes the mantle of membership of a stable category and is therefore identified (by the self and others) in terms of gender, ethnicity, culture, age, disability or other social classifications. The dominant discourse of sexuality is, of course, intimately implicated in discourses and practices related to the female and male gender categories, at the same time prohibiting or erasing the possibility of sexual practice by older people or those with certain disabilities. This may in part be due to the discursive connection between sexuality and women's bodies. Among the objects of cultural production is the manufacture of female desire for a more 'perfect' body, and as a result, body image dissatisfaction is widespread amongst women of all classes and cultures in Western societies. We may see female bodies as inscribed, in fact, by a range of discourses – gender, sexuality, consumption – inscriptions which provide women with desirable but unattainable and transient projects for their bodies and, therefore, for themselves as subjects.

But the state also has an interest in bodies, as Foucault shows in his studies of disciplinary regimes and systems of surveillance and normalization to be found in penal systems and in medicine (Foucault, 1973, 1975). It is concerned with the health of the bodies of its subjects, especially in the prevention of transmittable diseases such as AIDS, and in this concern the discourses of sexuality and the family play a central part. With the rise of capitalism and the need to provide a labour force of the quantity and quality necessary to ensure capital accumulation and profitability, the state turned to the issue of its role in promoting the well-being of its subjects. It began to give attention to those levels of the exploitation of the bodies of women and children in factories and mines which, through death and illness, would adversely affect the physical reproduction of labour power. Similarly, the state became concerned with infant mortality and with fertility, with useful, 'docile bodies', their reproductive capacities and their ability to engage in present or future productive labour. But how is this state objective of securing the efficient organization and performance of bodies achieved so far as the subject is concerned? With the growth of new forms of political power the repressive state apparatus of direct coercion gives way, as a central control mechanism, to ideological state apparatuses, as Althusser (1971) argues: the subject identifies with the discursive formation and experiences it as autonomy. Using as a metaphor Bentham's eighteenth century design for a prison – the Panopticon – which made prisoners subject to the continual gaze of a supervisor, Foucault comes to a conclusion similar to that of Althusser, namely that under modern forms of surveillance through dominant discourse, the subject regulates herself. Compared with the modes of control and coercion required before the Enlightenment and the rise of capitalism,

> There is no need for arms, physical violence, material constraints. Just a gaze. An inspecting gaze, or gaze which each individual under its weight will end by interiorizing to the point that he is his own overseer, each individual thus exercising this surveillance over, and against, himself. A superb formula: power exercised continuously and for what turns out to be at minimal cost. (Foucault, 1980: 155)

In writing a critical review of the use feminists have made of Foucault's work, Deveaux (1994), after quoting the above passage, explores the idea of 'self-regulating docile bodies' as an explanation of women's subordination to patriarchal control. For Deveaux (p. 227) there is a danger in such analyses of women's passive bodies as the object of cultural practices because they have the effect of 'diminishing and delimiting women's subjectivity, at times treating women as robotic receptacles of culture rather than as active agents who are both constituted by, and reflective of, their social and cultural contexts'. When we look at the question of agency and the possibilities of autonomy later in this chapter we will return to the issue of whether such theories of cultural determinism, characteristic especially of Foucault's early work, are too extreme and fatalistic in their depiction of the subject as powerless in the face of 'disciplinary techniques'. We can leave this question open at present but still recognize the usefulness of seeing state disciplinary power over the bodies of its subjects as a gaze, an inspecting, regulating gaze. The history of the welfare state in Western societies might be seen as the refining of this gaze, its technological development, its proliferation through specialization and professional expertise, its justification as necessary for the promotion of the subject's well-being. The physician's gaze at patients' bodies effected through an increasingly complex technology is concerned with their capacities for production and reproduction. The teacher's gaze is directed towards ensuring that the student is a productive worker, prepared for a world of labour, consumption, sexuality and family life. The social worker's gaze is directed at the bodies of the poor, the rejected, the objects of discrimination, aiming to bring order to disorder. The therapist's gaze is, perhaps, the most penetrating and most powerful, a gaze directed, as it were, *inside* the subject, searching for origins, for the very elements which constitute identity. For the representatives of state welfare in direct contact with the subjects for whose well-being they are concerned, observation of bodies is a crucial skill; 'the gaze' is both a literal description of social practices and a metaphor for the monitoring and surveillance of subjects undertaken by the state apparatus.

The Subject as Agent

Having identified some of the features of perspectives on the subject which focus on individual identities, needs and desires as socially constructed, we are in a position to move forward to confront the major problem which such accounts face. If individual subjects are constituted by the discursive formations which are embedded in the cultures in which they live, if they are bodies inscribed by social practices, if they, through a process of identification, experience their subordination as autonomy, then in what ways, if any, are they able to act upon the world in pursuit of their own intentions, become emancipated as subjects?

We have to acknowledge immediately that this is, perhaps, one of the most difficult philosophical and political questions to resolve in any entirely satisfactory way. Indeed, one might say that it is a question not possible to answer, because to argue for the existence of some level of individual autonomy is to invite the response that what we experience as autonomy, an experience apparently authenticated by our self-reflection, is an illusion, a self-evident perception which is no more than reflection of dominant discourse. 'Like all evident facts', Althusser (1971: 161) writes, '... "the evident fact" that you and I are [autonomous] subjects – and that this does not cause any problems – is an ideological effect, the elementary ideological effect'. If our perceptions of ourselves, as well as of our environment, are the result of the action of cultural forces upon us since birth, then we cannot attain a sufficiently critical distance to understand ourselves as subjects of dominant discourse. It is for this reason that Foucault's early work was directed towards the archaeological task of digging down into the cultural substratum of earlier centuries in order to reveal how knowledge and its uses were then constructed: it was not possible, he believed, to understand our own contemporary selves as culturally constructed.

To deny your own autonomy, deny your own critical distance from the discursive practices which constitute yourself, is a difficult position to maintain, especially for the intellectual. The philosopher, political theorist or sociologist committed to a fatalistic cultural determinism is caught in an unenviable paradox: how is such an intellectual able to understand his or her lack of autonomy sufficiently to give it voice, in spite of dominant discourses which tell us otherwise? More generally, how is radical critique made possible if the social order is so monolithic in its dominant discursive formations that dissent and resistance are rendered either impossible or at the very least, minimal and ineffective? Specifically, how do the changes in dominant discourse which Foucault reveals in his early studies of madness and punishment actually come about, except through some critique of the status quo? In his later work, Foucault in fact turned away from his earlier determinism and sought to balance the notion of power with that of resistance, a solution to the problem to which we will turn later.

One answer to the paradox of accounting for change in a determining social order is to exclude the human factor from any role in such change, to see change as a result of impersonal historical forces, the result of History. Some forms of Marxism appeared to advocate this solution to the problem of change: historical materialism was seen as a science which understood the dynamic effects of modes of economic production on social formations. In opposition to all forms of idealism, human consciousness was seen as determined by material existence. But Marx himself sought a solution by which all history was seen as 'the history of class struggle' and therefore as a result of human agency, albeit of a collective kind. In a famous passage Marx argued that humans produce change, but not under the historical and material conditions of their own choosing. Subjects enter a social world they didn't make, but they are able to act upon it provided they can understand how it is made, and in so doing, develop a revolutionary *praxis* to free themselves, at least to some degree, from the hegemony of ruling discourses. In *The German Ideology* (1970: 94–5) Marx and Engels refer to changes in consciousness as 'the alteration of men', a shift in subject identity necessary for revolutionary change: 'Both for the production on a mass scale of this

Communist consciousness, and for the success of the cause itself, the alteration of men on a mass scale is necessary . . .'.

In practice, intellectuals who otherwise pursue a determinist perspective tend either implicitly to exclude themselves from the myopia experienced by other subjects, a necessary conceit perhaps, or more generally account for this exclusion by reference to a theory, a metanarrative which enables the critic to explain the reality behind the illusion of autonomy and thereby gain autonomy. Thus Althusser (1971) argued that to understand that one was within ideology was a step towards being outside ideology in the reflexive embrace of a scientific materialism. It is not difficult to see how such a view of the possibilities of escape from a determinant world of discursive machinery and its forms of discipline might appeal not only to the zealot of a particular explanatory narrative, to the party apparatchik of the past, or the religious fundamentalist of the present, but to the intellectual as such. The élitism embedded in the exclusion of oneself or one's social stratum from the determinant effects of the social order is not pleasant to behold. Only the intellectual, it might appear, can attain the critical distance necessary to withstand the impact of cultural production, of the manufacture of desire or of the discourse of fixed identities. The rest of the population of subjects are rendered as impotent robots, passive in the face of the cultural practices inscribed upon them.

One arguably less élitist, though connected, way of approaching the problem of the possibility of autonomy within dominant discourses is sought by postmodern critics who retain a foot in the Marxist camp. Eagleton, for example, sees individuals in contemporary society as functioning simultaneously both as autonomous agents and as products of discursive power. He maintains a difficult balancing act when he writes that 'the subject of late capitalism, in other words, is neither simply the self-regulating synthetic agent posited by classical humanist ideology, nor merely a decentred network of desire, but a contradictory amalgam of the two. The constitution of such a subject at the ethical, juridical and political levels is not wholly continuous with its constitution as a consuming or "mass cultural" unit' (Eagleton, 1986: 145, quoted in McGowan, 1991: 162). This contradiction in the constitution of the subject is not a universal form of individual functioning, Eagleton maintains, but historically specific to the mass consumption society of late capitalism. The contradiction between autonomy and subjection cannot be resolved theoretically at present because it has yet to be resolved in the future through the mounting of resistance to the homogenization of dominant culture. McGowan, in his critique of Eagleton's position, remarks dryly that the 'theoretician/intellectual caught in postmodernity must wait upon history' (1991: 163). Although Eagleton cannot be accused of simple élitism, struggling as he is with the limitations on his own autonomy as literary critic because the critic can only think within the parameters of existing discourses, nevertheless, his commitment to a role in cultural and political emancipation leads him near to excluding

himself from the 'false consciousness' of the masses. McGowan's characteristically sharp comment pins down the problem precisely:

> The heroic critic who, like Moses, will lead the masses out of their captivity to the
> commodity is, Eagleton's work suggests, himself strangely immune to the
> workings of symbolic power. Eagleton's good critic is peculiarly innocent; once
> liberated into 'the counter-public sphere' that ideal criticism would create, any
> worries about criticism's institutional ties to 'ideological state apparatuses' are
> dispelled, while the alignment with some sort of 'universal interests' also seems
> assumed. Eagleton never explicitly makes these claims, of course, but I think that
> they are strongly implied. (p. 164)

Jameson, a Marxist critic who sees postmodernism as 'the cultural logic
of late capitalism', appears to take a more gloomy view of the possibility of
a relatively autonomous subject because the contemporary stage of capitalism – the global market – subjugates the individual to a mass culture in
which desire is commodified. In this situation, it becomes impossible,
Jameson (1984) argues, to maintain a critical distance. The capitalist system
is now so complex, so overwhelming in its subordination of nature and of
the individual subject to the logic of accumulation, that it becomes impossible to grasp hold of, intellectually, the totality of this world-wide system.
We can only think in fragments. Within the intestines of the monolith, the
Western subject of late capitalism is commodified and reproduced by mass
culture and loses the capacity for resistance. Whereas Eagleton searches for
the possibility of a certain social stratum – Left critics – being able as
individual subjects to maintain the critical distance necessary for resistance,
Jameson appears to consider this disengagement impossible. At the same
time, the liberating figure of the proletariat, the revolutionary working class,
is also abolished as a possibility because collective resistance inside the
monolith is no longer feasible against the penetrating force of mass
commodified culture. Perhaps, Jameson speculates, liberation will come
from the dominated populations of the Third World; in any event, only
collective action is likely to produce the transformations whereby the subject
gains or regains a degree of relative autonomy.

The answers to the question whether the subject, though socially constructed, is able to attain relative autonomy, have been so far either élitist or
gloomy. While intellectuals may be able, some suggest, to disengage
themselves from dominant discourses to sufficiently attain critical distance,
the masses are immersed in the mind-rotting sludge of commodified culture
in which they live a life of manufactured desire which they experience as
autonomy.

Such a view of the contemporary subject as entirely a *victim* has given rise
to political objections and theoretical formulations that attempt to return the
possibility of relative autonomy to the 'ordinary' individual subject, the man
or woman who is not part of an intellectual stratum.

In a review of the use which feminists have made of Foucault's work,
Deveaux (1994), as we saw earlier, begins with a critique of his early work
on 'docile bodies'. She objects to some feminists' depiction of women as

entirely moulded by patriarchal culture where their gender identity is supposedly adequately accounted for by drawing upon Foucault's docile bodies thesis. The account of the female subject as simply the passive victim of cultural power, Deveaux argues, 'blocks meaningful discussion of how women feel about their bodies, their appearance and social norms. It obscures the complex ways in which gender is constructed and the fact that differences among women – age, race, culture, sexual orientation and class – translate into myriad variations in responses to ideals of femininity and their attendant practices' (1994: 227).

In order to regain a notion of relative autonomy for the subject, it is important to shift attention from an exclusive focus on the major apparatuses of domination – the abstractions of the State, the world capitalist market, mass culture – and examine, rather, the micro-processes of power relations. Here, one is trying to render an account of the diverse everyday experiences of heterogeneous subjects as they struggle with the relationships between determining structures, that which is internalized from these structures, and what remains of their own intentions, albeit mediated in culture. One way forward may be to draw upon Foucault's later work in which the discursive determinism of the notion of passive bodies is superseded by one which opens up the possibility of resistance to dominating power. Power and resistance are, according to Foucault, implicated in each other; 'where there is power, there is resistance'. This is because power and freedom are not mutually exclusive – we are neither entirely socially constructed nor are we entirely autonomous subjects – but are in continuous interplay. Foucault writes:

> The relationship between power and freedom's refusal to submit cannot therefore be separated. The crucial problem of power is not that of voluntary servitude (how could we seek to be slaves?). At the very heart of the power relationship, and constantly provoking it, are the recalcitrance of the will and the intransigence of freedom. Rather than speaking of an essential freedom, it would be better to speak of . . . a relationship which is at the same time reciprocal incitement and struggle. (1983: 221–2)

For Foucault, then, power is not exercised without resistance, without insubordinacy and obstinacy, and we may see this resistance as an indicator that the subject is, in part, self-constituted, able under certain material and historical circumstances to act as a moral agent. We might, with Giddens (1984, 1990, 1994), go further and suggest that agents and structures are mutually constitutive, that there is, like the power/resistance relationship, a necessary interplay between them. In approaching the question of how to understand the different kinds of consciousness exhibited in studies of old people – self-confidence or fear, assertive optimism or depression – Leonard and Nichols (1994) argued for a theory of the subject in old age in which 'agency and structure are not antagonistic but are closely linked: structures are both determining and enabling. This is, after all, a necessary dialectic; subjects could not exist without the structures that provide possibilities and constraints, and structures could not exist without subjects who reproduce

and transform them' (1994: 8). This approach 'is not to be mistaken as a
reworking of naive Victorian ideas of "free will" as a way of providing
consolation in old age' (p. 7), the authors remark.

But if we are seeking for some space for the individual as agent, as
simultaneously both self-constituted and the product of discursive power,
having the capacity for resistance and dissent, then upon what basis in
consciousness is this recalcitrant subject formed? In particular, if the
analyses of the discursive powers of late capitalism, of the commodification
of desire, are to be accepted, as I believe they must, then how is resistance to
massive cultural onslaught possible? One piece of the answer might be
formed in returning to the Marxist notion of contradiction. In an earlier work
(Leonard, 1984), I sought, as part of a study of the social construction of the
individual, to identify the modes of avoidance, resistance and dissent which
subjects employ in the face of domination. Apart from drawing upon the
psychoanalytic conception of unconscious resistance, the idea of the development of individual capacities as a means of avoiding the psychological
effects of abstract labour (Sève, 1975), and the beneficial experience of
collective action, I introduced the concept of *contradictory consciousness*.

The idea of contradictory consciousness is based on the need to explain
how individuals come to resist the determinant social order, how it is that
opposition to it is mounted, individually or collectively. We can begin by
noting that late capitalism, like its earlier forms, is not a seamless, fully
integrated machine for the production of subjects, but is, in fact, continuously facing its own internal contradictions. These contradictions within
and between, for example, the economy, the state, the family and the forms
of mass cultural production – the work ethic and large-scale unemployment,
sexual diversity and familial ideology, mass consumption and environ-
mentalist critiques – imply that although we might say that subjects are
produced by the social relations characteristic of a specific social formation,
because these relations contain contradictions there is never a perfect fit
between the individual subject and the social order. Although dominant
discursive formations are, by definition, generally successful in ensuring that
subjects internalize a particular world view, nevertheless, because ultimately
such a view, reflecting the interests of international capital, for example,
contradicts many of the material interests of subordinate people, the grip
which dominant discourses have on their subjectivities is always imperfect.
This is not to say that these discursive formations are unmasked, are seen
through, that the subordinate subject manages often to gain a critical
distance from them; it is to suggest that structural contradictions and their
attendant struggles enter the consciousness of the subordinate subject as a
disturbance which points to the gap between dominant discourses and the
actual material experiences and practices of everyday life. As an example of
this gap, we might point to the acknowledgement by many women of the
contradiction between the dominant discourse of 'the good mother' and the
actually problematic experience of engaging in 'mother work'. The notion of
contradictory consciousness points to the internalization of contradictions

which the subject experiences as conflict or minimally as discomfort, the internalization of both compliance and resistance within the same process. This dialectic of the incorporation and repulsion of dominant discourses may explain how some forms of resistance may be expressed and also suggest how significant to the subject of late capitalism a reflexive ability might be.

What is problematic about the analyses of discursive power in late capitalism formulated by Eagleton and Jameson is not that they are unconvincing as narratives of commodification and mass culture, or as accounts of the limits set to the attaining of critical distance due to the linguistic parameters produced by dominant discourses; what is unconvincing is the idea of a totally monolithic social formation in which the economy, the state and ideological and discursive apparatuses all function in such a smooth integrated way that subjects incorporate and identify with the dominant social order to a degree which permits of no autonomy except an illusory one. Emphasis on the contradictions of late capitalism, on its failures effectively to control dissent, or on the possibilities and sites of resistance, is in no way intended to minimize the very great difficulties encountered in mounting resistance or in attempting to act as an agent in the face of discursive power. What this theoretical perspective permits, however, is the possibility of a continuation of the narrative of emancipation, reconstituted to fit the postmodern conditions of late capitalism, a possibility we will return to in the final chapter.

The Subject of Welfare

Our discussion of the subject has brought us to the point at which we are ready to place the analysis of social construction and relative autonomy, of power and resistance, in the context of the welfare state in late capitalism. If the welfare state is the product of modernity, of a liberal, humanistic individualism, then we can expect that the discourse of the welfare subject will embody these discursive characteristics. As we saw in the previous chapter, the subject within modernity was seen in terms of essentials, the central core of the individual after all environmental and cultural factors had been stripped away (Henriques et al., 1984). This universal, essential subject was then envisaged as rational ego, as self-determining 'economic man', a humanistic subject 'deemed to be the fundamental human atom, that is, the origin and sole active substance of sociality' (Woodiwiss, 1990: 2). Furthermore, the discourse on the centrality of the human subject, still dominant in the social sciences and in the administrative state practices with which they are implicated, leads to the assumption Woodiwiss suggests that 'the boundaries of groups and institutions are marked by lines that include some individuals and exclude others, hence, this obsession with classifying and counting individuals' (p. 3).

What kinds of lines separating subjects from each other became crucial to the development of the welfare state? Foucault shows us that the establishment of discourses based on the dividing practices emerging from the binary dichotomies of modern, Enlightenment thought had profound impact on state practices. Most convincing was Foucault's (1965) history of madness where he demonstrates how the division between reason and unreason, between sanity and madness, was a necessary precondition for the establishment of psychiatry. Only after its object had been identified – the mad effectively separated from the sane – could psychiatry as the bearer of reason enter into the domain of unreason. The welfare state in general developed historically upon such divisions, some of them to become the ground upon which whole professional disciplines formed: poverty distinguished from pauperism, health from ill health, good mothers from bad mothers, law-abiding from delinquent. The subjects of the welfare state find themselves located within these discursive constructs, their subject positions carrying with them a moral judgement and an incitement, in the present or in the future, to moral instruction by state apparatuses. But perhaps most important for the constructing of subjectivity within the area of state welfare has been the discursive division between the subject as dependent or independent.

The Dependent Subject

In the past twenty years, the rise of the New Right has made the issue of whether the welfare state induces dependency within individuals into a central political concern. We might expect that the issue of dependency on the state would, from a New Right perspective, be applied generally to dependency, for example, on public education, public transportation or public health services. In the political project of cutting state services in the interests of capital accumulation, the legitimacy of many state services has indeed been questioned, but the notion of dependency as a psychological and social malaise has been reserved primarily for dependency on state welfare payments, on social assistance. The reason for this focus is not, perhaps, difficult to understand: dependency on state financial support means the absence of dependency on the labour market, the latter being a form of dependency essential to the reproduction of capitalist social relations. 'The sovereign individuals of capitalism' sell their labour and, in return, secure a means of material existence which enables them to consume commodities and be the objects of the manufacture of desire. To be outside of one element of the market – the exchange of labour for wages – weakens the subject's allegiance to the *moral* necessity of paid work and permits escape from the social regulation involved in daily paid labour. At the same time, lack of dependency on the labour market results, in the case of those dependent on state benefits, in a reduced ability to consume. Having financial dependency on the state critically weakens the power of the discourse of work with its emphasis on family responsibility, competition and what are known by neo-liberal writers as the 'vigorous virtues' (Giddens, 1994: 39). In brief, dependency on the market is lauded while dependency on the state is criticized or even reviled.

The subject position of 'welfare dependent', then, is one in which the individual is likely to experience, alongside the benefits that result from welfare payments, subjection to a discursive formation which addresses her or him as an object of both negative ethical judgement and of moral reform. Negative ethical judgement, and its political manufacture and media dissemination, comes to legitimate increased state surveillance and, in the opportune political climate, cuts in state benefits. Moral reform is achieved when the welfare dependent becomes a dependent on the labour market, or in the case of the single parent mother, when the women becomes dependent on a wage-earning man. Many women, however, realize that dependency on the state when you are caring for several children is, however problematic, preferable to dependency on a man in the often embattled, dangerous and uncertain private domain of the family.

In order to understand more fully the discursive formation within which the subject position of 'welfare dependent' is situated, we must refer to the history of this discourse and its articulation in the ideological construct 'culture of dependency'. Although the political vanguard of the contemporary attack on welfare dependents consists primarily of neo-conservative, neo-liberal and other ideological strands of the New Right, we would be mistaken to assume that centrist and left-wing political forces were not also giving some attention to the 'problem of welfare dependency', even if reluctantly.

We can find the origins of the discourse on dependency in the apparently widespread political concern with poverty in the latter part of the nineteenth century. The concern focused not primarily on poverty as such but in part on the profligate and indiscriminate way in which bourgeois charity was dispersed amongst the teeming thousands of poor in the major industrial cities. The charity organization societies were created to combat and systemize, using 'scientific' criteria, indiscriminate charity so that the 'honest poor' might be given carefully regulated and scrutinized aid and instruction. The dishonest, degenerate poor, morally corrupted by their dependency, were characterized as 'paupers' and it was to contain, punish and reduce pauperism which both organized bourgeois charity and state intervention (such as the English Poor Law) had as their objectives. There can be little doubt that fear of civil unrest and of contamination lay at the root of political concerns about pauperism. The ground-breaking work of Stedman-Jones (1971) provides many insights into the way in which the discourse on the dependent poor haunted the bourgeoisie across the political spectrum in the later nineteenth century. Stedman-Jones's work provides the source of our analysis of the origins of the discourse on the 'underclass' and the 'culture of dependency' to be found in Dean and Taylor-Gooby (1992). Stedman-Jones maintains that the 'dangerous class' or the 'residuum' of unregenerate poor were universally seen by political leaders as likely to

contaminate the 'respectable working class'. The moral degeneracy of
pauper dependency was considered to be a social infection that the indus-
trious and responsible working class needed protection against. The aim, in
short, was to maintain existing class relations, 'the social relations of
production and reproduction and, in particular, of labour and the family'
(Dean and Taylor-Gooby, 1992: 29).

The punitive attitudes towards the 'residuum' match, a century later, the
moral condemnation contained in the contemporary discourse of the 'underclass' whereby those occupying the subject positions determined by the
receipt of state benefits for which they are judged undeserving, are conceptually herded together under the sign 'dependent'. The sign of 'dependency' is taken to mean, as we have seen, receipt of state benefits: the
opposite to dependency is not conceptualized as 'wage labour dependency'
but as 'independence', a term which signifies autonomy, industriousness and
self-reliance. The discursive constructs 'underclass' and 'culture of dependency' perform a certain function in the debate about the welfare state,
indeed they represent the latest challenge to the idea of welfare, a challenge
which originates with the 'residuum'.

The subject position of the poor dependent relying on state subsistence is
envisaged in dominant welfare discourse, especially in the United States, as
belonging to the 'culture of poverty' which reproduces itself from generation
to generation, transmitting values and corresponding practices – delinquency, immorality, violence and neglect. Membership of this conceptual
category has, therefore, real consequences for the subject identities of those
who belong to it: they are at the receiving end of continuous moral
condemnation. But the so-called intergenerational cycle of poverty which
makes the poor into some kind of 'underclass' is, Dean and Taylor-Gooby
argue, without real foundation because this 'class' comprises of a range of
different groups, all of whom experience poverty, including the long-term
unemployed, single parents and the elderly poor. They have nothing in
common, no shared culture or class consciousness, except the fact that they
receive state benefits over extended periods. The function of the discourse
on the 'underclass' is to direct attention from the structural forces which
determine the distribution of economic and social advantages – class, gender
and race relations – and how the state itself reproduces these distributive
mechanisms, by holding the poor responsible for their poverty; in other
words, by pathologizing them. The discursive formations which classify and
distribute subjects into the 'underclass' or 'the culture of dependency' are, in
essence, Dean and Taylor-Gooby observe (p. 44), 'conceptual repositories
for non-conforming social minorities' and furthermore, 'the irresistible
teleology which underpins the underclass notion is that the cause of the
underclass lies in its composition'.

If this description of the classification and distribution of troublesome
populations appears to parallel Foucault's accounts of the separation of
madness from sanity as a necessary precondition for the establishment of the
mental health profession, it is not difficult to see why. The discourse of

the residuum and the classification divisions that the discourse gave rise to might be seen as necessary to the establishment of the welfare professions, disciplines rooted in the claim that scientific judgements can be made on the basis of these classifications. Following Foucault's analysis, Dean and Taylor-Gooby (p. 45) suggest that:

> techniques once specific to penal or remedial establishments became inherent to power relations in general ... the underclass (or residuum) is indeed *par excellence* a symbolic device for the division and branding of the delinquent and the dependant and for their assignment of a very particular social location, status and identity. The underclass is a symbolic rather than an actual institution, capable of serving at a discursive level as a repository for those whom society would segregate or exclude.

But what are the consequences for the individual subject of this segregation and exclusion? Not being dependent on the labour market also reduces, because of limited resources, dependency on the market of commodity consumption. I argued earlier in this chapter that seduction to market dependency through the manufacture of desire may be seen as a primary mechanism of integration and social reproduction for the majority of populations in postmodern Western countries. Of course, market dependency is still necessary to recipients of state benefits but their severely limited purchasing power means that they cannot be fully absorbed into the manufacture of desire: for them *direct repression* is a major means of control. Segregation and exclusion into an 'underclass' are accompanied by their struggle to meet the most elementary needs, to survive materially, but it also requires subjection to state surveillance and regulation. Indeed, we might say that such repression demonstrates, both materially and ideologically, how alternatives to market dependency are profoundly subordinating. Dependency on the state, precisely because it involves the public and visible separation and supervision of a diverse population, performs the symbolic function of continuously making evident to the recipients and to the wider working class population the various social and psychological costs involved in becoming subject to a state social assistance system. In Foucault's imagery, the poor, by being subjected to the Panopticon gaze of state administrators and professionals, are thereby contained, made less likely to become what the Victorians and their present day successors most fear: a 'dangerous class'.

My analysis of welfare dependency argues that what is stigmatized and condemned by dominant discourses is dependency on the *state*, while dependency on the market is approved precisely because it is necessary to the dynamic of the capitalist system itself. But this market dependency goes by another name: it is called 'independence'. Such 'independence' is, in fact, a construct fostered by dominant discourses not only because market dependency is a necessary condition of life in late capitalism, but because it must counteract the perception that individual subjects are more convincingly seen as mutually interdependent. In developing a theory of welfare 'claimsmaking', Drover and Kerans discuss the place of self-determination in explaining the diversity of human needs and of human welfare. They are careful, however, not to confuse the notion of self-determination with the discourse of independence.

> The association of well-being and personal development with individuality, separation and autonomy may be, at best, a reading of the behavioural development of men in Western society, and at worst, a distortion of reality for everyone . . . [A] theory of [human] development based on interdependence proceeds along [a] path in which separation and individuation are replaced by relationship and differentiation. (1995: 7)

If the notion of independence is, at the very least, a Western cultural abstraction and might more strongly be seen as an ideologically induced illusion, then perhaps we must seek the possibilities of relative autonomy and critical distance not in the atomistic individual, but within the context of mutual interdependence and collectivity. We shall consider the significance of this context for the production of welfare subjects and their claims towards the end of this chapter. At this point, however, I want to return to the Foucauldian thesis on the state's 'gaze' at the bodies of its subjects in order to examine another aspect of the constitution of the individual within contemporary capitalist conditions.

The Body and the Gaze

We have already noted Foucault's argument that the modern state in the nineteenth century became increasingly concerned with the welfare of its subjects, a concern which focused upon their bodies in terms of procreation capacities, mortality, sexuality and disease. His studies of the history of madness (1965), the birth of the clinic (1973) and the development of prison systems (1975) all illustrate how this concern for welfare was manifested as an exercise of power over the body of the subject. We can say, further, that subjectivity is constituted by power, that it is in the interplay of power and resistance that subject positions are formed. The subjects of the contemporary welfare state assume, as objects of administrative and professional intervention, the subject positions of patient, client, learner, claimant or consumer and with each of these subject positions are implicated specific practices to which we will refer later. The expert and the subject meet, and in that meeting the exercise of power and the production of resistance results in continuous contestation so that the practices attendant on state intervention are always, implicitly or explicitly, covertly or overtly, sites of struggle.

The body we are giving attention to here might first be seen as a physical entity, *the anatomical body* – which is subject to surveillance and intervention. Thus, we might consider the physical body of the subject as the object of the gaze. The physician observes the body of the patient and in that observation uses the discipline of medicine and its technologies of testing and assessment in order to reveal what is wrong with it, under the body's surface. The prison guard or the practising criminologist observes the body of the prisoner and draws upon the disciplines of penology and psychology in order to maintain control and, if possible, to find out what is wrong with the prisoner in the hope of effecting rehabilitation into the world outside. This second example of how the body of the subject is observed through the gaze of the expert begins to reveal, however, a certain slippage in the meaning attached to the term 'body'. The body which is the site of the exercise of power appears to be more (or less) than the anatomical body; it is a body with a social and psychological history, a body with desires and expectations as well as a body taking up physical space. It is because people's physical bodies and their subjectivities are fused inextricably together that we might see the body as representing the subject, as a text which the professional observer reads for certain signs, signs which refer to what might be going on 'under the surface'. The conception of the body as a text might usefully refer to the term 'body without organs', a founding construct in Fox's (1994) postmodern analysis of health care and originating in the work of Deleuze and Guattari (1984). The body without organs, or BWO (Fox, 1994: 35–8), is not the anatomical body but rather a political surface upon which is inscribed the discourses produced by the gaze of the expert. This body without organs is the social body and as such is not simply passive under the gaze but is also a site of resistance.

What is it that is being resisted? Self-reflection alone might tell us that what is being resisted is the domination over our bodies (physical and social) which is legitimated by reference to professional knowledge. The gaze of power is the gaze of he or she 'who knows'. What we, the subjects, know is what 'lay persons' know, knowledge which must be discounted except when the subject's self-disclosure may be used to confirm or particularize the expert's knowledge. The professional refers to a 'discipline' for the legitimation of the power exercised over the body – to the discipline of medicine or psychology, for example – but these disciplines, paradigms which order and systematize theories, methods, techniques and results, are also disciplinary in another sense. They are the means by which the professions central to the welfare state of modernity, including physical medicine, psychiatry, nursing, social work, education, law and psychology, are able to discipline the bodies of subjects. The professions of welfare exercise *disciplinary power*.

We may take psychiatry as an example of this disciplinary power and note how the psychiatrist, aided by nurses and social workers, observes and interrogates the subject of psychiatric intervention in order to discover 'what is wrong'. The gaze and the questioning are the initial stage in the constitution of the subject position of *mental patient*. The aim of this first stage – the diagnosis – is to find a place for the subject within the existing classifications of types of mental illness which serve as a guide for the diagnostician as well as providing an indication of the treatments to which the body might be subjected. Once the classification has been made to the satisfaction of the expert in psychiatry, then the subject position of mental patient is further refined to a more specific identity, such as that of 'schizophrenic'. The classification may be resisted by the subject overtly or covertly, but what follows from the gaze, the questioning, the classification, is the disciplining of the body by treatment. The body is subject to monitoring and surveillance to ensure that medication is ingested, insights attained through individual or group therapy, or rehabilitation achieved through training and exercise. Over the subject position of mental patient a certain subtextual moral discourse is also exercised: the stigma of being 'a schizophrenic', for example, of being relegated to the population of the incurables, the 'mad', is deeply inscribed on the subject identity of the patient.

In the postmodern discourse on 'bodies without organs' as political surfaces inscribed by power, the inscription is achieved not only by the direct intervention of the external forces of the welfare state – professional and administrative practices – but also by *self-surveillance*. We have already noted Foucault's contention that self-discipline is ultimately the most efficient and cost-effective form of control; it is the control of subjects within modernity brought to the highest level of sophistication in which continuous adaptation is achieved with minimum expenditure. In 'The Subject and Power', Foucault writes:

> What is to be understood by the disciplining of societies of Europe since the eighteenth century is not, of course, that individuals that are part of them become more and more obedient, nor that they set about assembling in barracks, schools or prisons; rather that an increasingly better invigilated process of adjustment has been sought after – more and more rational and economic – between productive activities, resources of communication and the play of power relations. (1983: 219)

How is self-invigilation, as a rational and economical means by which power is inscribed on the body, actually achieved? First, we can identify a type of self-surveillance which is simply part of the regimen of treatment promulgated by the expert. Medicines must be consumed, exercise engaged in, dreams noted down, anger monitored, written work undertaken, roles practised, all of these activities undertaken outside of the direct gaze of the expert, but nevertheless guided by the expert's discipline (in both senses). But this delineation of self-surveillance as part of expert invigilation does not render an account of a more self-generated self-surveillance which the subject experiences more clearly as a form of autonomy. In this form we reflect upon and regulate our own conduct as an ethical subject – monitoring, testing and improving the self, according to self-imposed moral goals (Fox, 1994: 34; Rose, 1989: 241). Self-surveillance experienced as autonomy becomes, in effect, a moral virtue, as we can see most clearly in health promotion campaigns and programmes. Effective health care becomes increasingly a matter of self-discipline: a matter of diet, exercise, abstinence from smoking, control of alcohol intake, and engagement in safer sex practices. Similarly, discourses on 'fitness' engage the subject in a moral self-discipline which Fox (1994: 34) illustrates from a study undertaken by Glassner (1989: 187), in which the latter writes:

By becoming fit, persons are said to achieve a degree of independence from medical professionals and medical technology. They also achieve protection against temptations to alienated or marginalized forms of deviancy such as obesity, drug abuse and psychological depression, and a set of frames within which information from and about the body can be effectively reduced and catalogued.

Another form of self-surveillance, better described perhaps as *mother surveillance*, is that discipline and regulation which the discourses of motherhood expect women to exercise over their children, especially in the prevention of ill health, the promotion of healthy lifestyles, control over delinquent behaviour and, in general, socialization into good citizenship. Once again, I turn to Fox for an instructive example of what I (but not he) calls mother surveillance. He refers to Nettleton's (1991) study of the way in which mothers were recruited into the process of the monitoring and disciplining of their children's dental practices as part of a preventative health measure.

> The care of the self is elevated to a moral virtue which creates a subjectivity of motherhood in the subjects of its discourse, while formulating a liberal 'welfare mentality' of surveillance of the population of children's mouths and teeth. The mouths of the children are inscribed ... but also, too, are the bodies of the 'mothers', through the diligence with which they approach the task of sustaining oral hygiene. (Fox, 1994: 33)

We can see that 'mother surveillance' of their children also involves the self-surveillance by the women, a monitoring of their own practices of mother-work under the sign of the discourse of motherhood.

In many of the practices of self-surveillance carried out under the auspices and leadership of the professional disciplines, self-disclosure is considered a necessary precondition. Foucault (1988) traces the origins of contemporary self-disclosure back to the confessions required of the Christian church in order that the penitent could seek forgiveness of sins confessed and, in return, receive God's absolution. Confessing might be a practice undertaken through an intermediary, a priest, or directly in prayer to God: in either case, confession was a precondition of forgiveness, and as Foucault maintains, one of the main rituals for the production of truth. If confession has its origins in the religious practices of Western Christianity in the Middle Ages, it has since then become a crucial element in self-surveillance as a subordinating practice.

> The confession has spread its effects far and wide. It plays a part in law, medicine, education, family relationships and sexual relations, in ordinary, everyday matters and in the most solemn sites ... One confesses – or one is forced to confess. When it is not spontaneous or dictated by some internal imperative, it is extracted; it is driven out of the soul, or drawn out of the body. Since the Middle Ages, torture has accompanied it like a shadow and supported it when it began to falter: the dark twins. Like the most vulnerable of creatures, the bloodiest of powers have need of confession. Western man has become a confessing animal. (Foucault, 1988: 60)

How are we to understand the function and processes of confession in its contemporary form of self-disclosure within the power relations of welfare practices? The first point to note is that within the modern discourses of professional disciplines, the subject's self-disclosure is not understood as a narrative to be put beside the expert narrative of the professional. The two stories about 'what is wrong' are not given equal weight: the narrative of self-disclosure is viewed as the raw data of perceptions, desires, distortions and defence, to be fed into classificatory schemata in order that the professional expert is able to render a judgement. Self-disclosure is necessary to the professional assessment which is part of therapeutic practice, widely defined. But it also performs another function. Self-disclosure is more than simply telling a story about yourself in which you place before the gaze of the observer your version of your life, or part of it. There is a dynamic about confession which engages the subject in the attempt to constitute a new self. In religious confession, the detailing of the 'sins of the flesh', often highly charged accounts of sexual desire and forbidden sexual practices, was a necessary precondition of a commitment to be a new person, determined afresh to struggle against sin, to resist the temptations of the flesh. The parallel between this religious process of confession/renewal and contemporary self-disclosure is not difficult to see. Self-disclosure is, like religious confession, accompanied by a commitment to change oneself. The practice of self-disclosure takes place within discourses of health and well-being which require behavioural change: to be more assertive, less assertive, more reflective, less self-destructive, more nurturing, less demanding, more self-directing, less dependent. The changes that are expected to emerge from self-disclosure involve both the self-constitution of a new subjectivity and, at the same time, subjection to the discourse embodied in the gaze of the observer to whom the subject is bound in the very process of creating a new or changed identity.

Self-disclosure is a critical element in the regimes of self-care to which contemporary programmes of health promotion and personal well-being are directed. The individual subject is discursively constituted as 'independent' and therefore responsible for her or his own welfare. Such an emphasis on the care of the self resonates with widespread dissatisfactions with state forms of intervention and increasing attachment to the discourse of 'empowerment', the ideological success of the discourse of 'welfare dependency' and the apparent attractions of the illusion of independence. One consequence of the discourse of self-care and, under the sign of 'community care', that of mother surveillance and 'women's nurturing abilities', is that the state in Western countries is able to transfer to volunteers and unpaid care-givers many of the costs of direct welfare provision. The rhetoric accompanying this transfer often exploits the postmodern hostility towards the large organizational forms and professional domination of directly provided state services. Local voluntary services which purport to reflect the specific interests of diverse groups in the population and depend on informal care-giving and on self-care and self-regulation are often welcomed, or at least accepted, as a viable alternative to costly state services. The subject is reconstituted as 'an empowered participant in health promotion and community care'. Thus, the state in late capitalism is able, through the discourses and practices of self-regulation, to continue its exercise of power, but as Foucault maintained, in an increasingly economical way.

But perhaps there is a contradiction at the centre of this state strategy. The discourse of individual independence and personal autonomy becomes increasingly difficult to identify with and internalize when, under post-modern conditions of accelerating change and profound uncertainty, dependency on the state becomes a more widespread experience. In the context of unemployment and temporary, irregular and part-time employment, the labour market as another kind of dependency becomes, perhaps, more evident. At the same time, such situations of uncertainty may produce in the subject a contradictory consciousness which questions the atomistic individualism and belief in abstract family values which lie behind neo-liberal policies. The notion that dependency and, more importantly, interdependency are inherent in the constitution of the human subject may become more convincing as an alternative discourse. Although self-care may be seen as a technique of power when it is linked up with the local organization of care and the withdrawal of the state from some welfare activities, the experience of interdependence with others, of exchange relationships, becomes more sharply felt. An unintended consequence of the state's commitment to 'community care' may be, in other words, to undermine the dominant discourse on the constitution of the subject as an independent, autonomous entity and allow some strategic space for an alternative discourse on the interdependence of active human subjects.

The Interdependent Subject and the Collectivity

Interdependence is a common experience in all human societies. Becoming a human subject involves discourses and practices in which the interplay between subjects, their mutual dependence on each other – child and parent, teacher and student, sexual partners – are the means by which identities are formed. That these identities are contested, especially if they are experienced as 'fixed', is evidence supporting Foucault's 'agonistic' conception of power – a power which is the site of combat, or resistance. Between power and the intransigent subject there is a mutuality, an interdependence, and this is why Foucault's object of analysis was not 'power in itself' but power *relations* (Foucault, 1983). Power relations in Foucauldian terms, are also omnipresent, because power is exercised on the actions of others in a wide range of relationships. The phenomenon of power/resistance exists not only, for example, between psychiatrist and patient or teacher and students, but is also found in the struggles and conflicts between sexual partners. Of course, this omnipresence of power and its mutual interdependence with the obstinacy of resistance should, I believe, be seen as culturally constructed rather than as a universal characteristic of some unchanging 'human nature'.

If interdependence, whether benign or coercive, is our inescapable experience of the human subject which, in Western societies at least, has been

obscured by the ideological illusion of individual independence and autonomy, then upon what basis might the recognition of interdependence be
advanced as a political project aimed at counteracting this ideological
illusion? The substantive answer to this question will be attempted later in
Chapters 6 and 7: at this point, I want to lay some groundwork by turning
back to reconsider the notions of self-care, self-surveillance and disclosure
in the context of *collectivities* of subjects.

In Foucault, self-surveillance and confession are seen essentially as
expressions of power relations in which the subject engages in the monitoring and reconstituting of the self under the direction of another's power,
albeit contested. What cannot be satisfactorily explained in Foucault's
account is the process whereby self-disclosure and the reconstitution of
identity is undertaken within a collectivity, such as a feminist women's
group. Consciousness-raising has been the term used to describe this
collective practice of the struggle to reconstitute the self through a 'process
of transforming the hidden individual fears of people into a shared awareness of the meaning of them as social problems, the release of anger, anxiety
and the struggle of proclaiming the painful and transforming it into the
political' (Mitchell, 1975: 61). In this collective practice, where there is
recognition of mutual dependence as a condition for the functioning of the
group and where, therefore, there is not one 'detached' observer, one expert
gaze, it is in the act of self-reflection and of speaking and listening to others
that the subject constitutes him- or herself and recognizes the emergence of
a new and possibly even unstable identity. It has been through such a
process of *conscientization* that popular education movements in Latin
America have striven to connect the misery and fatalism of peasants' lives to
the imperatives of political and economic power in an oppressive social
order. The collective practice of self-disclosure and the development of
critical consciousness enable individuals who occupy subordinate subject
positions to reveal to themselves the oppressive conditions of their existence, an understanding which is systematically denied by the dominant
discursive formation which had previously constituted their subjectivities. It
is upon this basis that alternative explanations of the social order may
emerge, explanations which challenge the discourse of fragmented individualism and begin to articulate a different discourse, one which maintains
that interdependence is at the core of human subjectivity.

3
Culture

In deconstructing the universal and unitary humanist modern subject, postmodern critique offers, in its place, diverse and multiple subjectivities. These subjects, conceptualized now in their difference, are perceived as constructed by cultures marked in turn by their diversity. The modern notion of culture thus becomes problematic. Problematizing culture, critiquing essentialist ideas about culture, focusing on the diversity and subordination of the Other under the conditions of late capitalism, all contribute to debate on the production and reproduction of welfare discourses and practices.

In the previous chapters, the term 'culture' has served to express a number of different meanings revealed in the phrases 'the cultural logic of late capitalism, the commodification of culture, the production of mass culture, the politics of cultural difference, the cultural construction of subjectivity, cross-cultural communication'. As these and other similar phrases have been used in my arguments, I have allowed the context of discussion to signify to the reader one particular meaning rather than another. But now it is necessary to make the distinctions clearer in order to specify the issues which will be discussed in this chapter.

The first meaning we can identify here is that which is the object of ethnography: cultures as particular ways of life of specific societies or groups, systems of meaning which give form and order to individual existence. It is in this sense that we speak of the subject as culturally constructed. In his classic introduction to anthropology, Kluckhohn (1953) defines cultures as 'the total way of life of a people', but goes on, Geertz (1973) points out, to add ten further definitions which refer to ways of thinking, feeling and believing, learned behaviour, standard orientations, normative regulation, techniques of social adjustment, an abstraction from behaviour, and other descriptive phrases which attempt to grasp the range of meanings which anthropologists give to the concept. Unsurprisingly, the notion of culture is currently subject to debate and contestation within the wider context of the postmodern challenge to the knowledge claims of the social sciences; claims to the *truth* of descriptions and analysis of 'other' cultures are now obviously problematic. Furthermore, the challenge to the humanist notion of an essential, self-determining subject requires a definition of culture as the *determinant* of subjectivity. Here, Williams's (1981: 13) succinct definition serves his critical purpose, culture being 'the signifying system through which necessarily (though among other means) a social order is communicated, reproduced, experienced and explored'. In a similar vein, Geertz (1973: 5) refers approvingly to Max Weber's belief that 'man [*sic*] is an animal suspended in webs of significance he himself has spun'.

To speak of culture as a signifying system by which the social order is communicated and reproduced, takes us close to the *second* meaning of the term, namely that which denotes artistic and intellectual production. Here, we are referring to the social practices, products and consumption of literature, visual arts, music, theatre, film and television. One of the forms of signification by which culture (in the anthropological sense) is expressed and reproduced is that of artistic production, practices which represent, intentionally or not, a way of life, its struggles, problems, conflicts and possibilities. The issue for debate here is precisely which artistic activities can be counted as cultural products. Western modernity has rested on a definition of High Culture, a hierarchical conception in which only the products evaluated positively by élites, through purchase or patronage by private individuals or by state institutions, would count as worthy aesthetic objects. The challenge to the idea of High Culture, to prioritizing 'serious' novels, conservatory music, or 'straight' theatre, comes from the political analysis of who is excluded from these cultural discourses. Whose voices are unheard? Specifically, a limited, hierarchical definition of artistic culture has tended to exclude the work of women, of ethnic minorities, of working class populations, and of subordinate strata in general. Another closely linked challenge to the prioritizing of High Culture is the massive growth of intellectual and political interest in popular culture, more pejoratively known as mass culture. Here, emphasis is placed on mass produced cultural forms – pulp fiction, genre novels, popular cinema, fashion, high-rating television shows, videos. We have referred already to the central regulating role accorded to mass culture by critics of late capitalism such as Eagleton, Jameson and Bauman and we will return to their analyses later in this chapter. At this point we merely note the contention that artistic production, widely defined to include the mass media, is a central mechanism in the reproduction of the culture (way of life) and forms of subjectivity of late capitalism.

One of the major features of the transformations taking place in late capitalism is, we have argued, a substantial shift in the idea of welfare towards a more punitive, residual conception, although always in a context of dispute, struggle and resistance. It is a shift which has profound implications for both dominant and subordinate cultures in Western societies, including an apparent return to nineteenth century ideologies of individual self-reliance and a decline in a belief in the virtues of collectivity and solidarity. In these wider cultural changes and the self-absorbed subjectivities in which they are manifested, the transience and uncertainty characteristic of the experience of these changes are powerfully represented and reproduced symbolically in artistic production and media culture. The social needs expressed in the claims made on state welfare reflect both the impact on individual subjects of the manufacture of desire and the pejorative discourse on 'welfare dependency' and the 'culture of poverty' in which the mass media play a crucial role. The provision of welfare in the widest sense – education, health care, social security – takes place in the context of increasing cultural diversity, a consequence of the diaspora of cultures resulting from the migration of populations across the globe, especially into the cities and other large urban areas of metropolitan capitalist countries. Modernity had its own characteristic ways of responding to the cultural Other: neo-colonial, racist, culturally imperialist. The question posed by the postmodern emphasis on respecting *difference* is what sorts of needs might be considered as being *general* and what is *specific* to each difference. Even where a need is considered to be a general, 'universal' one, such as the need for ante-natal care, how might this need be differentially responded to, taking account of the specific cultural discourses and practices within which the user of ante-natal services is embedded?

A further question here is whether 'respecting cultural differences' in the provision of state services necessarily involves the suspension of cultural critique. Is 'respect' equivalent to the approval of all the cultural practices of the Other, or are we obliged to make ethical judgements on them? Does the making of such judgements mask the extent to which we are still locked into the arrogance of ethnocentric culture while claiming moral legitimacy by reference to a universalistic notion of 'human rights'? These are among a number of issues which we will need to consider if we are to understand the relationship between ways of life, artistic production, and the discourses and practices of welfare. We will examine, first, the concept of culture as a way of life, subject it to a postmodern critique and then explore the various political implications of this critique for the provision of welfare.

Deconstructing Culture

In Chapter 1, we considered the postmodern challenge to the modernist idea that theory represents the real, that the real is fixed, is knowable and that by the application of reason, the truth about the real world can be discovered with increasing accuracy. This challenge which results in a crisis of representation and of the authority of Western knowledge claims, has, as we might expect, substantial impact on cultural anthropology. Postmodern anthropologists disclaim the modernist assumptions of truth and of theory as 'representing' other cultures, in part because modern anthropology is said to invent, through its academic discourses, the phenomena – rituals, practices, structures, beliefs – which it is attempting to study. Rosenau illustrates this argument by reference to the Maori of New Zealand:

> Early anthropologists studying the origins of these people offered histories, sometimes constructed on the basis of dubious documents, that have subsequently been woven into the Maori myths so thoroughly that today the distinction between truth and invention as concerns their origins disappears altogether. (1992: 87)

In postmodern anthropology, truth about cultures can no longer be discovered or theorized about; instead, it offers narratives, a person's stories, so as to evoke for the reader a glimpse of another culture. Although cultures cannot be *represented*, their structures of signification may be interpreted through description. 'What we call our data are really our own constructions of other people's constructions of what they and their compatriots are up to' (Geertz, 1973: 9). Narratives, in other words, never 'speak for themselves' in an unmediated way but are always interpreted by the listener, the reader, the ethnographer or the state official. But a critique of the modern beliefs in truth, certainty, fixed identities and knowable social regularities not only challenges anthropology, but more importantly for the purposes of the argument, it suggests a deconstruction of the idea of culture itself. If meaning is, as with Derrida, continuously deferred, if discourse is contingent and invented rather than resting on a solid, permanent foundation, then we must ask whether the discourses within cultures and about cultural practices are similarly unstable, impermanent and continuously invented. 'Traditional culture,' Hanson (1989: 899) writes with reference to Maori culture, 'is increasingly recognized to be more an invention constructed for contemporary purposes than a stable heritage handed on from the past.' Cultures are not, a postmodern argument might go, bounded by hard, impervious shells, inside of which 'traditional culture' thrives until such time as the shell is broken and the culture destroyed by another invading culture, because all cultures are surrounded by porous, receptive membranes, continuously reinventing themselves as they adapt to changing circumstances. To understand and evaluate this kind of argument, we must place it in the context of the power relations between cultures and most specifically, within the history of colonialism.

If the idea of 'traditional culture' is a product originally of Western anthropology, a means of conceptualizing the exotic, the Other, more significantly it may be seen as a product of what Rosaldo called 'imperialist nostalgia'.

> Curiously enough, agents of colonialism – officials, constabulary officers, missionaries and other figures from whom anthropologists ritually dissociate themselves – often display nostalgia for the colonized culture as it was 'traditionally' (that is, when they first encountered it). The peculiarity of their yearning, of course, is that agents of colonialism long for those very forms of life they intentionally altered or destroyed. The relatively benign character of most nostalgia facilitates imperialist nostalgia's capacity to transform the responsible colonial agent into an innocent bystander. (1989: 69–70)

This contemporary nostalgia for 'traditional culture', for exotic 'Native' arts and rituals, has its roots in part in the modern discourse on progress. Modernity's self-appointed task of bringing 'civilization' to the Other, required a view of such other societies as static and traditional, thus highlighting and legitimating the progressive change and innovation which Western colonizing societies could confer on non-Western cultures. At the same time, the destabilizing effects of continuous change produce an ambivalence about 'progress', about the ambiguous benefits of late capitalism, and lead to a yearning for a 'simpler' past, supposedly embedded in one's own cultural history or in the 'traditional' cultures of other peoples. The role of the mass media in the production of nostalgia is a significant cultural phenomenon, often attempting to portray an 'age of innocence' in our 'own' past or that of others. Thus films and television which depict 'the long Edwardian summer' before the 1914–18 war, that valorize the traditional, precolonized cultures of North American aboriginal people, or evoke the 1950s as a period luxuriating in 'family values', all respond to this yearning. The politics of nostalgia for 'the world we have lost', for 'the way we were', are clearly complex and contradictory, especially for subordinated cultures where reference to traditional and authentic cultural identity is seen as an important weapon in the struggle for equality, justice and respect in the context of the cultural arrogance and institutional racism of dominant society. It is because claims to tradition and authenticity are often made by those representing emancipatory struggles, for example over the control, planning, adequacy and delivery of welfare services, that deconstructing the discourse on culture must be approached with considerable care.

In a study of 'cultural essentialism', upon which I have drawn in my subsequent arguments, Fleming (1995) points to abstraction as the epistemological starting point of what she refers to as culturalism, an abstraction through which culture is separated from the present and 'made into a timeless attribute of peoples that determines the character of the relationships into which they enter with others' (Dirlik, 1987: 13). The alienation of 'culture' as a pure, authentic set of practices originating in the past, although linked, as we have seen, to Western ethnographers' search for the exotic and different, plays a contemporary political role. The problem lies in the danger of 'fetishizing' the differences between minority groups and dominant society as differences of *culture* rather than as differences due primarily to the multiple oppressions of racism, gender and class. In contrast to a view of culture as homogeneous and 'authentic', postmodern critique suggests that narratives about a culture are always partial, contested and emergent. Culture as a system of signification is always in a state of flux, an activity which involves development of new practices, although the members of cultures typically experience these significations as entirely 'natural' rather than as socially constructed. As socially constructed, cultures are continuously being invented, as the title of the book by Hobsbaum and Ranger (1983), *The Invention of Tradition*, makes clear. The authors argue that countries and peoples who are striving to be self-determining often invent historical traditions that convey to themselves and to others a continuity with a long distant past.

The fact that narratives of 'the past' are often inventions should not, however, worry us. Those committed to emancipatory struggles are able to embrace politically useful myths and fictions as an inevitable part of rendering a narrative of the history of resistance to oppression. The point is to avoid the trap of so prioritizing cultural difference and uniqueness that the possibilities of establishing solidarity with other oppressed populations is thereby substantially reduced. It is an issue to which I will return later in the book.

Culture, Difference and Critique

A postmodern deconstruction of the discourses on culture as authentic and traditional opens the door to the interrogation of cultural practices. If cultures are not homogeneous social entities but rather systems of signification within which the subject is able to achieve an identity and sense of belonging, then we must acknowledge that these signification systems of discursive practices are themselves arenas of contestation and struggle. The symbolic production and reproduction of cultures does not operate as a smooth, effortless and conflict-free process because dominant meanings emerge as the result of historical processes of internal and external struggle, of power and resistance, of subordination and subjection. So the differences between categories of people that exist *within* a particular culture may be the result of inequality and exploitation, a situation in which domination masquerades under the sign of 'respected' difference. It is this understanding of cultures as sites of power and resistance which, it is argued, may enable us to critique features of cultures, our own or others', which appear to show us that the treatment of one part of a population (distinguished usually by gender, age, class, sexuality, ethnicity or some other characteristic) is based upon a morally unacceptable disadvantageous difference. A question which immediately presents itself is who exactly is the 'us' who is making the moral judgement on a cultural practice of another society or people? If the 'us' who judges the Other is of the majority white culture of Western societies, then considerable moral subtlety is required to make such a judgement if it is to be defensible.

Some Western countries, Canada most recently, have formulated policies based on a critique of the cultural practices of Third World countries which affect the status, health or well-being of women. Claims for refugee status on the basis of the experience of persecution by virtue of the claimant's female gender are now accepted in Canada. In addition, legislation now specifically forbids the cultural practice of clitoridectomy, the mutilation of a female child's clitoris, taking place in Canada. These policies claim legitimacy by reference to the universal human rights of women and a morally and politically justified critique of oppressive patriarchal practices wherever in the world they may appear. Specifically, in the case of the ban on clitoridectomy, they proclaim that there are limits to the toleration of cultural differences insofar as they are judged to affect adversely the health and welfare of Canadian residents and citizens. We must note in passing that Canada has an official policy of 'multi-culturalism'. A similar claim to universality, though reflecting a different politics, was made by the radical feminist writer Daly (1979), when she attacked a wide range of oppressive cultural practices in Europe, North America and Third World countries. These practices, as Jordan and Weedon (1995) point out, are named as those of a universal patriarchy which consequently demanded a universal resistance on behalf of all women. Daly writes specifically of the practice of clitoridectomy, and in so doing, defends herself against charges of racism:

I have chosen to name these practices for what they are: barbaric rituals/atrocities. Critics from Western countries are constantly being intimidated by accusations of 'racism' to the point of misnaming, non-naming and not seeing these sado-rituals. The accusation of 'racism' may come from ignorance, but they serve only the interests of males, not of women. This kind of accusation and intimidation constitutes an astounding and damaging reversal, for it is clearly in the interest of black women that feminists of all races should speak out. (Daly, 1979: 154, quoted in Jordan and Weedon, 1995: 545–6)

Here Daly claims to be able to speak out in the interests of the female 'Other' by reference to a notion of universal oppression, universal struggle and ultimately universal rights. The fact that postmodernism is incredulous when faced with such universalizing metanarratives demonstrates, perhaps, the problematic consequences of cultural relativism. Not only have feminists claimed political legitimacy by reference to a concept of universal human rights, but so also have socialists, anti-racists and others engaged in emancipatory battles. But if all discourses – including those on cultural difference and human rights – are culturally constructed, how can a claim to speak within a universalizing discourse be justified? It is a problem which emerges continually in the policies and practices of state welfare under conditions of cultural diversity. For example, family practices reflecting diverse cultural mores often entail a set of gender and age hierarchies which result in the punishment of children, social restrictions on women and girls, and lack of communication on family problems, which are perceived as problematic, or more simply, *wrong* by health, education and social service professionals employed by institutions reflecting the majority white culture. Would we be forced, in these circumstances, to return to the solace of transcendental universals in order, like Daly, to justify our judgements and likewise defend ourselves against the charge of racism, or more mildly, cultural insensitivity and ethnocentrism? In the face of the normative paralysis which may face postmodernist academics deprived, through extreme cultural relativism, of any universal standards of moral behaviour, we can turn to the notion of 'interactive universalism' (Fleming, 1995: 51). An interactive theory of culture, Benhabib (1992) maintains, accepts that there are many different modes of being human, but distinguishes between the *fact* that such differences actually exist from an evaluation of these differences. We are not required, in other words, to endorse as morally and politically valid all the cultural differences which human societies produce.

If we set some limits to cultural relativism in the policies and practices of state welfare, limits required by moral judgements that recognize but do not necessarily endorse all cultural variations, are we thereby forever constrained by our own ethnocentrism? Perhaps we can never know or understand a culture other than our own because understanding a culture is a lived experience of 'effortlessly belonging'?

In a paper on 'The Uses of Diversity', Geertz (1986) expresses concern about a resurgence of ethnocentrism amongst Western liberal intellectuals who are reacting to the collapse of moral self-confidence in the face of the crisis of the knowledge and certainty which underpinned modernity. Confronted by a cultural relativism which allows for no universalizing moral judgements, and exemplified in 'the desperate tolerance of UNESCO cosmopolitanism', there is a reaction in the direction of 'anti-anti-ethnocentrism'. This reaction, which argues for the moral validity and superiority of Western liberal values and its democratic institutions both for the culturally specific societies of the West and for any other societies that might wish to follow a similar path, provokes Geertz's response:

> Any moral philosophy so afraid of becoming entangled in witless relativism or transcendental dogmatism that it can think of nothing better to do with other ways of going at life than make them look worse than our own is destined merely toward making the world safe for condescension. (1986: 111)

In a reply to this attack, Rorty (1986) defends the anti-anti-ethnocentric position against the 'wet liberals' who, in a time when our truths are being endlessly deconstructed, fear that they are being irrational and probably viciously ethnocentric whenever they cannot appeal to *neutral criteria*. The point, of course, is that with the collapse of the certainties of the philosophy of the Enlightenment, neutral criteria for moral judgements are no longer available to us. Rorty is surely right to insist that we avoid 'witless relativism' by maintaining our capacity to make moral and political judgements in a context of knowing more about cultural diversity. The problem with Rorty's position is that he sees the *existing* institutions of dominant white Western countries as the tested vehicle for the tolerance of plurality and diversity, coupled with a belief in the vehicle's superiority over all others. For him, postmodernists have no need for transcendental ethical guarantees because history has proved that the Western bourgeois liberal way is simply *the best*. The smug arrogance of Rorty's defence undermines what is otherwise a compelling argument: in the absence of universalistic values, we are still obliged to act as moral agents, to develop, where we can, critical practices which may question and disrupt established discourses, including the discourses which celebrate cultural diversity.

But celebrating cultural differences and being prepared to critique them *almost at the same time* is exceptionally difficult, which is why the critical judgement element is often avoided. This is because the power of critique is usually unevenly distributed amongst cultures: the critiques established by dominant cultures carry with them the power of actual intervention within minority and subordinated cultures. The history of cultural critiques emerging from dominant majorities invariably reflects the universalizing arrogance of colonizing modernity. For example, current Canadian governments, as we have seen, justify state intervention by reference to the incompatibility of certain cultural assumptions and practices with the universal welfare rights of women and children. Until recently, however, Canadian governments directly intervened in the family structures of Aboriginal communities, removing children and placing them in distant residential schools with the intention of culturally assimilating them into dominant white culture. The disastrous cultural, social and personal losses suffered by Aboriginal people as a result of this now discredited and abandoned social policy of ethnic genocide, which was experienced alongside other oppressive welfare policies and practices, must lead us to wonder how moral judgements can ever be validly made 'in the interests' of the Other.

The alternative to modernity's universalizing cultural domination which carried within it the philosophical seeds of racist ideology, is to pursue a notion of *cultural pluralism*. This is cultural pluralism as a form of *politics* rather than as a type of play where emphasis on cultural diversity takes the often transient and nostalgic form of festivals and similar events to celebrate the surface textures of difference. In contrast, a postmodern politics of cultural pluralism targets racism and begins with an acknowledgement of the monolith within which diversity attempts to survive. Before we can examine the possibilities of cultural resistance, of differences accommodating themselves to each other, we must confront, as we have attempted in the previous two chapters, the massive forces of homogenization released by the productive technologies of late capitalism. Before we venture into any optimism about the possibility of pluralism, we must face the monolith head on. Describing postmodernism's sometimes paralysing perspective, McGowan writes:

> Late capitalism constitutes the totalized terrain of contemporary life; the name of the despised totality is different in [different] postmodern texts, but the spectre of patriarchy, or Western metaphysics, or disciplinary power, or some other dominant social form haunts the postmodern imagination. This fear of a distopic totality is sometimes even embraced, partly in the heroic spirit characteristic of Nietzsche's and Freud's determination to face the worst truths without flinching, partly as a weapon to use against the hopes for autonomy found in modernist and avant-garde [artistic] work, partly as a refutation of the liberal insistence that capitalism is not only compatible with, but actually productive of, pluralism. (1991: 16)

If McGowan is right in his interpretation of postmodern theorization about the saturating economic, political and cultural practices of late capitalism, and if we are not to fall into despair in the face of them, then we must equally not expect cultural pluralism to be achieved within existing social structures. But can we instead see cultural pluralism as a *process* of struggle for change, as a first prefigurative step in establishing the kind of politics which might mobilize populations in the direction of cross-cultural solidarity? Later we will consider this cultural politics in detail, but for now we need to ask how different cultures, especially those living beside each other, can communicate between communities views about the moral implications of some cultural divergencies without arrogance, as an alternative to resorting to 'witless relativism'.

Cross-cultural Communication and Racism

We have to admit immediately that the prospects for effective and peaceful communication of similarities and differences between cultural communities, ethnic enclaves or populations with different 'racial' origins, look, as we approach the end of the century, decidedly bleak. Whether we take the example of ethnic violence in Bosnia, racism in North American cities, xenophobia in Europe or armed conflict in Somalia, the story looks the same, even though each has its own specific origins and features: different cultural, ethnic or racial communities frequently experience great difficulty in coexistence. One reason for this state of affairs may be found in the imbalance of power and therefore of resources between different cultural and ethnic groups. 'There are virtually no societies in the world where different ethnic groups are wholly equal to one another. Ethnic division, and some other kinds of differences, such as religious ones, are normally also differences of stratification' (Giddens, 1994: 243).

In situations of marked inequality between dominant and subordinate cultures, one form of politics presents itself as a strong option: segregation as a necessary element in emancipation and symbolic community identity (Klaff, 1980). Here, the demand emerges, for example, for culturally and racially specific services – education, health, child care, social services – because dominant services are perceived as incapable of overcoming the institutional racism that lies at their core. The discourse on segregated services emphasizes *not* communication between cultures as part of a process of social integration, but equality and rights. In essence, the struggle is seen as needing to take place not primarily over the issue of 'cultural sensitivity' or the celebration of difference, but over the power of neo-colonialism and racism. So far as the allocation of state finances is concerned, this focus has significant implications, as Daenzer suggests:

> The redistribution of resources to maintain or strengthen cultural identity has the effect of shadow boxing with a fierce giant, and thus sustaining inequality. Further, resources which are applied to celebrating differences are utilized at the expense of money and political initiatives which should be directed at structural reforms which alter substantively the traditional distribution of power. (1994: 36)

Placing racism, equality rights and the distribution of power as central elements in a political agenda directed to the discourses and practices of welfare, is, I believe, essential even if we were to reject at this juncture the necessity for a wide range of alternative, segregated services. For most populations of ethnic, cultural and racial minorities, maintaining difference while participating in mainstream services relevant to their needs is still a central political objective. They want or accept the maintenance of difference but without the hierarchy which is rooted in colonialism, as the postmodernist African American, Cornel West, maintains in his vision of a possible pluralism despite racial differences:

I cannot envision, within the logics of the modern West with its legacy of slavery, societies that do not have racial differences. Consequently, our social emancipatory visions and projects have to acknowledge the irreducibility of racial differences but fight against a translation of such differences into hierarchical social relations and symbolic orders. So we will not get beyond the play of differences and binary oppositions. The question is how we arrest the political and economic translation of such differences into hierarchical relations. (1988: 30; McGowan, 1991: 17)

If we acknowledge the centrality of the pervasive problem of the racism rooted in modernity's slavery, colonialism and exploitation, we are still left with the different but related issue of cross-cultural communication, moral judgements and the problem of a relativity (which attempts, presumably, to be intelligent rather than witless). Devising principles of communication that do not replicate the hierarchy of modernity's discourse directed to the Other becomes essential if we are to attempt to develop cross-cultural criteria for truth, validity and morally acceptable behaviour. To develop cross-cultural criteria based not on transcendental universals but on consensus, demands that we develop cross-cultural tools of adjudication through dialogue and, Nicholson (1992) maintains, thereby establish a means of explicating the criteria for truth *embedded in social practices*. 'To speak of criteria of truth immanent to the practices which generate them is to focus on the situational elements which make proof possible or not. This approach suggests an alternative mode for interpreting relativism: relativism becomes the situation which results when communication breaks down. Thus relativism becomes a life possibility rather than a theoretical position' (Nicholson, 1992: 86). Communication may break down as a result of differences of cultural traditions, rules, notions about the legitimacy of claims, but such difficulties may be eventualities which can be avoided, depending on the rules agreed in any dialogical engagement, Nicholson suggests. Cross-cultural communication is a politics of conversation, and its discursive rules would include a number of injunctions: *first*, to attempt to avoid implicit ethnocentrism in adjudicating truth claims, and so preventing a deterioration of dialogue into authoritarian assertion; *secondly*, to give no priority to culturally specific forms of communication, encouraging every form to be expressed, such as speech, music, dance, ritual; *thirdly*, to acknowledge that Western political and moral values are not grounded outside of human history but are socially and historically constructed and cannot be taken as self-evident universal preconditions of communication; they may, however, be *argued* for and compared to alternatives.

Typically, a postmodern approach to cross-cultural communication offers *no guarantees*; once the universalistic assumptions of modernity are abandoned, we must accept that we live under conditions of uncertainty. If we conclude that communication between cultures – on political structures, on human rights, or on the appropriate policies and practices of state welfare – must be conducted as dialogue rather than hierarchically directed assertions of the Truth, then continuous exploration, experimentation, historical contextualization and the understanding of power relations becomes the way to proceed. This, often slow, process depends above all on the ability of participants in cultural dialogue to listen to the many narratives that may be offered as relevant to a particular issue for decision, especially those previously hidden, excluded and subordinated. If, as I have already suggested, cross-cultural communication based upon pluralistic equality cannot be achieved within the social structures of late capitalism, then we must see the process of cultural dialogue as a prefigurative social practice through which we might move towards greater solidarity amongst presently subordinated populations in the interest of their/our greater short-term wellbeing and their/our longer-term emancipation.

Is this tentative, provisional, open-ended approach to cross-cultural communication sufficient to fuel a cultural politics based on demands for equality and justice? Perhaps we need to acknowledge here a problem identified by both feminists and black political critics (hooks, 1991): postmodernism, by its incredulity towards metanarratives, disempowers subordinate populations at the very point at which they need to demand emancipation in the name of universalistic notions of justice and equality. Living with uncertainty may be the ethically appropriate contemporary condition for those whose previous (and still surviving) tradition was based on the certainty of an ideologically legitimated oppression. We might say that the dominant strata of white Western cultures, including professionals, administrators and intellectuals, have surrendered, through their domination of the Other, the right to any certainty. But what of those whose very social and material conditions of life have historically been subject to the endless experience of debilitating and destructive uncertainty: those living in poverty, under the imprint of institutional racism, or suffering the abuse of male violence? These are amongst the very populations to which an emancipatory form of welfare should be directed, and they surely require an increase in certainty rather than uncertainty.

It is with these problems in mind that we turn to two examples of attempts to reintroduce limited notions of universality which we might be able to appropriate for the purposes of a cultural politics of welfare. The first argues for the need to distinguish between ideological discourse and 'undistorted communication', and the second proposes a theory of human need which could be considered 'transcultural'. We can see at once that both of these ideas will constitute a challenge to the postmodern scepticism embedded in the notion of discourse determinism and the cultural construction of needs.

Let us turn, then, to Habermas (1981, 1987) and his theory of communicative action in order to evaluate what it might render for us. Habermas recognizes that the traditional role of the philosophies of modernity is at an end and that now philosophy, including Marxism, must 'take a linguistic turn'. In particular, the Marxist paradigm of production must be replaced or supplemented by a paradigm of communication: under the contemporary conditions of late capitalism, critical focus, Habermas argues, must be given to the production and reproduction of ideology, a focus obviously similar to postmodern critics' concern with the problem of dominant cultural discourses and the manufacture of desire. But Habermas's approach to the problem is different, as Rorty points out in his discussion of the debate between Habermas and Lyotard. Habermas's response to Lyotard's deconstructive unmasking of 'grand theories' is that:

> Unmasking only makes sense if we preserve at least one standard for [the] explanation of the corruption of *all* reasonable standards. If we have no such standard, one which escapes a 'totalizing self-referential critique', then distinctions between naked and masked, or between theory and ideology, lose their force. (Rorty, 1985: 161; emphasis in original)

What standard has Habermas in mind? What might enable us to distinguish between an emancipatory theory and dominant, masked ideology or more specifically between a critical cultural politics and a state's policy of 'celebrating multi-culturalism'? Habermas is attempting to reclaim Marxism in the form of a critical social theory appropriate to late capitalist conditions. In a commentary on Habermas, Roderick (1986: 157–8) remarks that 'critical social theory traditionally has been concerned with identifying and dissolving relations of power masked by ideology, so as to make it possible for human beings to make their own history with "will and consciousness" and achieve social arrangements based, not on unreflected and hidden power, but on open and equal discussion and real consensus.' How can such critical discussion (including cross-cultural dialogue) be achieved *outside* of the distortions, manipulations and oppressions of ideology? Can emancipatory struggle have a normative foundation so that the critique of ideology is not itself simply *another* ideology? Postmodernists would answer no. Habermas maintains, on the contrary, that as ideology is 'systematically distorted communication', it should be possible to develop 'undistorted communication' as the normative basis for emancipatory struggles, a form of communication which is based upon a competency which humans have to reach agreement as a result of their universal 'nationality'. We can see clearly that Habermas is demonstrating here his commitment to attempting to salvage what remains of the Enlightenment project of modernity in the context of the postmodern critique of transcendental guarantees. How successful is he, and more important perhaps, is his theory useful to us? Let us examine his argument step-by-step (Roderick, 1986: 158).

Ability to communicate in 'ordinary language' presupposes that it is possible for at least two subjects to reach an understanding/agreement in which it is further possible to distinguish between a genuine and a deceptive understanding/agreement. An agreement is genuine insofar as it is based on 'the force of the better argument', a condition which can only exist if communication is 'free of hidden constraints', involving a symmetrical distribution of chances amongst participants to speak ('select and employ speech acts'). All of these preconditions are met in an 'ideal speech situation' characterized by the ideas of freedom, truth and justice. Such a situation contains the 'practical hypothesis' that such situations of free and undistorted communication *ought* to be brought about. This normative *ought* provides, finally, the basis of a critique of ideology as systematically distorted communication.

This summary cannot, of course, do justice to the complexity, subtlety and detail of Habermas's argument. None the less, it is possible to see at once some of the problems and questions which such an argument raises and have been variously debated amongst his critics and supporters. Among the questions and comments we might make would be included the theoretical priority given to understanding and agreement, when it is possible (especially between different cultures) for subjects to arrive at misunderstanding and disagreement. The 'force of the better argument' prevailing sounds uncomfortably like a ratification of the kind of theoretical discussion engaged in by white male intellectuals intent on excluding from the discourse reference to personal narrative, expressive communication, and the experiences of subordinated subjects and their forms of language. The normative *ought* at the conclusion of this argument seems to contain more weight ('freedom, truth and justice') than can be carried by the formal requirements of undistorted communication. Why not express the values of freedom, truth and justice in terms of potential emancipatory discourse arrived at through, for example, a commitment to solidarity, culture-bound and historically contingent, but no less valid as a human project in the world? The answer, of course, is that Habermas is still seeking a universal normative justification for an emancipatory project, a justification which appears to hover uncertainly between the dogmas of transcendental guarantees and the tentativeness which accompanies cultural relativism.

Habermas's work cannot, I believe, help us to gain normative or empirical certainty when we engage in a cultural politics of struggle for more equality and justice in the field of welfare and elsewhere. However, examining the preconditions and assumptions of cross-cultural communication, attempting to unmask hidden ideology, seeking symmetrical participation and building a critique of dominant structures and ideologies in the name of shared values are critical activities for which we would find support in Habermas's enormous output of work.

What kinds of certainty do we need to have none the less in order to engage in a cross-cultural politics of emancipation? If the reintroduction of a universalizing rationality into the competence required for unmasking cross-cultural communication, as Habermas proposes, is unsatisfactory, to where can we turn? I referred in the first chapter to Doyal and Gough's (1991) work in developing a theory of human need and we return to it as our second example of the reintroduction of notions of universality upon which we may be able to draw.

Doyal and Gough maintain that it is possible and desirable to identify human needs which are universal and transcultural: all human beings have basic needs for physical health and autonomy which are the preconditions for human action and interaction. For those who are critical of existing social systems and the distribution of welfare within them, the authors argue (1991: 2), the following beliefs seem imperative:

1 Humans can be *seriously harmed* by alterable social circumstances, which can give rise to *profound* suffering.
2 Social *justice* exists in inverse proportion to serious harm and suffering.
3 When social change designed to minimize serious harm is accomplished in a sustained way, then social *progress* can be said to have occurred.
4 When the minimization of serious harm is not achieved, then the resulting social circumstances are in conflict with the objective interests of those harmed.

The italics in this quotation are in the original, and signal the intention to do combat on behalf of the concepts of justice, progress and objectivity embedded in the critical discourses of modernity. Acknowledging that universalistic discourses on 'common human needs' have been used to legitimate many different kinds of domination and abuse in socialist as well as capitalist countries, Doyal and Gough maintain that a notion of objective human needs is still *morally* necessary. 'It is the belief that the satisfaction of basic needs has normative *precedence* over the satisfaction of wants that generates condemnation when such needs are not satisfied' (p. 3). Unless we have some notion of objective human need as the basis of political struggle for justice and equality in the distribution of welfare, Doyal and Gough argue, then we are left with the neo-conservative belief that individuals know what is best for themselves and that the mechanism of the market best meets these subjective preferences. When physical health and autonomy, however, are identified as needs basic to the conditions necessary to enable humans to act as moral agents, the authors argue that we are provided with a sound basis for social policy, for moral judgements on our own and other societies, and presumably, for the consensus necessary for cross-cultural communication. It should be added that Doyal and Gough do not deny the existence of culturally specific needs, nor that basic needs will be manifested in different cultural forms, but maintain through many indicators and measures the irreducible objectivity and universality of basic human need across cultures, traditions, peoples.

How are we to respond to Doyal and Gough's strong and compelling presentation, supported by an array of cross-nation data? The answer lies, I believe, in our response to their suggestion that 'without the concept of objective human need and the moral work of which it alone seems capable [a] move from "is" to "ought" would not be possible' (p. 3). But is it true that the idea of basic human needs requires the transcendental guarantee of objectivity in order to enable it to perform the function of generating the moral and political outrage necessary to an emancipatory struggle? We have already discussed the argument that the rejection of universality does not require us to abandon moral judgements. We can go further, in fact, and agree that the concept of basic human needs is an invaluable moral premise upon which to build solidarity amongst culturally different populations: justice and equality in meeting basic human needs are the moral norms which should surely guide such solidarity. But does the moral discourse of emancipation and human well-being require a certainty beyond that of a culturally generated set of values? I suggest that it does not. The fact that a belief in basic human needs is culturally constructed as a discourse and practice which intervenes in a world of injustice and suffering, does not lessen its impact. Our most cherished beliefs remain open to debate and dispute, but we can hold on to those that appear to survive cross-cultural interrogation, and as moral actors we remain obliged to follow the good as we see it. 'Not enough!' say the modernists, 'We need objective guarantees for our certainty.' For me, acting on the belief that all human beings have some needs in common is moral certainty enough. I believe, further, that exploring basic human needs cross-culturally through dialogue, provides a basis of sufficient certainty both to establish a critique of existing welfare and begin a process of struggle for the transformation of welfare.

Culture, Art, Politics

In looking at culture as a way of life, a system of significations which provide for individuals and communities a sense of place and often a location of conflict, emphasis has been given to the issue of *difference* as between subjectivities, identities and perceptions of the world and of 'the good'. This postmodern emphasis has been put in contrast with modernity's commitment to order, control, unity, *homogenization* and the binary dichotomies which have prioritized Us over Other, Male over Female, White over Black, Heterosexual over Homosexual. These hierarchical divisions are, postmodernist critics argue, embedded in the form of modernity represented by capitalism both as a mode of production and as a totalizing cultural system. Furthermore, these dichotomies of inclusion and exclusion perform the function of distracting attention from the existence of ambivalence and contradiction which continuously, in the name of the suppression of difference and multiplicity, express themselves in the lives of individual subjects and of communities. 'The repression of contradiction both within the self and within the social body favours integrity and unanimity over difference and multiplicity' (McGowan, 1991: 19).

How is this control, through the attempted maintenance of hierarchical conceptual divisions and the repression of contradiction, actually carried out under capitalism? Part of the answer lies in the economic institutions and practices of capitalist production itself – capital accumulation, work discipline, division of labour and other means of economic reproduction. Capitalism as an historically distinctive economic mode of production was the appropriate target of critique in the nineteenth century and the first half of the twentieth. But by the end of this century, a period of the late capitalism of global markets, control becomes vested increasingly in the mass media, in the 'culture industry', in advertising and more generally in the manufacture of desire. Here, media and artistic production can be seen to represent the culture of late capitalism understood as a way of life. The two meanings of the term 'culture' become increasingly fused together in the following discussion, which is focused on the role of the media and artistic production in both representing and challenging contemporary capitalist culture. The maintenance of control and the repression of difference, are, I suggest, the central issues to be faced in any attempt to reconstruct welfare as an emancipatory project.

The postmodern argument that late capitalism has developed new and more saturating forms of control turns on the analysis of the ways in which the *images* to which the subject is exposed perform the function of controlling, manipulating and shaping anticipation and desire. Control of the workplace, although still necessary, fades into relative insignificance compared with control over the consumption of commodities, involving as it does the consumption of social identities and the presentation of the self in everyday life. The mass-produced cultural images of late capitalism, women's bodies as signifiers for example, exist separately from and often prior to the signified objects which will be produced, consumed and desired. It is partly because of the dominating power of mass cultural images that the postmodern stand against the application of hierarchical categories in the arts gains a political edge. The traditional exclusion of mass culture from High Art no longer holds water, not only on the philosophical ground which rejects universality and élitism in aesthetics, but on the more immediately political ground that mass culture is a central control mechanism and therefore demands critical attention and contest. In Western culture High Art was 'pure', white and predominantly male; it was homogeneous and part of a 'great tradition' – the literary canon, the masterworks of the great painters, the unbroken line of eighteenth and nineteenth century classical composers of genius – all reflected the universalizing discourse on what was aesthetically superior and, by implication or directly, what was inferior. Postmodern cultural critics do not deny the significance of the work produced and subsequently categorized as High Art, nor the contradictions which it contained, but they emphasize its exclusions, its denial of difference, and specifically, its rejection of the images, sounds and narratives produced by women, minorities and the working class. But more importantly in the context of a discussion of mass culture, postmodern critics see the production of images within the popular media as a crucial battleground of contemporary politics.

The media is an appropriate focus for our attention because it is the major vehicle for the production and distribution of culture, and it is, *par excellence*, in Baudrillard's (1983) words, a culture of excess. Here, the separation of the signifier from the signified is most evident, in that the image itself is more powerful than the explicit message. In television, in particular, the viewer is exposed to a presentation of innumerable, fleeting images in which the distinction between 'reality' and simulacra becomes increasingly blurred, and the 'real world' becomes a staged spectacle, its 'events' determined as newsworthy by their suitability for continuous

reproduction on the television screen. Furthermore, the screening of television's *own* events can be seen as taking precedence over other elements of
the 'real world', for media events, as Dayan and Katz (1987) suggest, 'are
not descriptive of the state of affairs, but symbolically instrumental in
bringing that state of affairs about'. The terms in which the cultural
meanings of the transient images of television are described reflect in many
postmodern critics a moral outrage and political revulsion which is captured
in Bauman's approving commentary on Baudrillard:

> For Baudrillard, society itself is now made to the measure of television: history is
> nothing but spectacle. History is a debauchery of signs, an endless play of
> simulation, drama and grotesque political minuet, and immoral promiscuity of all
> forms. One can no longer speak of the distortion of reality: there is nothing left to
> measure the image against. This is a soft, disjointed, insubstantial reality, of
> which Sartre's Roquentin said that 'everything is born without reasons, prolongs
> itself out of weakness, and dies by chance'. (Bauman, 1992: 33)

If television is the epitome of the culture of postmodernity – a culture
without universals, hierarchies, élite aesthetic judgements – we can see how
its apparent superficiality and *meaninglessness* can lead to a pessimistic and
despairing response of the kind to be found in the work of Jameson and
Eagleton already referred to. Against the guarded Victorian optimism of
Matthew Arnold's view that culture (as High Art) was a means of defence
against the anarchy which modernity produces, we might easily see the
culture of late capitalism as being anarchy itself. However, this culture is not
meaningless, even though it is packed with a multitude of transient images;
its meaning, after all, must be found in its role in the production and
reproduction of discourses and practices salient to the construction of
contemporary subjectivities. I want to look at this role of production and
reproduction in terms of the contradictions to which it gives rise and the
spaces that are available for resistance, especially in the context of discourses on welfare.

Modernity, as we have seen, gave authority to the creator of High Culture,
the writer, the artist, the composer. *Modernism*, the artistic movement which
emerges from the late nineteenth century, gave to the artist the supreme and
unchallengeable role not any longer as practitioner of a classical 'great
tradition' but as the innovator of a revolutionary cultural practice, member
of the avant-garde. In this latter role, the author of an artistic product
remains the authority, just as she or he did in the earlier history of Western
artistic production: from Bach to Debussy, from Shakespeare to Pushkin,
from Michelangelo to Van Gogh, all exercising upon us their authorship, all
giving rise to attempts to understand what *they* mean, how *their* message to
us, as recipients, can be understood. Contemporary postmodern criticism
rejects this authority of the author, whether part of a classical tradition or
part of an avant-garde. Umberto Eco, commenting on his novel *The Name of
the Rose*, writes that 'the author should die once he has finished writing, so
as not to trouble the path of the text' (1983: 7). Although I shall use the
terms *author* and *text*, these terms should be taken to signify not only writer

and what she or he writes, but more generally, to distinguish between the cultural producer and the product – artist and painting, composer and score, director and film or television programme.

Within the cultural traditions of modernity, the sovereignty of the author of a text was clear: the author was the privileged interpreter of the text and so the reader, viewer or listener (or critic) had a fairly straightforward task, namely to understand and appreciate the intentions of the author. Within these assumptions the text was relatively unproblematic in itself once the meaning of it to the author was established. How might this authorial meaning be assured? The answer lay, in part, in understanding how the author's subjectivity was socially constructed and, for the critic, this required an investigation of the economic, political and cultural forces to which the author was exposed and how these forces intermeshed with a specific biography of family influences, education, sexual identity and other elements of personal history. Interest in the authority of the author remains strong, as we can see by the popularity of biographies, especially those of cultural figures. Perhaps they will help us to understand the establishment Christianity of T.S. Eliot's poetry or the meaning of madness in the latter years of Van Gogh's life. In any case, the final arbiter of meaning is the author, who assumes the right to lead, to educate, to enlighten and to critique. This leadership role may, with admittedly an expansion of meaning, be seen as that assumed by radical documentary film-makers or by cultural establishments such as the BBC.

The greater the status accorded the author of a text, the lower, we might assume, will be the status of the reader. Moreover, the professional critic of literature, film or other cultural products will be seen as entirely parasitic on the work of 'the master'. But what if there is no fixed meaning in a text? If Derrida's contention that meanings are indeterminate, that language permits of multiple understandings of a text, is convincing, then we can see why some postmodern critics celebrate 'the death of the author'. If there are no universal aesthetic or literary standards, if the priority given to authorial meaning is another manifestation of the knowledge/power relationship of Western culture, then not only is the author's meaning simply one amongst many, but the reader's (and even the critic's) interpretation of a text is equally valid, and some would argue even more significant. Within a less radical understanding of authorship, which I share, the author has not died or been killed because to claim the right to state a meaning is oppressive, but survives in a diminished form. The author's interpretation of the text is one amongst many and can claim no priority over that of the reader.

It is when we turn to the reader or the viewer that we can begin to glimpse the contradictions which lie in the realm of cultural production. Whatever authorial intentions might be, whatever meanings are *intended*, the readers of the text supply their own meanings. These meanings are, of course, limited by the linguistic parameters which define a discourse (including its rules of inclusion and exclusion) but none the less a variety of potential meanings is available. This is especially so under contemporary cultural conditions which conflate 'reality' with simulacrum, 'original' with copy. The notion of authorship is itself in decline in the context of various forms of media production. 'There is no author in the modern sense for commercial ads, television scripts, radio dialogue or the speeches delivered by political candidates or elected presidents. In each case the author (ghost speech writer, advertising agency, screenwriter or producer) may generate a text, but she or he has little control over it and is seldom given much recognition' (Rosenau, 1992: 29). In television, elements of external control over an 'author's work' begin with audience ratings, then the reactions of sponsors and advertisers and finally the decisions of senior network managers. What is the response of the viewer to the author(ity) of television programmes? It is here that we meet a contradiction.

If the author, along with other forms of authority, is diminished, challenged, unmasked by cultural critics, what of the rest of the population of Western countries? How do they view cultural authority insofar as such authority continues to exist? This is not a question that can be answered with any degree of certainty or precision, but we might speculate, alongside Smart (1993) and Giddens (1994), about the choices that appear to be available under present conditions. We have already identified the most significant experiential quality attached to living under postmodern conditions – everlasting uncertainty. For many, probably most, people this is a material uncertainty generated by economic recession, unemployment, short-term contract employment and cuts in state provisions resulting in higher costs required to maintain previously established lifestyles but with fewer resources. Economic and social uncertainty go alongside each other, especially affecting the attachment previously felt towards various forms of solidarity – political parties, labour unions and other experiences of collective belonging. If postmodern consciousness reflects the failure of modernity, in its different forms, to deliver on its promises of continuous *progress* in economic and social life, and if, instead, we experience an apparent collapse in the moral authority which was once the prerogative of ruling classes and states, then a crisis appears before the individual subject. One resolution lies in a flight to new (or old) certainties, to various kinds of *fundamentalism* – religious, political, cultural. In a world of global communication and the exposing of cultural diversity, traditions and the authority upon which they were based are increasingly subject to challenge and debate, 'discursively forced into the open' in Giddens's words:

> The defence of tradition only tends to take on the shrill tone it assumes today in the context of detraditionalization, globalization and diasporic cultural interchanges . . . Defending tradition in the traditional way means asserting its ritual truth in circumstances in which it is beleaguered. (1994: 85)

If fundamentalism is the chosen path of escape from postmodern conditions of uncertainty and the collapse of universalizing authority, then attempts must be made by fundamentalists to establish *alternative* cultural texts: books, music and, most importantly, television programmes. The rapid growth of religious and political fundamentalism in America, especially the 'born again' Christianity associated with the radical Right, has resulted in a massive increase in television channels and programmes that address the subject with the reassuring authority of certainty and moral conviction. The strong association between these traditionalist discourses and practices and attacks on the fragile remnants of the welfare state make fundamentalist cultural products especially significant to us.

The other path open to the subject bombarded by the conflicting, transient and morally diverse messages and images of mass culture is to attempt to live with the confusion and uncertainty. To maintain an ability to tolerate this bombardment requires a certain *distancing*, a form of consumption which involves a Brechtian alienation effect. It is not possible to consistently *believe* in the signifying images, nor in the commodities (material and cultural) with which they are tenuously connected. Although there is a monolithic quality to the mass of cultural products, their commodification and their role in the manufacture of desire, they also meet a certain *resistance*. It is a resistance which may emerge from satiation after the consumption of an overabundance of mass cultural products, but it is mostly to do, I suspect, with the contradictory consciousness experienced by the consumer, reader, viewer of the text. Insofar as the dominant discourses of mass culture contradict the interests of those in subordinate subject positions, then a disturbance enters consciousness which signals the existence of a gap between the definitions and meanings promoted by mass culture and the actual material experiences of everyday life. A process of attraction/ repulsion may characterize much of the consumption of mass culture and accounts for the scepticism and even cynicism with which it is greeted.

To point to the possibilities of resistance to the predominantly legitimating messages of late capitalist cultural production, is not intended to underestimate their enormous power. We must acknowledge that they are primarily directed, as we have seen, to the manufacture of desire and dependency on the market. It is because of this predominant economic/ political discursive intention that network television, especially in North America, has so little to say directly to those who do not qualify as appropriate targets for the manufacture of desire – those living on welfare payments and low incomes generally. It has much to say to them, however, about those who occupy the more favoured position of not being immersed in poverty. Such favoured others – the individuals and families featured in television sitcoms – represent predominantly a combination of material security and 'family values' which can be taken, indirectly, as a commentary on the excluded 'other', those 'dependent on welfare'. Even here, however, the popularity of the American television show *Roseanne*, a comedy which provides often ironic observations on material necessity, class and family values, indicates, perhaps, that the possibilities of resistance may exist even in sitcom land. Outside of sitcom land, documentary television and film-makers are still able to occupy a space within which to expose the degradation which dependency on the market as well as on the state may require people to submit to – an exposure which always carries with it a possibility of resistance.

Alongside resistance, which is the contradiction presented by exclusion and difference when confronted with power, I want to turn to another contradiction situated within cultural commodities themselves, which we can name *reversal*. Here, the dominant meanings we can assume were intended by the author(ity) are open to new interpretations in which subordinate voices can reverse the intended meaning. This postmodern perception of the fragile and unstable nature of meaning deserves sustained attention here in order to open up the possibilities of resistance even in the most hostile cultural terrain.

To illustrate this process of reversal we can take as the subject matter the filmic depiction of female violence in a context of the violence against women which dominates the social reality within which women live their lives. How can we explain the fact that as violence against women escalates – battering, rape and murder – films about murderous, sadistic *women* emerge as a significant cultural trend in Hollywood productions of the 1990s? Beginning with the film *Fatal Attraction* and continuing with such films as *Basic Instinct, The Hand That Rocks the Cradle* and *Body of Evidence*, there has developed a genre which depicts frenzied attacks on average American males and their yuppie families by strong, powerful, sexually dominant and psychotic female killers. Describing a climactic scene in the 1992 film *Basic Instinct*, Pidduck (1995) writes: 'Wielding a K-mart ice pick with wild abandon at the apex of sexual ecstasy, Sharon Stone gave ''castration complex'' a new lease on life in 1990s post-feminist North America.' Much feminist critique has been directed at this and similar films, often populated by lesbian and bisexual female murderers, pointing to their role in a wider homophobic and anti-feminist backlash. What is also depicted in many of these films about female killers are the inadequacies, stupidities, sexual vulnerability and lack of authority of the male leading figures, reflecting, it is suggested, the masculine anxiety and paranoia embedded in the political and social backlash against women who dare to usurp male power and authority. At the same time, of course, reversing the male and female roles of perpetrator and victim of sexual violence and murder operates as a denial, in fantasy, of the brutal abuses to which women are exposed.

There is, however, another step in the discussion of role reversal which leads to different ground. In exploring the ambiguities of role reversal to be found even in a film as demonstrably anti-feminist, if not anti-women, as *Basic Instinct*, Pidduck quotes approvingly from Halberstram's study of film violence and resistance:

> Role reversal never simply replicates the terms of an equation. The depiction of women committing acts of violence against men does not simply use 'male' tactics of aggression for other ends; in fact, female violence transforms the symbolic function of the feminine within popular narratives and it simultaneously

challenges the hegemonic insistence upon the linking of might and right under the sign of masculinity. (Halberstram, 1993: 191)

What is being argued here is that role reversal allows for unpredictable fantasy to emerge for female film audiences, because instead of the reality of victimization there takes place an imagined contact or even identification with turning the tables, acting out a pent-up rage and revenge. Pidduck suggests that indulging in the fantasy of role reversal, imagined quite differently from the meanings intended in the 'authorized' text of the film, offers 'moments of wicked escape, even the critical distance and humorous release of irony'. In her concluding comment on *Basic Instinct* and the character played by Sharon Stone, Pidduck continues:

> Catherine Trammell, with all her impossible verve and absolute sexual confidence, her ability to turn a room full of seasoned cops into so much quivering jelly, even her tight grip on the proverbial castrating ice pick, provides moments of supreme pleasure for the feminist spectator – a fleeting but potentially empowering fantasy of transcendence to bolster up our imaginary reserve. (1995: 72)

What this example of the potential for resistance to dominant cultural discourses suggests is the possibility provided for alternative meanings to be generated by the reader of a text. Distancing irony, scepticism and reversal are all means by which we might repulse, neutralize or even turn to our oppositional advantage, texts which maintain us in subordinate positions as subjects. This possibility emerges, especially in the process of reversal, from the decline of authorial power, a decline which, by extension, threatens all experts and leads to a questioning of administrative and professional power, as we shall see in the next chapter.

It would be misleading, however, to draw this chapter to a close on an over-optimistic note of resistance, if only because at present resistance to dominant cultural discourses, although it exists in the attempts made to challenge the representations of gender, class and race, remains relatively subdued. We shall explore this collective cultural resistance in the later chapter on politics: here we have focused on readers' resistance, as individual subjects, to discursive cultural formations that confront them. When we consider the representations of the welfare state in the media, it is clear that there exists a hierarchy of moral evaluation of the users of state services: education and health care consumers generally ranking highly as predominantly deserving, and the recipients of social security welfare payments occupying the lowest position of esteem as generally undeserving. The fact that health and education services are universal and have been used by middle class consumers, whereas income support has been used predominantly by the working class poor, is obviously critical to the moral evaluations communicated by the media. Older people are usually excluded from the opprobrium meted out to social security recipients and most negative attention is given to single mother families. This negative moral evaluation is further refined through the filter of institutional racism, the stereotypical recipient of welfare payments often being characterized as a 'single black mother'.

How do welfare recipients respond to the overwhelmingly negative media portrayal of their situation, a representation rendered, as we have seen, in terms of dependency, inadequacy and moral failure? Here we might hope to find signs of resistance to the dominant discourses of mass culture, evidence of a contradictory consciousness which shows awareness of the conflict between dominant ideologies of welfare and the actual material experience of living on welfare. Alternatively, we might expect that the process whereby subjects identify with and internalize dominant discourses plays itself out in this instance, and that welfare recipients, ground down under the weight of daily struggle for a minimal material existence, show few signs of resistance.

Some insight into the complexity of the reactions of welfare recipients to dominant media representation of them is to be found in the study by Dean and Taylor-Gooby (1992), to which we referred in the last chapter. Their findings can be used to illustrate an aspect of contradictory consciousness in which conflicting discursive statements can be made without any obvious sign of discomfort. Writing of their interviews with British social security claimants of working age, Dean and Taylor-Gooby (1992: 136) found that these welfare recipients subscribed, on the whole, to mainstream cultural values about people who live on welfare, and 'often manifested the sort of popular prejudices and punitive attitudes to be found throughout the population, and were predominantly uncomfortable with if not actually resentful of their status as social security claimants'. That welfare recipients are unhappy with their dependency on state income support and the stigma which it attracts is unsurprising; that they are able to hold contradictory views about social security and its users is more significant at this point. Dean and Taylor-Gooby suggest that the holding of these contradictory views illustrates 'the ways in which everyday "common sense" is capable of accommodating conflicts between general ideas and situated judgements; between popular and personal perceptions' (p. 137). After providing an illustration of one man's contradictory beliefs, the authors continue:

> Other respondents, having said that their own benefit levels ought to be increased and described how difficult it was for them to find or to undertake paid employment, nonetheless went on to say that it would be a 'good thing' if the social security system was phased out so as to force people to fend for themselves or to find work. (p. 137)

The 'common sense' beliefs embedded in daily life are the product of culture in the two senses in which we have used the term. 'Common sense' is constituted of the unreflected meanings, definitions and assumptions which come with effortlessly belonging to a culture. In late capitalism, the media and popular mass culture generally play a significant, and some would say dominant, role in the sedimentations of taken-for-granted views about the world as part of the construction of subjectivity. It is because the media plays such a significant part in the representation of welfare discourses and practices that we need to give popular culture increased attention. In particular, we must focus on those media (such as newspapers) where corporate control ensures the continuous reproduction of anti-welfare messages. It is clear that these messages have their impact not only on wider populations, but specifically on the recipients of welfare themselves. Under postmodern conditions of crisis and change, however, where the challenge to long-held beliefs emerges as a state of chronic uncertainty, then 'common sense' itself begins to change. For those who do not take the path to fundamentalism, a new common sense, more reflective, may be born. It would be a common sense which included not only a capacity for adaptation to difference, but also a scepticism which lay at the root of the ability to resist the various kinds of cultural domination which we have discussed in this chapter.

4

Organization

Whenever the welfare state is attacked for generating or denigrating cultures, from the Right, for example, for encouraging a culture of dependency, or from the Left for failing to respond to cultural diversity, dispute invariably includes attention to problems of organization. In these political debates the terms *organization* and *organize* appear to be used in two, related senses. The first term is a noun, referring to welfare organizations, the agencies that plan and deliver services and are typically referred to, especially if they are government-controlled bodies, as bureaucracies. The second is a verb, and refers to a process whereby the state organizes both its resources (including what have become known as 'human resources') and its recipient populations in an attempt to fulfil its policies and, perhaps, prevent *disorganization*. One of the things the state does in organizing its activities is to create organizations, so in practice, the noun and the verb are closely linked together. Distinguishing the uses of the terms serves the purpose of emphasizing a dual focus for this chapter, one which considers both structures and processes.

The organization of state welfare as structure and process has, as we have seen, been subjected to Foucault's powerful critique. It is a critique that we can use as a starting point before moving on to consider, in the light of postmodern perspectives, the characteristics of modern organizations and especially the Weberian discourse on bureaucracy. As the organization of the emancipatory enterprise of modernity was predicated on the development of *expertise*, the issue of the role of experts in welfare organization will be the focus of a following section of our discussion. Next, we will examine the possibilities of developing distinctly *postmodern* organization, taking account of the argument surrounding such an enterprise, and finally we will address the issue of whether organizations can be *alternatives* to bureaucracy.

In his studies of the modern state's organization of populations, Foucault (1965, 1973, 1975) characterizes such organization as the exercise of 'disciplinary power' involving the development of apparatuses of control and surveillance. The nineteenth century sees the emergence of new systems whereby various populations were classified, separated and subjected to discipline and, where necessary, punishment. These new regimes of control were developed within a welfare discourse which was committed to both the prevention and the eradication of many of the social and physical ills which were the direct consequences of early capitalist industrial growth – rural depopulation and the development of large cities breeding squalor, crime and disease. The early state responses to these problems of social disorder settled the paradigm of expert intervention which would later characterize the surveillance functions of the state welfare apparatus. Early on, Foucault writes, 'people appear who make it their business to involve themselves in other people's lives, health, nutrition, housing; then out of this confused set of functions there emerge certain personages, institutions, forms of knowledge, public hygiene inspectors, social workers, psychologists' (1980: 2).

The new techniques of surveillance and control which emerge in the modern state's concern with the health, education and welfare of, especially, the working class, are not neutral mechanisms, nor only simple tools of repression. The new structures, organizing principles and forms of expertise represented a moral commitment to *improvement*, to social progress. The reformers and philanthropists who established new organizational forms of welfare – charity organization society leaders, public health and sanitation officers, public housing advocates – were intent on strengthening the collective moral backbone of the poor *in their own interests*, and, of course, the interests of a bourgeoisie threatened by physical and social contamination from the dangerous classes. In Althusser's (1971) terminology, the Repressive State Apparatus could, with the emergence of sophisticated forms of care, control, surveillance and therapy, take a back seat within the state's panoply of powers, and the Ideological State Apparatus, which reflected this new sophistication, could come to the fore.

Modern Organization

The complex organizational forms and processes which developed under capitalism from the nineteenth century onwards and also under state socialism in the twentieth century, may be seen as epitomizing the whole project of modernity. Order, rather than disorder and confusion, progress and innovation rather than stagnation under the sign of tradition, and, above all, rationality rather than irrationality and superstition, these were the hallmarks of the discourse of modernity which was sedimented into concrete forms of practice: modern bureaucracy. No discussion of bureaucracy and the contradictions to which it gives rise can fail to acknowledge the foundation work undertaken by Max Weber. Although he identified the discipline of the bureaucratic form as a scientific advance, a central vehicle for modern progress, Weber was pessimistic about where this 'advance' would lead. On the one side, *rationalization* was a superior form: universal standards, division of labour, rule-governed behaviour and clear hierarchical structure, all brought the order which modernity needed to supersede the *anciens régimes* of pre-modern, feudal times. On the other side, Weber saw bureaucracy as an 'iron cage', objectifying the subjects of its discipline and order and turning into a monster, as Clegg notes:

> While it was indeed technically superior to other forms of administration it was still a human product. Yet, in his view, its humanity was fatefully compromised

by its technical functioning. Although the efficient bureaucracy was a human creation it was one over which control was rapidly lost. Rational calculation has become a monstrous machine. All significations of humanity, those 'relations which are important to us due to their connections to our values' (Weber, 1947: 76) are devoured and denatured by the triumph of human ingenuity. (1990: 30)

In the name of reason and progress, modernity, we might say, imposes upon the world, through economic exploitation and colonialism, a universal organizational form which permits of no distraction from its objectives, and annihilates all claims to difference. Weber, like Freud, was a cultural pessimist who saw the monolithic growth of bureaucracy as both necessary and unavoidable, even though it subordinated subjects to its impersonal rules. Freud similarly saw 'Civilization' as based upon instinctual repression, the price to be paid, however reluctantly, for modern progress. Both reflected that romantic ambivalence towards capitalist industrialization and its consequences which was present throughout Western cultural discourses in the nineteenth century. Later, some of that ambivalence was lost, especially by socialist commentators who saw bureaucracy as so specific to capitalism that they failed to fully acknowledge its triumph as the state form which subordinated its subjects in the name of socialist progress. At the other end of the political spectrum, the protagonists of efficiency and effectiveness showed none of Weber's ambivalence and are still prepared to exclude the possibility of a variety of organizational forms in the interests of a universalizing discourse on organization (Clegg, 1990; Donaldson, 1985). Weber's ambivalence and scepticism return today to lend apparent support to the critique of modern organization by Foucault and those postmodernists who have followed his path, an ambivalence which has been replaced by outright hostility, as we shall see later.

The strength of modern bureaucracy, Weber argues, lies in its essential characteristic and principle: its authority is based upon rationality rather than upon tradition. Rational authority is a legal form of domination, 'a system of rules that is applied judicially and administratively in accordance with ascertainable principles . . . valid for all members of the corporate group' (Weber, 1947: 341). Although this is a hierarchical organizational form, it is a hierarchy based upon abstract *principles* (demonstrated expertise, etc.) which govern the relationships which exist in the organization – personal relationships themselves are subject to the rationalization process whereby all members are equal under the rules governing their specific behaviour. The emphasis on rule-governed behaviour contrasts with pre-modern or traditional organizational forms where personal characteristics and cultural mores are seen as the determinants of behaviour. The emphasis on the authority of rules, on a concept of universal law, was crucial to the legitimization of a strong nation state and a triumphant colonialism. Modern bureaucracy was the organizational form which enabled the capital city to ensure that its state authority was effective throughout the land, even being felt in the most distant and peripheral regions. Imperial authority, likewise, sought to replicate its bureaucratic form as a central feature of its self-appointed civilizing mission, bringing, eventually, models of education, health care and legal justice to societies considered 'primitive' or less 'advanced' than the colonizing West, but potentially able to be 'improved' in the name of Progress. Whether we are speaking of the elimination of local forms of community-based education as part of the establishment of compulsory state education for the English working class, or the removal and re-education of Aboriginal children in Canada, or the domination of Western medicine in colonial countries, the vehicle for scientific and cultural progress was modern bureaucracy. Kinship, friendship, personal influence, were, like corruption and nepotism, to have no place in the enlightened bureaucracy: only impersonal rules were to govern the structures and processes through which modernity was to bring its enlightenment to the world.

We can appreciate, within its historical context, how convincing was the case for modern bureaucracy. It was a structure based upon equality before the law, upon the notions of order, reason and justice. The power of the ideology embedded in bureaucracy, the source of its legitimization, is to be found in the fact that members of bureaucracies more or less willingly submit to their subordination. Why do they do this? The answer lies in the belief, amongst organization members, that orders must be obeyed because they are based on *rules* rather than personal power or desire. The rules are objective and can therefore claim obedience because the person exercising authority is also obeying the rules, and that 'obedience is due not to the person who holds authority but to the impersonal order which has granted the person this position' (Clegg, 1990: 35). But convincing as the case for bureaucratic authority might be, legitimating as it does a particular form of 'progress' and a corresponding form of organizational subjectivity, Weber, among many others, pointed to the negative consequences of the rule of rationality:

> The outcome of this process of rationalization, Weber suggests, is the production of a new type of person shaped by the dictates of modern bureaucracy. Such a person, whether in business, government or education, is one with a restricted, delimited type of personality. Characteristically, this is the specialist, the technical expert who increasingly, Weber feels, will come to replace the ideal of the cultivated person of past civilizations. (Clegg, 1990: 36)

This is a romantic pessimism which looks at the past, at pre-modern societies, and at early capitalism as the ground in which a subjectivity not yet dominated by material goods could grow. Early capitalism, Weber maintained, was infused with the spirit of Calvinism, a religious asceticism, but 'victorious capitalism, since it rests on mechanical foundations, needs its support no longer . . . and the idea of duty in one's calling prowls about in our lives like the ghost of dead religious beliefs' (Weber, 1930: 182).

If bureaucracy, for Weber, is the objectifying tendency of modernity made manifest in organization, it is also a technically superior means by which capitalism can achieve its triumphal progress. This technical superiority makes it unstoppable, for it is able to serve a range of different moral and political ends, including those of totalitarianism, in both its Stalinist and

Nazi forms (Bauman, 1992). Such a view of bureaucracy as fully implicated in structures of domination is the perspective which emerges with post-modern critique. No longer are we speaking of ambivalence or even of the contradiction of modernity, of the interaction between emancipation and domination demonstrated in its essential organization form. Now we speak of disciplinary power, surveillance and control as the central imperatives of bureaucracy, especially in its role of implementing the policies of the state.

We will see that postmodern critique focuses primarily upon the micro-processes of knowledge, power and resistance in organization. It is a critique which should be first contextualized by reference to feminist and Marxist commentary on the place of bureaucracy in the wider social order. Whereas postmodernism gives attention to organization as a manifestation of the emancipatory/oppressive project of modernity, feminism and Marxism focus on the particular forms of modernity represented by the terms patriarchy and capitalist domination. For feminists, modern organization reflects and pro-motes the dominant masculine culture centred on power, hierarchy, objectifi-cation and, in general, instrumental values. Bureaucracies reflect the gender relations that exist in the wider patriarchal society so that, typically, men tend to occupy the most senior positions in organizational hierarchies and women the most junior. Where, in a minority of cases, women achieve senior positions, they experience overwhelming pressure to conform to the 'masculine virtues' involved in the competitive struggle for power, but their assertive behaviour is generally reinterpreted as a form of pathology: aggression, manipulation, 'bitchiness'. Marxists see bureaucratic organ-ization as reflecting class relations. The class structure is replicated in organizational forms that typically place representatives or supporters of the bourgeoisie in dominant positions which reflect the interests of capital and the bourgeois state apparatus. State welfare organizations are concerned to reproduce existing class relations. In the field of childcare, for example, the relations which may exist between three women – a single poor mother whose child is experiencing material and social deprivation, a working class foster mother, and a middle class social worker – can be characterized as a *class relation* as well as an example of gender subordination to patriarchal power. We will need to keep these gender and class perspectives in mind as we read the postmodern critique, and return to them in later chapters where I develop an argument about the politics of new forms of welfare.

Postmodern Critique of Bureaucracy

Weber's conceptualizations of bureaucracy as 'the iron cage' – necessary but deadly – have undergone substantial revision by modern organization theorists. Research on organizations has shown that bureaucracies are less than perfect representations of Weber's bureaucratic principles, that ration-ality is less secure, uncertainty and pluralism of intentions more prevalent than Weber's pessimism envisaged. Modern organization theory, however, has usually remained fixated on 'efficiency' and has been unable to treat seriously the possibilities of a wide variety of organizational forms (Clegg, 1990: 41–74). But if we stand outside of mainstream organization theory and adopt a postmodern reading, then the discovery that organizations are unable to practise exclusively within a discourse of reason becomes, perhaps, more understandable.

> Genealogically, the development of organization theory since Weber can be seen as a fragmenting and discontinuous movement to explain and rationalize organization. Morgan (1986) documents these discontinuous perspectives as a series of 'images of organization': machine, organism, brain, culture, psychic prison, and so on. We might perhaps see in these contested perspectives, rhetorics for comprehending and controlling something which, according to modernism, should be rational, but continually fails to achieve this objective. (Fox, 1994: 47)

If we followed Foucault's (1965) lead in his investigations of how the discourse of madness was based upon the splitting of reason from unreason, we might see the discourse of organization as preconditioned by a need to separate order from disorder, predictability from unpredictability, organiz- ation, in fact, from disorganization. The pervasive fear of disorder, unpre- dictability and disorganization can be glimpsed most clearly, perhaps, in the organization of the users of state welfare services. These users – patients, clients, recipients, students – characteristically queue up, or wait in line as parts of an assembly process designed to counteract any tendencies to radical individuation or the expression of organizationally 'problematic' intentions. Human actors must be depersonalized to the extent that they are appro- priately prepared for the relatively passive status of someone being acted upon 'in their own interests', by those inside the organization. The categor- ization, classification and recording on computer of users of services is designed, one might argue, to hold at bay a continuous tendency towards disorganization. The range of techniques available to ensure the effective organization of users – measurement of cost-effectiveness, time manage- ment, speeding up or increased 'client through-put' – are predominantly designed to fit the user into the preferred structures of the expert, and do so in the name of efficiency and rationality and as a defence against the ever- present fear of their opposites.

Later in this chapter I shall discuss the possibility of a 'postmodern organizational form', but here, in order to continue to focus on the perceived threat of disorganization, I shall attempt to elaborate a postmodern critique of modern organization. 'All organizations are mythologies constituted discursively to serve particular interests of power, and contested by other interests of power' writes Fox (1994: 49) in his strongly Foucauldian approach to the organization of health and health care. It is a perspective which, with its focus on discursive inscription, usefully identifies the many 'dangers' which organization is intended to guard against. I build upon it substantially in what follows (1994: 49–50).

Unpacking the notion of *organization as discourse* leads us back to the distinction we made earlier between structure and process. If we focus on organization as process, then we can see it as reactive or remedial, existing only in relation to disorganization. Organization is thus the means by which unity and continuity are privileged and conflict and discontinuity denied or bracketed off as 'problematic'. Once again, we see that modernity's 'principle of non-contradiction' (McGowan, 1991) enables such denial to take place, rather than contradiction being incorporated into a conception of organization as process. A central contradiction in the process of organization is that of the struggle between organization and its subject. If we see organization as a discursive text which inscribes humans, constituting their subject positions as welfare recipients, hospital patients, or therapy clients, then we can acknowledge that such inscription always takes place in a context of resistance, subversion and contestation. A text, as we have argued in the previous chapter, is always open to reinterpretation because the authority of the author (of organization as text) is continuously disputed as new meanings emerge.

If, as I have argued, organization *constitutes* subject positions, though always in a context of resistance, then we must put aside the humanist pessimism which underpinned Weber's picture of modern organization as deforming and alienating a prior, essential human subject through imprisonment in the 'iron cage' of bureaucracy. Subjects are constructed, we are arguing, in discourses, including discourses of organization, in a way that enables a subject's actions to become meaningful, a mode of objectification that provides the ground where power/resistance takes a beneficial turn and can lead to the empowerment of the subject. Such empowerment is not easily gained, of course, because resistance to the power of dominant discourse is everywhere opposed, and we can assume that organization will attempt to suppress and eliminate resistance through the various techniques of subjectification (diagnosis, classification, exclusive professional language, surveillance, medication, therapy) which organization has available. But power/resistance may be seen as operating not only at a conscious level. In previous work (Leonard, 1984) I have drawn on psychoanalytic theory to provide an understanding of both the internalization of ideology and unconscious resistance, as similarly Althusser (1971) draws on Lacau in order to explain the subject's identification with dominant discourses. In attempting to understand more fully the relationship between modern organization and the subject, it would be necessary, using a similar set of ideas, to explore the interaction of desire, identification, internalization and resistance at the level of the unconscious.

> Organization may act in the unconscious. (This point is so contradictory to the modernist conception of organization as a rational activity to achieve some end or other, that unconscious organization is likely to be redefined as something else: paranoia, oedipal fixation, sociopathic activity.) The unconscious is seen as a barrier to effective organization (Morgan, 1986: 229). This is one of the ways the unconscious is suppressed in modernism, and in modernist social science. (Fox, 1994: 50)

Fox is here pointing to the subversive character of the psychoanalytic concept of the unconscious, its challenge to reason as well as its role in the understanding of repression. To be an effective member of a modern welfare organization demands subordination to its universal rules, and in so doing requires the repression of desire and the renunciation of forms of subjective identification which might interfere with the necessary objectifications of the clients of the organization. In studies of the phenomenon of 'burnout' in human service organizations, we find attention given primarily to the professional employee as 'problematic' and the low morale, depression and declining productivity which are said to result from such problems. Little attention is given, on the other hand, to the role played by the organization of human service clients, as objects of discipline and surveillance, on the psychic resilience of the employee in the face of a continuous bombardment of evidence of racism, poverty, sexism and other forms of subordination (David, 1995). The 'burnout' of professional employees indicates a contradiction within modern organization which cannot be acknowledged; unconscious resistance, like conscious subversion, must be seen as pathology and as therefore suitable for exclusion and, if possible, treatment. The form of rationality – order, categorization, control – which is central to the discourse of modern organization cannot be seriously questioned. To question this rationality in the name of desire and of difference is to be subjected to the stigma of pathology – the principle of non-contradiction remains intact. 'Resistance to discourse is that which organization seeks to suppress through its technologies of subjectification. Desire (that which is beyond discourse), where it challenges discourses of power, is the most feared and oppressively dealt with object of organizational discourse' (Fox, 1994: 50).

Although it is necessary to acknowledge that the professional employees of health and social services are subject to the instrumental rationality of organization, our major focus here is on the objectification practices to which the patient, client or user of services is required to submit. In this situation, and it is the most common one, it is the professional who exercises power and the service user who submits to, but also resists this power. Resistance to the power of organization as manifested in professional practices is generated by the contradictions which are experienced by the service user when faced with the *care and control* strategies of the professional. The challenge to professional power may be understood, in part, as an example of the 'death of the author', where the readers/users insert alternative readings into the discursive professional text which is presented to them. If meaning is always unstable, always deferred, then professional author(ity) is always insecure, always requiring reassertion in the face of conflicting meanings, demanding organization in response to the continuous threat of disorganization.

If the maintenance of the power of organization always takes place in a context of resistance and struggle, how does this power/resistance process manifest itself? The power of organization can be seen most clearly in the documentation of the service user. In social service agencies, for example, the client's *file* is the material expression of, typically, a process of referral, interviewing, telephone calls, a range of narratives, including those of the client, an assessment of the nature of the problem(s) presented, an interpretation of issues which may be perceived as lying 'below the surface', and finally an intervention plan and an ongoing record and evaluation of the intervention itself. The clients' issues may be voiced in the file but are frequently reinterpreted into problems or needs which conform to the legal, clinical or organizational categories already laid down before the file was opened. The power of the file is, in effect, the power of the discursive formation to which the client is subordinated. The clients wait in line and are acted upon 'in their own interests' by the bureaucracy which organizes them, their multifarious wants reduced to the manageable entity of a set of defined items requiring attention. To describe the file and its meaning in terms of control and subordination is not to suggest that social service agencies are typically Kafkaesque in their heartless anonymity, though some may be. The file objectifies and controls while *at the same time* it represents a commitment to human caring on the part of those engaged in organizing clients. What we must recognize is that social service organizations reflect the contradiction between care and control, the management of resistance in the face of bureaucratic power.

How does the client's resistance to the power of the file manifest itself? In offices and behind desks the personnel of the agency hold the file, consult it on the monitor screen, grasp the printout and gaze at the client. The client can read the contents of the file, check that the basic data is accurate, argue against interpretations and assessments, but cannot *own* the file, cannot remake it in accordance with her or his own narrative. Resistance to the file may take the overt form of disputing its contents, placing an alternative meaning on events recorded there. But usually in state social service agencies resistance is more covert. For most social service clients their relationship to this element of the state apparatus is a class, gender and ethnic relationship: the state's representatives may have a legal power, as in the case of child protection, or the power to give or withhold resources, typically, from poor women. Furthermore, the state, in its commitment to human caring through organization, represents dominant culture, so that the process of power/resistance may be understood as a form of cultural politics. Covert resistance may be manifested as a calculated surface conformity, or a slowness to disclose, or an expression of desire where the client attempts to speak subject-to-subject, breaking down organizational objectification and disrupting the discourse represented by the file. These forms of resistance, but most especially that which proclaims itself as desire, are the most dangerous to organization.

Another illustration of the power/resistance process in the state organization of the well-being of its populations can be gathered from an ethnographic study reported by Fox (1994) of the organization of postoperative ward interactions between surgeons and patients, a context in which opposition may be seen to exist between surgical healing and the injury which surgery causes and where the surgeon's power is expressed in efforts to privilege the discourse of surgical healing and exclude that of surgical injury. Although the authorial text of the postoperative ward round centres on the opportunities it provides for the assessment of patient progress, the monitoring of junior staff, the overall management of the case, and some input by the patient, there is a detectable subtext which can be understood as a power/resistance process. The surgeon's authority depends upon the continuing display of expertise and the compliance of the patient: the organization of the ward round may be seen as the mechanism by which the surgeon's power is continually reinforced, and challenge and resistance continually reacted against and usually defeated. The other participants in the surgeon's ward round – nurses, doctors, the patient – are all potential threats to the surgeon's power because the relationship between surgical healing and the injury inflicted on the patient by the surgeon in the process of surgery is always open to interpretations alternative to those of 'surgical success'. The patient, Fox (1994) demonstrates, uses the ward round to express resistance to the dominant discourse of successful healing, raising questions and complaints about the operation and its consequences, about pain, about readiness for discharge, and about the extent of the surgical injury inflicted. These patients' comments are in the public domain – they are witnessed by others – and so the surgeon is quick to avoid, dilute or ignore them. The organization of the surgical postoperative ward round is, essentially, designed to overcome such expressions of resistance to the surgeon's power, to respond to the perceived threat of *disorganization*.

What is significant in the two examples of the power/resistance process of organization is that they show that power is both achieved and challenged *discursively*. In the social services file, people acquire the subject position of client, and their lives are turned into writing, a text co-authored by social services staff which can be challenged by the assertion of alternative meanings. Of course, in certain circumstances (such as in child protection and mental health services) the direct coercion of the law is available, but predominantly the power of control and discipline is achieved through the maintenance of a certain discourse which reinforces the authority of social services personnel. In the case of the ward round, power 'does not derive from coercion of the patient, nor from the surgeon's position in a hierarchy, status or professional culture, but through the practical demonstration of expertise in achieving "successful" cases of surgical outcome' (Fox, 1994: 57). The type of resistance we have addressed may be called the *micro-resistance of everyday life*. Wider and more institutional forms of resistance based upon alternative ideologies and knowledge claims may usefully challenge dominant discourses and we will consider these forms of resistance in a later chapter. Micro-resistance, on the other hand, is not an organized resistance but its opposite: it attempts to disrupt the organization of the subject, contest its status as a docile body on which expertise is inscribed. It is an ever-present threat to organization, one which demands continuous vigilance.

The Modern Expert

The power of organization and the ubiquitous presence of resistance to it is, I have argued, a discursive process whereby alternative intentions and meanings occupy a contested arena. It is an arena which above all else is concerned with the constitution of knowledge, because knowledge may be seen as central to the imposition of power. For Foucault (1991) the term 'discipline' is used to signify the duality of knowledge: disciplines are both bodies of expertise (medicine, education, psychology) and also the strategies of power by which subjects are organized and controlled. It is because the idea of expert knowledge has been so central to the development of the welfare state that we need to give attention to, first, Foucault's examination of the rules which have governed the growth, maintenance and reproduction of discourses of knowledge. For Foucault (1991: 135), the production of discourse 'is at once controlled, selected, organized and redistributed according to a certain number of procedures, whose role is to avert its powers and its dangers, to cope with chance events, to evade its ponderous, awesome materiality'. These procedures include, most importantly, rules of exclusion whereby divisions are drawn which demarcate what is true knowledge from that which must be set aside, placed outside the boundaries of knowledge. As we have already seen, such a division silences the voices of those who are subjected to knowledge/power in the interests of reason or progress or science duly articulated through the voice of the expert. Foucault's study of madness (Foucault, 1965) explores, as we have seen, the way in which a discursive division opposed reason to folly so that the speech of the mad was considered null and void. But this division, Foucault argues, has not really died with the establishment of psychiatry, but simply takes on another form. Within the contemporary state apparatus of mental health services, professionals learn to decipher the speech of the mad, to listen to them and to subject them to the gaze of reason manifested in the power of the expert who is 'listening to speech invested with desire, crediting itself – for its greater exultation or for its greater anguish – with terrible powers. If we truly require silence to cure monsters, then it must be an attentive silence, and it is in this that the division lingers' (Foucault, 1991: 136, 137).

The narrative of the patient, the client, is listened to, but is not received as a form of knowledge to be placed alongside the professional knowledge of the expert: it is subject to *interpretation*, evidence of the patient's mental condition which contributes to the expert judgement delivered as a differential diagnosis or a psychosocial assessment. The eruption of desire, which is so dangerous to the organization of the social world, is tamed and controlled, first through the attentive listening of experts and then, many times, through pharmacological intervention. But we might see the division between madness and folly, or reason and unreason, as simply an example of a more profound division and exclusion, namely that represented by the opposition between *the true* and *the false*. The professional knowledge of the expert of modernity is based upon the assumption that it is possible to separate true from false by reference to some transcendental standards or guarantees – philosophy, reason, science – as the basis upon which the expert judges and controls those who are subject to the disciplinary gaze. Foucault demonstrates that the true/false dichotomy in the development of scientific knowledge is a historically and culturally constituted division. The exclusion of the false has been, Foucault maintains, essential to 'the will to knowledge', but it is an exclusion which can be pinned down with some precision if we consider as an example the work undertaken, particularly in England at the turn of the sixteenth century, to establish a scientific schema of possible, observable, measurable and classifiable objects. This scientific work represented a will to knowledge

> which imposed upon the knowing subject – in some ways taking precedence over all experience – a certain position, a certain viewpoint, a certain function (look rather than read, verify rather than comment), a will to knowledge which prescribed (and, more generally, all instruments determined) the technological level at which knowledge could be employed in order to be verifiable and useful (navigation, mining, pharmacopoeia). (Foucault, 1991: 138)

The discourse of universal and objective Truth, separated from the False, was the foundation upon which professions came to be established and provided the state with the disciplines necessary to ensure the well-being and organization of its populations. The practices which supported these disciplines of medicine, psychology, social work and public administration among others, became embedded in state institutions such as schools, universities and libraries and private sector enterprises such as publishing. These practices performed the functions of reproducing and distributing the knowledge/power of the disciplines and provided a foundation upon which could be built the processes of control of entry, accreditation and certification which characterize the professionalized occupations that staff the health and welfare services today.

Belonging to a profession means having a 'licence to practise', being the privileged bearer of expert knowledge, and being able to make statements and render judgements within a specific disciplinary discourse. These disciplinary discourses – psychiatry, health care administration, psychotherapy, educational counselling, for example – operate upon discursive rules and mechanisms of exclusion which seek to guarantee the validity of any authorized statement made within them. To belong to a professional discipline, in other words, statements must fulfil certain conditions; they must refer to a specific range of objects and they must fit into a certain theoretical field. Statements within the discipline of social work, for example, especially those made in reports to state institutions – hospital teams, schools, the juvenile justice system, for example – are required to refer to the individual circumstances of subjects, not broad structural factors such as racism or class exploitation. Furthermore, such statements must be expressed in the professional language of the discipline, a world of pathologies, family dynamics, parental deprivations, material insecurities or identity crises. This language is sufficiently understood by the other human service occupations to which social work must relate to ensure the necessary exchange and communication. But to maintain disciplinary *boundaries* it is also necessary to speak within a technical discourse legitimated by reference to theoretical constructs or models claimed to be a distinguishing feature of the discipline. The bounded, theoretically justified technical discourse is an especially significant feature of professional education where socialization of new entrants into the discipline requires identification with the institutionalized objectives of the profession. In professional practice, therefore, three discursive variants are required: statements made *within* the boundary of the profession, statements made *across* the boundary directed to other related occupations, and statements made to the *subjects* of the discipline, those whose well-being are asserted to be its objective. Inevitably, all three discursive variants contain their own rules of exclusion: for example, omit or translate into 'common sense' language, the technical discourse of the profession when making statements to the patient or client and avoid making statements which invade the territory of another profession. These discursive variants, although justified in terms of the necessity for communication, face the contradiction that a central purpose of disciplinary discourses is to privilege the knowledge and power of its members. Thus those outside the discipline – patients or other professionals – may need to be exposed from time to time to hearing or reading the exclusive and esoteric technical language of the discipline in order to produce an acknowledgement of its particular truth.

Disciplines induce 'voluntary' subordination of those who enter its field of caring through systems of ritual of which technical language is only one part. Foucault (1991: 144) suggests that professional discourse involves 'imposing a certain number of rules upon those individuals who employ it, thus denying access to everyone else. This amounts to a rarefaction among speaking subjects: none may enter into discourse on a specific subject unless he [*sic*] has satisfied certain conditions, or if he is not, from the outset, qualified to do so.'

The maintenance of exclusion, the denial of access to those not certified to speak 'authoritatively', discursive rules that organize disciplinary power, are part of a ritual which we can observe daily within health care, social service and social security systems. Take, for example, the organization of a case conference in a hospital department of psychiatry. Some of the more overt forms of ritualized hierarchy and distance characteristic of some hospital departments – the white-coated procession of the consultant and his or her subordinate staff, the use of screens, sometimes the talk across the patient as a passive body, an object – these practices are absent in a psychiatric case conference. But the hierarchy and exclusion remain as a reinforcement of the power of the psychiatrist, first in relation to the other professionals in the mental health team – nurse, psychologist, social worker – and secondly in relation to the patient. In the 'multidisciplinary' team, the psychiatrist remains the central figure, responsible for clinical diagnosis and for the treatment plan, including medication. The psychiatrist's perspective on mental illness, its aetiology, genetic origins, classifications and prognosis, will tend to determine the discourse of the team, especially in the case conference. Alternative theories of mental illness, such as those which might be held by a social worker, will tend to be excluded from discussion, though they may be communicated in some form directly from the social worker to the patient outside of the confines of the case conference. The patient at the case conference is, of course, the object of the professional gaze of the others. The patient's narrative will be listened to, under optimum conditions, with respect but primarily for the evidence such a narrative may provide in order to sharpen a differential diagnosis and to detail a treatment, discharge and after-care plan. We have discussed, in an earlier illustration of patient–doctor encounters, the vulnerability of the professional to the challenge of alternative interpretations which endanger the power of the expert. In the example of the psychiatric case conference, desire, taking the form of a struggle for power, is omnipresent. Compared with the cardiac patient, the psychiatric patient's narrative of the 'illness' and the possibility of the patient arguing for the significance of cultural difference in understanding the 'condition', are a threat to psychiatric authority and to the demands of patient compliance. The psychiatric case conference is always, potentially, a dangerous place where the challenge to a medical model of mental illness, to the 'objective' assessments and classifications of modernity, is an ever-present possibility. It is an arena where resistance to disciplinary power may be mounted.

In our discussion of the role of the professional expert in the welfare state, we have focused on a central contradiction: that the caring provided by the expert is founded on a relationship between knowledge and power which creates the subjectivities and inscribes the bodies of those who are cared for. Where there is welfare, in other words, there is expertise directed to the organization and control ('in their own interests') of those who are subject to its gaze. The welfare state describes many of its functions as directed to caring: health care, childcare, after-care, psychiatric care, and so forth. The organization of this care is 'the organization of technologies of expertise, the (attempted) organization of subjectivity itself' (Fox, 1994: 65). Under conditions of postmodernity, expertise is increasingly challenged, it meets more frequently the resistance of everyday life as deference to authority itself weakens. This erosion of authority is also accompanied, however, by a proliferation of new kinds of experts providing private contractual advice which, it is argued (Rose, 1989), may have more impact in reconstructing subjectivities than the more hierarchical expertise of state authority: coercion and overt social control give way to a more profound internalization of expertise. Is this what postmodern expertise will become: internalization without surveillance and control? We will turn to this question when we examine the idea of postmodern organization later in this chapter.

Before we turn to the question of whether it is possible to speak of a postmodern organizational form, we need, I believe, to acknowledge the

significance of the relation between experts and their education in universities. We have noted already how expertise is founded on the link
between knowledge and power and how the accreditation of professionals
serves to establish and reproduce the power of the expert. Knowledge
production and the certification of experts take place primarily in universities, places where the human services professionals learn to exercise
power and diffuse or avoid resistance. The central role of universities in the
constantly expanding claims of experts has the effect of increasingly
excluding from debates about welfare the politics of the daily experience of
receiving welfare, of being a patient or client, because such experiences are
already spoken for by the research and education of experts: the political
becomes decomposed into aspects of the technology of the professional
care-givers and administrators. This depoliticization process in the face of
the expansion of expertise has its roots

> in an ideology of professionalism [which] made possible the growth and prolifera-
> tion of private monopolies of expert knowledge such as law, medicine, and
> engineering in the late nineteenth century and after. By appropriating to them-
> selves certain fields of discourse, professionalizing groups were able to convert
> knowledge into a form of property and constitute themselves as agents of the
> state, entrusted with the task of defining human needs and supplying services
> within their various fields. (Haskell, 1984: xxi)

We can see that this development of professional power, this occupation
of spaces previously recognized as political, was founded, especially in the
twentieth century, on alliances with universities. Universities legitimated the
power of professionals by ratifying their knowledge claims and their
commitment to 'social progress', and they socialized those outside (as well
as inside) universities into deference to their knowledge-producing activities
and the epistemological assumptions upon which they were based. The
triumphal alliance between professions and universities, especially in an era
of mass higher education, masks the class, gender and race relations
embedded in this alliance. Entry into a profession depends upon certification
by universities and other higher education institutions, a process which
dominant educational and professional discourse renders as requiring intellect and years of hard study: IQ + Effort = Merit. Such a meritocratic
discourse deflects attention from the politics of entry into professions and
universities, a politics of differential access determined by the social
relations of class, gender and racism.

Postmodern Organization

Postmodern critique of modern organization, like feminist and Marxist
perspectives, often takes as given the monolithic character of contemporary
organization, especially in its state bureaucratic form. State bureaucracies, it
may be argued, are ultimately based upon accountability to elected politicians responsible, in Western democracies, for the policies (and often the
concrete practices) of these bureaucracies. In the provision of health,

education, social service and social security programmes, the professional autonomy of the expert is always constrained and limited, not only by the level of organizational responsibility carried or the human and material resources available, as is the case in the private sector, but by the political will of those who claim (with varying degrees of credibility) to represent the electorate. We might speculate that it is this requirement of political accountability that explains the difficulty which faces state organizations in attempting to move too far away from the hierarchical, pyramidal form of the classical bureaucracy.

Nevertheless, under the pressure of critical intellectual analysis (such as in the sociology of health care) combined with the interventions of community activists and consumer groups, some efforts have been made to move towards less hierarchical, more community-based and participative forms of human service organization. The political criticisms directed to monolithic welfare organizations have resulted in experiments in new conceptions of care, in efforts to reduce depersonalization and dependency, and in attempts to strengthen the voice of the consumer (especially in health and education services).

Do these recent developments signify the beginning of a breakdown of modern organization and its eventual replacement by something different – organization appropriate to the postmodernity of late capitalism? We should, I believe, be cautious in claiming that these changes are in any way prefigurative. Organization in the welfare state is subject to many conflicting discourses reflecting the various interests of the actors involved – politicians, administrators, professional and non-professional employees and the users of services. Organization as a set of signifying practices, concerned continuously with the relation between power and resistance, is always subject to challenges to its rationality and meets these challenges by inventing new organizational practices which attempt to keep disorganization at bay. With this reading of organizational change, increased flexibility and representation are the means by which the micro-politics of knowledge/power/resistance are managed through new practices which aim still to maintain the modern discourses of rationality, science and order. This, of course, is a sceptical reading: arguably valid as critique but reluctant to engage in a metanarrative of possible futures, such as that which might be involved in developing a notion of postmodern organization. I can understand this reluctance, but do not fully share it. It is for this reason that I intend, at this point, to explore the concept of postmodern organization and later return to it when I attempt to suggest, in tentative terms, the lines upon which the project of welfare might be constructed in a form appropriate to postmodern times.

To examine the idea of postmodern organization requires a shift in theoretical perspective. The postmodern *critique* of organization explored so far has rested on the premise that organization is process and not structure, a process which we may describe as a discursive system which constitutes subjectivities in the context of struggle signified by the terms 'knowledge, power and resistance'. The shift which we now make is to consider organization as structure as well as process, and to ask whether in the postmodern conditions of late capitalism, new organizational forms are emerging which reflect these conditions. In Chapter 1, I referred briefly to the argument that the economics of late capitalism in the context of world market forces and the growth of new technologies are moving in directions characterized by the terms 'flexible production and accumulation', and I shall develop this argument in the next chapter. We have also considered the contention that the idea of postmodernity might also encompass changes in culture and politics. Are these economic, cultural and political changes manifested not only in the kind of criticisms of modern organization already considered, but also in actual changes in organizational forms themselves? In order to begin to answer this question I shall draw upon the work of Clegg (1990), which though it focuses on the organization of capitalist enterprises, including Asian and especially Japanese ones, is open to a critical reading relevant to public health and welfare agencies. It is a reading also drawing on Marxist ideas and which will require us to question traditional Western ideologies of individual professional accountability and relative autonomy and ask where a notion of organizational flexibility might take us.

We begin this discussion by recapitulating the essential characteristics of modern organization as identified by Weber and his successors. Modern organization was a rational form of practice which, in spite of its dangers, represented a moral commitment to progress. This progress depended on the release, Marx and Adam Smith both contended, of new forces of production which would create new wealth and greatly improved standards of living. These new forces of production and the corresponding relations between capital and labour, depended for their effective exploitation on a central organizational principle – the division of labour. Whereas in pre-modern or early capitalist periods, the labour of the worker comprised of the unity and continuity of a range of skills, including the conception, planning, designing and actual manufacture of a product, modern productive organization fragmented, split and radically subdivided these tasks. In place of the craft worker, gradually gaining more skills (and more material rewards and social status) with progression through the occupational stages of apprentice, journeyman, master, comes the factory. Here, the worker becomes an appendage of the machine, carrying out a single predetermined task. We may see this as a deskilling process (Braverman, 1974) which, in modern organizations, has been a central feature of the management of both labour and production. As the work process is increasingly fragmented, a crucial division of labour emerges, that between intellectual and manual work. The intellectual work, the creative, planning and designing functions, previously activities all performed by the craft worker, are now removed and carried out by the senior strata of the organization: planners, designers, managers.

In the modern organization, management emerges as the central organizing principle of the division of labour. What is organized is differentiation, complexity, and the ever-present threat of disorganization consequent on a crucial contradiction, namely the existence of a labour force collected together and always resisting individually or collectively their objectification and exploitation. This form of modern organization achieved its apotheosis in Henry Ford's plant, the prototype of a system of mass production and radical differentiations of single tasks which became the American model upon which Western capitalism prospered for fifty years.

If modern organization was based, above all, on *differentiation*, and, Clegg argues, economically successful Asian enterprises are characterized by substantially less differentiation, then may we see emerging organizational forms based on *de-differentiation*? The typically Japanese organizational model – flexible, multi-skilled, team-orientated – may of course be seen as primarily a consequence of historical and cultural differences between Japan and Western countries, a product of 'non-individualistic capitalism' (Abercrombie et al., 1986). The Japanese example is not, after all, the result of postmodern critique and can hardly be called a postmodern organization, but may help us to realize that different organizational forms are possible and that cross-cultural comparisons might be useful.

Although drawing on examples of contemporary alternative forms of organization – Asian and others – may be valuable to us, my intention here is to focus primarily on postmodern critique itself, as identified already in this book, and to ask whether it provides a basis for new ideas for the organization of health and social welfare services. This is not a question which some postmodernists, rooted in scepticism and pessimism, would care to ask, let alone answer, but I choose to differ from them.

Postmodernism questions all hierarchical and functional divisions, deconstructing them to reveal their embeddedness in the production of knowledge and power. Thus, postmodern cultural politics challenges the differentiation between High Art and popular culture, and between the centrality accorded to Western art and the marginality of the art of the 'Other'. Postmodern literary criticism challenges the authority of the text and of the author, and denies definitive interpretation based upon superior knowledge, giving to the reader an equal role in debates about meaning. Postmodern political and philosophical analysis, following Foucault, challenges a hierarchical division between Western scientific rationality and the narratives of those excluded from dominant discourse. Postmodern cultural studies might be seen as rejecting the disciplinary boundaries which exist in academia, because these boundaries are culturally constructed on the basis of untenable knowledge claims supported by oppressive relations of class, gender and ethnicity.

What we can propose here as a basis for discussion is that directly, or by implication, postmodernism denies the validity of differentiation, division and boundary. The question, therefore, is whether we can detect already signs that organizational differentiation is eroding and that occupational and professional boundaries are decomposing or we can envisage such de-differentiation acting as an emancipatory element in the organization of welfare. Clegg (1990) argues that such de-differentiation is, in fact, taking place in non-state organizations using examples from Sweden, Germany, Australia and Japan to make his point, and quoting the work of Heydebrand (1989) who speaks of a shift in the mode of administration to an organization which tends 'to be small or be located in small subunits of larger organizations; its object is typically service or information, if not automated production; its technology is computerized; its division of labour is informal and flexible; and its managerial structure is decentralized, eclectic, and participative, and overlapping in many ways with non-managerial functions' (p. 327).

If this organizational form is increasing in its prevalence, as organization studies writers suggest, we need to ask whether such trends are observable also in public sector services. Only speculation is possible at this stage. Despite the requirement of political accountability which may have the effect of slowing down a process of de-differentiation, there appear to be some signs, however meagre, that such changes are taking place. Community health care, for example, may now be organized into small programmes, each directed to a specific objective, while teams of mental health professionals from different disciplines may now work together in ways which substantially blur, if not transcend, the boundaries that traditionally separate them. But at the same time, we could find more examples of traditional bureaucratic modes of organization with strict boundaries still thriving. We should be wary, also, of claims that the monolithic bureaucracy, typical of large state services such as the British National Health Service, are being replaced by more flexible, humane and indeed fragmenting systems and that these might be considered examples of postmodern organization. For the patient or client, furthermore, the monolith remains an experiential reality, so caution is necessary:

> We must not make the error of subsuming the modern discourse of organization within its postmodern critique. The discovery that a fragmenting care system is perceived as monolithic is precisely how we can explore what organization is about. The value of the postmodern perspective is that it stands beyond the discourse it criticizes, to demonstrate the discourses of rationalism and its associated bureaucratic forms as the generative motivation behind modern health care. (Fox, 1994: 60)

We may read this warning (with its ambitious claims for a postmodern critique) as suggesting that increased flexibility, decentralization and informality may still be experienced as hierarchical and bureaucratic because such changes are simply short-term strategies for maintaining power and counteracting resistance and disorganization. Certainly, we must also remember that the purpose of organizational change in the capitalist enterprise, whether American, Japanese or European, is to increase the rate of profit and maintain labour regulation under global market conditions. The *purpose* of organizational change in 'postmodern directions' should not, in other words, be confused with some radical, emancipatory intention: such changes reflect the need to adapt to a changing environment while maintaining the maximum level of control. One such change may be identified as a *shift in consumption.*

We have discussed already, in a previous chapter, some of the consequences of a massive increase in the central function of cultural production in the economies of late capitalist countries. We have described this function as the manufacture of desire which leads to an unprecedented dependency on the market in the constitution of contemporary subjectivities. But in constituting our subjectivities within a mass culture, we are not being addressed in the language of uniformity, of the mass consumption of identical products, but in the language of *individuality*. In sculpting our subjectivities in response to the messages of the media, we are looking for a means by which to express, in the performance of everyday life, both our uniqueness as persons and also our group and community affiliations. The products we have available to us for consumption reflect increasing differentiation: diversity of identities can be met by a parallel diversity of personal consumption. Our representation of ourselves in everyday life – how we dress, what we eat, what we own, how we travel – reflects increasingly our choices amongst a wide of range of possible subjectivities communicated to us through the mass media. Multiple cultural representations of gender, sexuality, ethnicity and class are reflected in multiple products, some of them – clothes and cars, for example – especially carefully calibrated to fit into a particular social segment of the population. The diverse socially constructed wants which are reflected in the consumption demands of late capitalism cannot be met by the classic form of organization based upon mass production: in place of the single black Model T Ford of yesterday we have today the one hundred Toyota models which can be purchased in almost any colour.

What is most significant in these changes in consumption is that while they are characterized by increased *differentiation*, the capitalist organizational response to these demands, compared with earlier models of organization, is through a process of *de-differentiation*. We might say that the dialectical relationship between consumption and production demands new organizational forms in which the cost benefits previously associated with large-scale systems are allied to a high level of flexibility in meeting a 'niche in the market'. This results, as we have seen, in the decomposition and recomposition of skills, the disappearance of rigid job boundaries and the development of new forms of identification and surveillance. Changes in the consumption of products and services follow a particular logic in the dominant discourses of late capitalism: increased emphasis on social diversity, personal identity and individual choice. Dependency on the market is recoded, within dominant discourses, as rejection of dependency on and interference by the state, and of the supposed sovereignty of the consumer. These political messages often resonate with a certain kind of 'postmodern' politics which also emphasizes diversity, identity, choice and a profound suspicion of the state apparatus. They are messages which are increasingly affecting the organization of state welfare provision.

If the consumption of state health and welfare services is being expressed increasingly in terms of diversity and choice, then we can see that organizational adaptation to this expression will become increasingly required; the pressures to some degree parallel those which are producing change in the private sector. Indeed, we might suggest also that the ideologies of capitalist organizations are infiltrating directly into public sector services under the banner of the need for increased efficiency, consumer choice and community participation. The idea of community participation is typically expressed not primarily in terms of community democratic control but through the provision of volunteers, in future likely to be drawn from a population of the skilled unemployed or under-employed, who are likely to be seen as able to replace many state-provided paid professional positions.

It is as the result of a range of discourses, contradictory in their fundamental politics but unnervingly similar in some of their expressions, which is placing pressure on state organization to change. In particular, radical Right rejection of the idea of government concern with the well-being of subjects, coupled with a radical cultural politics of diversity and identity, produce new challenges to the notion of expertise. The postmodern deconstruction of public expertise as the expression of state power and control resonates both with neo-liberal rhetoric about the advantages of consumer choice expressed through market forces, and with a cultural politics critique of the Eurocentric arrogance of state bureaucrats and professionals. The combination of these political pressures, odd bedfellows though they might be, is likely in the longer run to accelerate the de-differentiation of expert positions and skill boundaries within state health and welfare organizations. Within the field of professional expertise, however, a politics of power struggles exists, so we cannot assume that 'rationality' will triumph. Occupations that have common boundaries, that are organized together into teams, for example, do not necessarily submit to a sharing of professional space and skills as a result of consensus between them. In both hospital and community health and social service settings, a powerful and well-established nursing staff can appropriate some of the functions of social workers. Whether the result is an improvement in the quality and flexibility of service provision is a matter of debate: what seems clear, however, is that such occupational boundary shifts are often more the result of a process of power/resistance, than one of agreement.

The context of any shift in the organization of expertise is bound to be one of resistance and defence as well as using opportunities to increase power. One defence is actually to increase the number of boundaries between different kinds of expertise so that while responses to diversity may appear to multiply, new forms of professional specialization are claimed which act as barriers to de-differentiation. In examining a recent proliferation of specialist social work journals, for example, Chambon (1994) refers to a general increase in the partitioning of information into discrete areas of expertise, a trend, so far as publication is concerned, that appears to be open to expansion without limits, other than that of the market. It is, she suggests, a problematic expansion of increasingly narrow definitions of expertise:

> To their credit, a number of these new outlets legitimize a space of debate for previously marginalized voices (women, racial and ethnic minorities). This is not the case, however, with most of these new ventures. A potentially questionable outcome of this trend, which needs consideration, is the promotion of restricted spaces of knowledge as self-contained objects. Unlike the more traditional branching off into new fields of knowledge that characterizes the emergence of new disciplines, the recent multiplicity is a plurality of closed objects, rather than avenues of inquiry. Positions are being conquered while no new field is being created. (1994: 63)

Our discussion of the idea of postmodern organization has, to this point, underlined the need to be cautious before suggesting that organizational transformations are taking place, especially in the public sector. Furthermore, reflection on the politics of postmodern organization suggests that such changes that are taking place – greater flexibility and the restructuring or decomposition of a rigid division of labour – should be viewed in the context of struggles over power. Attempts to increase the participation of patients or clients may be seen as resulting in professional countermoves, such as increasing the expert's claims to specialized knowledge, as a means of re-establishing boundaries. Where boundaries appear to weaken or become blurred, especially the boundaries between professional and non-professional, paid employee and volunteer, or service provider and service user, we are bound to ask two questions: do these boundary changes result in actual changes in practices, and who benefits or loses from these changes? These questions may be seen as pointing to the wider political issues that need to be raised: in whose interests would 'postmodern' organizations be formed in the public sector and are they *alternatives* to modern bureaucracies or simply new ways of exercising the rule of knowledge/power with its mechanisms of control and surveillance?

The Politics of Alternative Organization

One perspective on the organizational changes which accompany postmodernity is to see them as beneficial: increased flexibility, the breakdown of previous rigidities, the empowerment which comes from replacing top-down supervision with horizontal group accountability, all may be seen, optimistically, as precursors of a new critical pluralism. This is the position taken by Clegg (1990), who uses the model of Swedish social democracy to point to postmodern possibilities:

> The 'Swedish model' is not culturally specific but institutionally produced . . . A party of labour in government, a strong and centralizing union structure and peak tripartite institutions in which priorities and policy commitments can be hammered out concerning wages, investment, skill and capital formation, and industry policy all point to the possibility of developing a broader organizational world. It would be a different organizational world, in some formal respects not too dissimilar to the modernist organizations we know so well. In some other respects,

however, it would be different. It would be a world of organizations replete with political possibilities for postmodern development. It would be an organizational world of enhanced skill formation and de-differentiation, facilitated in its further realistic development by the de-differentiation of the relations of private capital formation as a modernist hallmark. (Clegg, 1990: 233)

Clegg is speaking here of the democratic and emancipatory potentials of a strong central power structure which, through the development of collective capital formation, is able to promote industrial democracy, redistribute wealth and achieve greater equality. Swedish social democracy, in other words, is replete with the metanarratives of modernity and has the structures which it is proposed enable social progress to be achieved. Organizational innovation takes place in the intestines of this modernist organic body. It is an attractive proposition for 'moderate' socialists, as Clegg concedes, but has it anything to do with *postmodernism*? Perhaps the proposition should be seen as surrendering to the temptation of using the term postmodern as an equivalent of organizational innovation and flexibility, rather than recognizing such changes as essentially a continuation of the rationality of modernity itself. If we compare Clegg's approach with that of Bauman, whom Clegg refers to positively, if conditionally, then we can see that for some postmodern scholars the notion of a postmodern organizational *structure* is an oxymoron.

In his exposition of the major elements of a sociological theory of postmodernity, Bauman (1992) focuses not on the traditional concern with order, but on the postmodern habitat in which autonomous agents act in an environment characterized by chronic indeterminacy, ambivalence and contingency. It is not a sociological perspective that would be able to speak of postmodern organization within a social democratic state of centralized planning:

> The postmodern habitat is a complex (non-mechanical) system for two closely related reasons. First, there is no goal setting agency with overall managing and coordinating capacities or ambitions – one whose presence would provide a vantage point from which the aggregate of effective agents appears as a 'totality' with a determined structure of relevances; a totality which one can think of as an *organization*. Second, the habitat is populated by a great number of agencies, most of them single purpose, some of them small, some big, but none large enough to subsume or otherwise determine the behaviour of others. (Bauman, 1992: 192; emphasis in original)

Bauman's vision is one of an ongoing transformative change, the collapse of all the certainties of modernity as they succumb to deconstruction, and especially to the deconstruction of organization as rational, ordered authority. These are changes inadvertently instigated by modernity itself but previously seen as failures; sociologists, Bauman suggests, can theorize these changes but also work for them in seeing them as positive. 'The postmodern condition can be therefore described, on the one hand, as modernity emancipated from false consciousness; on the other, as a new type of social condition marked by the overt institutionalization of the characteristics which modernity – in its designs and managerial practices – set about to eliminate and, failing that, tried to conceal' (Bauman, 1992:

188). I propose that we draw upon Bauman's perspective here and try to understand the notion of postmodern organization not as structure, but revert to the usage earlier in this chapter: organization as process. We can then see that what is considered failure within the dominant discourses of organization and expertise – indeterminacy, contingency, disorganization – become, instead, the preferred characteristics of (postmodern) organization as signifying discursive processes. It is a process embedded in an understanding of power/resistance as manifested in all social interaction and as therefore a source of empowerment as well as resistance to power.

If modernity carries, as Bauman argues, the seeds of its own deconstruction, can postmodern (dis)organization as a process be seen as prefigurative, as one element of a renewed emancipatory project of welfare? A substantive answer to this question will be attempted in the final chapter: here I want to lay the ground by referring to two contrasting political positions relevant to the question. First, we can acknowledge the power of traditional Marxist argument which points to the futility of small- or middle-scale changes when the overall mode of production, and the relations to which it gives rise, remains untouched. This is a critique which Clegg (1990) considers and dismisses when he describes the 'Swedish model', and quotes from Ramsey and Haworth's (1984) attack on so-called 'radical reform':

> The division of labour (particularly of mental and manual work), the experience of control in the workplace, the production of goods for use rather than exchange, and the very relations embodied in the nature of the state must all be transformed. To seek incremental changes as if these dimensions were separate spheres or their development could be raised notch by notch, we believe, is an absurdity as a means to create socialism in the real world of class struggles. To change ownership and leave the division of labour intact and unchallenged, for example, merely recreates capitalist relations of the workplace. (Ramsay and Haworth, 1984: 314)

Although this is a general argument against reformism, including organizational reform, its point is most effective when applied, as the authors suggest, to changes in the ownership of enterprises – rationalization – which leave all other social relations intact. It is an argument which may be judged weaker if we consider 'reforms' aimed at developing alternatives to the authority, control and social relations of modern capitalist forms of organization. The issue of prefigurative change in organization can, in fact, be explored further if we look at a second position: that espoused by what may be termed 'collectivist organization'.

As an alternative to modern bureaucracies, we can see in the small community-based collectivist organization, the ideal type of a prefigurative form and process. In a study of American collectivist work organizations which included a free medical clinic, a legal collective, a food cooperative, a free school and an alternative newspaper, Rothschild-Whitt (1979) was able to contrast the characteristics of these organizations with those of bureaucratic structure. A postmodern perspective was not utilized in this study, but what became known later as postmodern critique of modern organization is evident in the ideal type of practice characteristic of what is described as collectivist-democratic organization, a form which under contemporary conditions most resembles feminist alternative social agencies – rape crisis centres, women's health collectives and shelters for abused women.

Rothschild-Whitt identifies eight dimensions within which the characteristic features of a Weberian ideal type of bureaucracy would show its typical form of rationality: authority, rules, social control, social relations, recruitment and advancement, incentive structure, social stratification and differentiation. In each of these dimensions, the collectivist-democratic organization attempts to occupy a position at the opposite pole to that held by a bureaucratic structure. In considering the ideal characteristics of a collectivist-democratic type of organization in the eight dimensions, we will be struck by the elements of postmodern critique which were already evident here. A postmodern reading follows the ideal type of collectivist-democratic organization described by Rothschild-Whitt (1979: 517) below:

Authority: resides in the collectivity as a whole; delegated, if at all, only temporarily and subject to recall. Compliance is to the consensus of the collective, which is always fluid and open to negotiation.

Rules: minimal stipulated rules; primacy of ad hoc, individuated decisions; some calculability possible on the basis of knowing the substantive ethics involved in the situation.

Social controls: primarily based upon personalistic or moralistic appeals and the selection of homogeneous personnel.

Social relations: based on the ideal of community. Relations to be holistic, personal, of value in themselves.

Recruitment and advancement: employment based on friends, social-political values, personality attributes, and informally assessed knowledge and skills. Concept of career advancement not meaningful; no hierarchy of positions.

Incentive structure: normative and solidarity incentives are primary; material incentives are secondary.

Social stratification: egalitarian, reward differentials, if any, are strictly limited by the collectivity.

Differentiation: minimal division of labour; administration is combined with performance tasks; division between intellectual and manual labour is reduced. Generalization of jobs and functions; holistic roles. Demystification of expertise; ideal of amateur factotum.

These ideal type characteristics of collectivist-democratic organizations differ dramatically from the ideal characteristics to be found in bureaucracies. Two points about these collectivist organizational characteristics need to be made. First, that they are ideal types, theoretical constructs representing the characteristics aimed for by organization members. In practice they cannot be fully realized because internal organizational dynamics and the material and cultural environment places constraints on the possibility of achieving complete congruence with the theoretical model. Secondly, we can identify a number of problems which face this alternative way of organizing the delivery of social welfare and health services. Democratic, participative decision making takes a great deal of time, compared with hierarchical decision making, so that in practice many decisions may have to be delegated to individuals and the participative process thereby weakened.

Because membership of a collectivist organization demands a high level of commitment, the experience of belonging often brings with it a level of emotional intensity and internal tension which in turn can produce a stressful work environment. Interacting as subjects, in other words, can have certain emotional costs which are avoided in the impersonal, objectifying world of bureaucratic rationality, although such a world carries, of course, its own costs – those associated with structured subordination. The subjectivities of collectivist organization members have invariably been constructed within the dominant discourses of gender, class and race, and these discourses remain as significant internalizations. The resistance to power which collectivist organization membership may be assumed to represent, is a site of struggle between dominant and subordinate discourses *within the subjects themselves*. In practice, therefore, although collectivist members may be striving to learn new attitudes and behaviours consistent with the values of solidarity, cooperation, sensitivity, respect and other collective virtues, the dominant cultural pressure to individualism, competitiveness, the attainment of power, deference towards authority and expertise will continue to have its effects. Finally, the wider political and economic environment of bureaucratic rationality, fiscal constraint and the measurement of cost-effectiveness makes the survival of alternative organizations always problematic because with few exceptions they depend upon external funding.

None of the problems of collectivist alternative organizations will come as a surprise: they are the everyday experience of people working in such organizations. The question for us at this point is whether such alternative organization developments, outside of the state apparatus but usually funded by it, can help us to understand the notion of *postmodern organization*. Some of the ideal type characteristics of collectivist-democratic organizations identified by Rothschild-Whitt may be read as postmodern critique and resistance to bureaucratic rationality. They can be seen to represent a critical resistance to hierarchical authority, universalistic rules, organizational control through supervision and surveillance, impersonal objectification, specialized expertise, and rigid division of labour. Collectivist organization represents, to some degree, the effort to deconstruct the organizational form of modernity and reconstruct, in its place, an alternative. That this alternative is a minority, unstable and often transient form of organization is hardly surprising considering the social forces that are ranged against it. But it continues to survive in what might be described as a postmodern form, namely as a vehicle for identity politics, the struggle to achieve, for specific populations of the Other – women, cultural and racial minorities, gays and lesbians, people living in poverty – justice, equality and welfare. These alternative organizations, while usually aiming to challenge the state and its dominant discourses to recognize and respond to *difference*, tend themselves to be relatively *homogeneous*. Moral commitment to furthering the material interests of a particular segment of the population lies at the root of such organizations and so their members will tend to share a set of common beliefs and often other characteristics, such as culture, race, gender or sexual identity. This relative homogeneity of membership is a necessary condition of achieving consensus in decision making as well as mounting politically consistent forms of resistance. In comparison, modern bureaucracies, at least in theory and to a limited extent in practice, are able to operate effectively with a diverse social, cultural and political member- ship because they do not depend upon consensus in making decisions and because stratification and material incentives provide the means of maintain- ing compliance. The political problem which we might identify as crucial to organizations committed to the value of diversity but based, in their membership, on homogeneity, is how such organizations are able to form long-term alliances with other organizations based on a solidarity which transcends differences. We return to this question in a later chapter.

In pursuing the notion of postmodern organization we have considered both structure and process. My reservations about the idea, emerging from contemporary developments in capitalist enterprises, of postmodern organiz- ation *structures*, stem from an acknowledgement that such changes are not intended to be transformative, but rather to maintain and reproduce, in a new form, the fundamental and dominant social relations of modernity. On the other hand, I have argued in favour of exploring the idea of organization as process because here a postmodern reading of organization as discursive signification allows us to develop critiques of knowledge/power and sub- jectification and, perhaps, invent strategies of resistance which build upon the resistance of everyday life. The example of alternative collectivist organizations may, despite their many problems, provide us with an entry into empowerment strategies to be used in attempting to think through the kinds of organization of welfare compatible with but also resisting the postmodern conditions of late capitalism.

5

Economy

When we speak of living under postmodern conditions, in contexts which are experienced as affecting and often destabilizing identities, cultures and forms of organization, we are aware always of a subtext: the discourses on the economic which seek to explain the transformations in our lives. These economic discourses take many forms – modern and postmodern, Left and Right, pro Welfare State and anti Welfare State – and continuously impinge on and contextualize the issues we have already examined, including the commodification of culture, the manufacture of desire, and the development of flexible organization, three crucial markers of the changing circumstances within which arguments about welfare are conducted.

A Discursive Shift

Faced with 'the new, ruthless economy' (Head, 1996), Western governments speak no longer with conviction about economic progress and rising living standards as the fruits of modernization but use Hobbesian and Darwinian phrases to urge us to come to terms with the fact that the competitive life is nasty and brutish and that we are immersed in a life or death struggle for economic survival. In this struggle, the old ideas which ruled the modern welfare state – universality, full employment, increasing equality – are proclaimed to be a hindrance to survival. They are castigated as ideas which have outlived their usefulness: they are no longer appropriate to the conditions of a global capitalist economy where investment, production, labour and consumption are all characterized by flexibility, transience and uncertainty.

Although there are many variations in this dominant economic discourse, from the ideological enthusiasm for compliance with market forces, characteristic of the new Right, to the reluctance and heart searchings of liberal and social democratic attempts to balance welfare with globalization, the message is essentially the same. It is a discourse in which discussion of the government *deficit* often plays a crucial role in posing the question 'How can the economy support a welfare state?' The answer is formulated as consisting of a number of dilemmas facing governments where the financing of welfare exceeds revenues from taxation. The choices presented by such governments are: to cut the level of public services, to raise taxation levels, or to allow the deficit to continue to rise. Of these three alternatives, raising taxation on individual incomes or corporate profits is perceived as politically problematic, while the escalation of debt-servicing costs, especially if they exceed the rate of growth of the economy, is seen as effectively excluding the option of deficit financing (Mendelson, 1993). This leaves cuts in public services or their privatization as the only alternative left, and this is the option which is now predominantly pursued by what might be called the *reluctant welfare dismantlers*, to be contrasted with the more ideologically driven *enthusiastic welfare dismantlers*.

We might, of course, attempt to deconstruct the dominant economic discourses on welfare so as to reveal the discursive rules underlying them, what is included and what is excluded, who speaks about the economy and within what processes of knowledge, power and resistance. A thorough-going deconstructive critique is, I believe, necessary but beyond the scope of this chapter. What can be attempted, however, is a beginning exploration of some of the assumptions underlying discourses on the economy, which will involve discussion on globalization, flexible accumulation, 'post-Fordist' production methods and the consequences of these developments on employment, unemployment, wages and class relations. The purpose of this uncovering and exploring of economic discourses and practices will be to indicate for later discussion the sites of resistance to late capitalist economies which might still be excavated as places where new approaches to human welfare might emerge. There can be little doubt that the economic discourses of the reluctant or the enthusiastic welfare dismantlers have a profound impact on the construction of subject positions of those most affected: patients, clients, taxpayers, wage earners, unemployed workers, welfare recipients. They are discourses in which the ideological formation of rationality and necessity, as interpreted by the expertise of those who can speak with authority, are both supported and challenged by expressions of desire, of anger, resentment, envy, guilt. The elderly recipients of social assistance, for example, are subjected to a discourse which speaks of the fiscal 'burden' of an ageing population and of the economic consequences of a demographic shift in the proportion of 'productive' compared with 'non-productive' citizens.

What contemporary discourses on the economy most clearly emphasize when they speak to the subject is that expectations that the state will be able to ensure the subject's well-being, or that of his, or her, children, are now no longer reasonable. The notions of community and solidarity, the liberal aspirations upon which the welfare state was founded, must give way to the economic reality of individual competitiveness and survival. Any form of Keynesian intervention by the state is, in other words, dead and buried:

> ... there is now no economically plausible Keynesian strategy that would permit the full realization of social democratic goals within a rational context without violating the functional imperatives of the capitalist economy. Full employment, rising real wages, larger welfare transfers and more and better public services can no longer all be had simultaneously – because growth rates are inadequate and because the distributive claims that capital is able to realize have increased. (Scharpf, 1991: 58, cited in Kerans, 1994: 124)

The death sentence pronounced here is not, as Kerans points out, that of a radical Right champion of the sovereignty of market forces. Scharpf is speaking sympathetically of the prospects of European social democracy and argues that capital is now able, through changes in international economic institutions, to exercise such power over national governments that they are unable any longer to pursue, even if they wished to, full employment and a universalist welfare state. In the old Keynesian welfare state, identities were constituted through exposure to a different expert view of the prospects for the well-being of the population, one which spoke in the confident tones of endless economic growth and social progress. Here is Donnison, a leading academic expert on social policy and, for a time, Chair of the British Supplementary Benefits Commission (which administered social assistance), speaking to bankers of the prospects of the social democratic welfare state as seen in 1970:

> Eventually it should be possible to maintain the process by which policies for the equalization of income, wealth and living standards extend freedom and promote innovation and development which ensure the continuing economic growth that makes further progress towards equality possible. (Donnison, 1970: 23)

We are now subjected to an entirely different authoritative view of the prospects for prosperity, equality and the state's role in our well-being. What has happened in a period of just over twenty-five years to produce this discursive shift? What are the features of the 'new economy' in terms of discourses, institutions and practices and how do they impact on the theories and practices of welfare? We can begin this discussion by identifying and dealing with key phrases in the discourses on the new economy: globalization, flexible accumulation and post-Fordism and 'lean production' methods. These phrases and others, such as 're-engineering' and 'time–space compression', all refer to elements in what is assumed to be an overall process of transition in capitalist economics which has taken place since about the mid-1970s.

Globalization

Because capitalism as a mode of production is essentially growth-orientated, and because economic growth is a precondition of increases in profitability and accumulation, capitalist enterprises have always, in their drive for markets, fuelled a globalizing process. This logic of capitalist development, however, has been transformed and accelerated by a number of major changes in the past twenty years. The first change can be found in the emergence of an increasing number of powerful, non-Western capitalist economies, beginning with Japan's reconstruction after the Second World War and subsequently encompassing other Asian countries, including Taiwan, South Korea and Hong Kong. Add to this China's commitment to capitalist forms of enterprise, and we have emerging a range of Asian economies with which the West is structurally linked through investment,

production and consumption. International corporations with 'home' bases
in Japan, the USA or Britain are able to shift capital investment in such a
way as to take maximum advantage of an increasingly global market,
especially for high-tech products, a market supported by a global system of
cultural communication. Globalization as a total process has been further
reinforced by the collapse of state socialist societies in Eastern Europe and
the former Soviet Union. These societies are in the process of being
transformed into various kinds of capitalist economy, some appearing
'advanced' and some showing the features of undisguised brutality more
characteristic of the entrepreneurs of early capitalism. We can now say that
there exists with the end of the Cold War a world capitalist economy
continuing to expand into every corner of the globe and meeting virtually no
organized political resistance, because no viable alternative to capitalist
economies any longer appears to exist.

Two technical and organizational developments have been critical to the
global expansion of capitalism. The first is the growth of information
technology and its control by corporate interests.

> Access to and control over information, coupled with a strong capacity for instant
> data analysis, have become essential to the centralized co-ordination of far-flung
> corporate interests. The capacity for instantaneous response to changes in
> exchange rates, fashions and tastes, and moves by competition is . . . essential to
> corporate survival . . . (Harvey, 1990: 159)

Access to the latest scientific, technical, financial and cultural knowledge is
so crucial to maintaining a competitive edge in a global economy, that this
knowledge itself becomes, Harvey maintains, a key commodity. It is a
process of commodification which demonstrates clearly the relation between
knowledge and power, and the extent to which knowledge acquisition has
become part of the global competitive struggle. The organized production
and commercialization of knowledge have had a major impact on those
institutions traditionally responsible for the generation of knowledge, for we
witness, in Harvey's (1990: 160) words, 'the uncomfortable transitions in
many university systems in the advanced capitalist world from guardianship
of knowledge and wisdom to ancillary production of knowledge for corporate capital'. Furthermore, alongside the exploitation of technical knowledge-
production for the purposes of corporate advantage in the global market has
emerged an increasing concentration of control over the creation and
dissemination of popular culture – television, newspapers, books and performances. Popular culture not only serves as a means by which desire can be
manufactured and market dependency ensured, but also maintains corporate
image and influence, especially through the sponsorship of events (sporting
and musical, for example) which keeps the corporate name constantly in the
public eye.

The second and related development which has been central to the process
of globalization is the reorganization of the world financial system and with
it a massively enhanced ability to manage financial coordination. Harvey
(1990: 160) identifies this development as 'a dual movement, on the one

hand towards the formation of financial conglomerates and brokers of extraordinary global power, and on the other hand, a rapid proliferation and decentralization of financial activities and flows through the creation of entirely new financial instruments and markets'. The deregulation and simultaneous reform of the financial system become necessary to the survival and high levels of profitability of financial centres within a global market context of instantaneous communication where time, currency and the geographical location of markets cease to be an impediment to trading. As time, space and national boundaries are progressively dismantled as obstacles to capital accumulation, so capital is able to achieve more rapidly and with greater ease what it has always been impelled to pursue – investment in the most lucrative markets. The global financial system allows for the rapid transfer of capital to the most profitable investments from the less profitable ones. Thus regions of the world able to operate at the lowest labour costs and with the most cost-effective and undisrupted production methods, are highly valued centres of investment. High wage, high cost, unionized sectors of the global economy experience the withdrawal of capital and the shutdown of plants unable to produce a competitive level of profitability. The development of global financial systems has, without doubt, increased the instability of national capitalist enterprises now rendered vulnerable to investment decisions made and immediately acted upon in distant parts of the globe. As national boundaries become increasingly irrelevant to the movement of finance capital, so the nation state finds it increasingly difficult to control its own financial and monetary policy. This state of affairs produces conflict between national governments and transnational corporations, because the state

> is called upon to regulate the activities of corporate capital in the national interest at the same time as it is forced, also in the national interest, to create a 'good business climate' to act as an inducement to trans-national and global finance capital, and to deter (by means other than exchange controls) capital flight to greener and more profitable pastures. (Harvey, 1990: 170)

The development of global financial centres, together with revolutions in communication technology, both alongside other trends, tend to weaken the power of the nation state *vis-à-vis* corporate capitalism. The state no longer holds a monopoly of power and it is this shift, a major consequence of globalization, that is argued as the central issue in the fiscal crisis of the welfare state: the discourse on the contradiction between the market and social investment. Western governments are faced with the problem of managing the social consequences of globalization – unemployment, increasing deficits, the widespread growth of uncertainty and apprehension – factors which progressively polarize incomes and substantially affect class relations and are part and parcel of the dynamic of the new capitalist world economy. Apart from the obvious effects of large-scale, long-term unemployment on income levels and therefore consumer spending, the ruthless and near frantic search for ever higher levels of profits has a direct impact on production methods, skills and the wage levels of those who are employed.

Before turning to these latter developments when we examine the emergence of the discourse on 'lean production', there is one further feature of globalization which requires attention at this point. Globalization as a process of capitalist development is evidenced, we have seen, in markets, consumption, technology and the role of the state, but it is also a feature of the growth of poverty.

Although there are millions of poor people inhabiting the affluent Western societies of North America and Europe, we need to address here the plight of the global Other. Giddens (1994: 98) remarks that 'over 20 per cent of the world's population lives in conditions of absolute poverty, if such be defined as a situation where people cannot regularly meet their most basic sub- sistence needs'. How are we to understand the growth of global poverty? Although the causes of this dramatic increase in world-wide poverty are undoubtedly complex, it is not difficult to point to the critical significance of a *relationship*, of that between 'First World' and 'Third World' countries, between the economies of North and South. The dynamic of capitalist development is historically based upon accumulation, the exploitation of labour and technological innovation, features which have a polarizing effect on the distribution of wealth, income and life chances. In the context of globalization, it is clear that the capitalist world profits from the impov- erished condition of the 'Third World', for it is this latter world which continues to provide cheap resources just as it did in the days of colonial rule.

The exploitative relationship which exists between North and South has not, on the whole, been ameliorated by attempts at economic 'development', because the process of modernization may also lead to impoverishment, in either absolute or relative terms. Modernization as the central element in the dynamic of capitalist development may lead not only to economic poverty but also to cultural impoverishment. This is clearly the case with Aboriginal populations world-wide, where the destruction of cultural histories and identities in the name of modern economic development has produced a pattern of socio-economic impoverishments and cultural losses which are only now beginning to receive some recognition in the West. To understand global poverty, we must, in other words, recognize once more the continuing destructive effect of the modern discourse on progress and the institutions and practices with which it is implicated. Although careful to avoid, in his attempt to reconstruct a political discussion 'beyond left and right', allocat- ing exclusive blame for global poverty to corporate capitalism, Giddens (1994) advocates an 'alternative development' model, and identifies as a central issue the questioning of endless 'modernization' and 'economic growth', and cites Paul Ekins as part of his argument:

> On the one side are scientism, developmentalism and statism, backed by the big battalions of the establishment: modern technology, and the institutions of world capitalism and state power. On the other are the people, principally the 30 per cent of humanity that is disposable as far as the modern project is concerned, but aided

and abetted by many from the other 70 per cent who regard this project as ethnically, socially and environmentally intolerable. (Ekins, 1992: 209)

Whether a counter-attack on the triumphalism of modernity in the name of ecological survival, social justice and the elimination of preventable global poverty would gain the mass support suggested here by Ekins may be open to question. Certainly, it would require a wide-ranging political movement which at the present time looks problematic in a postmodern world of diversity and identity politics.

Flexible Accumulation/Post-Fordism

If the development of a global market of finance capital, of products, consumers and communication technology characterizes this present stage in late capitalism with its polarizing tendencies in terms of wealth and poverty, then how might we conceptualize the transition in terms of a *before* and an *after*? Just as the term 'postmodern' has served, not without considerable dispute, to signify a social condition of uncertainty, transience, the commodification of culture and a questioning of Enlightenment values, might we use a similar term to point to an *economic* transition, a state of affairs which, it is argued, has existed since the end of the international boom in the early 1970s? An answer to this question can be explored through the idea that the past twenty-five years or so represents a change in the *regime of accumulation* (how capital allocates its product between consumption and accumulation) and an accompanying change in social and political regulation (especially how the worker is organized and socialized for the purposes of capitalist production) (Lipietz, 1985, 1987). Briefly, what is argued for in this paradigm of accumulation and regulation is that the crises of capitalism which led to the recession of the early 1970s – inflation, stagnation, decreases in profits – created the conditions for new economic institutions and practices. These new developments involved greater flexibility in financial systems, production methods, marketing strategies and the organization of labour, and because of the compression of time and space (especially characteristic of financial markets) were accompanied by greater capital mobility and the globalization of consumption. Increased flexibility in production, organizational restructuring, the growth of unemployment and part-time employment created a climate of uncertainty and fragmentation which, it may be argued, crippled the collective strength of labour to resist, and left it in a much weakened bargaining position. The development of new discourses on entrepreneurialism, on nationalism, on cultural production, and on market dependency, might all be seen as contributing to social regulation whereby people's abilities to undertake work are converted into a labour process of value to capital. The disciplining of labour power to the purposes of capital accumulation, Harvey writes, 'entails, in the first instance, some mix of repression, habituation, co-optation and co-operation' (1990: 123), a process 'that has to be renewed with the addition of each new generation of workers into the labour force'. In the language of postmodern critique, we may draw upon this Marxist analysis of accumulation and social regulations to point to the struggle which capital continually faces in creating the new subjectivities of workers and consumers necessary to the maintenance and reproduction of an economic system dependent on a modernizing process of continuous growth and innovation.

Another way of signifying an economic transition which has occurred since the 1970s is to identify the *before* as Fordism, and the *after* as, of course, post-Fordism. These periodizing designations have the advantage of strongly linking methods of Fordist production (the standardized assembly line manufacturing regime symbolized by Henry Ford's Michigan plant) with a set of interconnecting social relations including:

> the link between the systems of mass production and mass consumption, the role of Keynesianism and the welfare state in underwriting long term growth and profitability, and the integration of trade unions, on an industrial and later national/corporate basis, in the management of the post-war Fordist economy. (Rustin, 1989: 56)

The term 'post-Fordism' can be used to designate many of the features of contemporary late capitalism to which we have already referred in this and previous chapters: the impact of new communication technology and a speeding up of knowledge production, product diversification and the increased market dependency of consumers, flatter organizational hier-archies and greater lateral communication. What is clear from the attempts to summarize the changes which have taken place between the Fordism upon which mass production, strong trade unions and the Keynesian welfare state were based, and the present is that we now experience differences in almost every aspect of our economic, social and political life. Although we must be careful not to homogenize and over-simplify the contrast between present and past and to recognize, for example, that elements of Fordism continue to operate in some sectors and some countries *alongside* post-Fordist develop-ments, nevertheless, attempts to identify the features of the new economies and their link to postmodern cultural discourses (scepticism, uncertainty, emphasis on diversity and a renewal of intense individualism) are useful undertakings. They are useful because the abstraction involved in such attempts at understanding, although rejected by some postmodernists as metanarrative goulash, is the one way in which we can hope to gain any critical distance from the contemporary experience of chaos and uncertainty, especially so far as discussing the economy is concerned. In defending his attempt to theorize postmodernism in a 'totalizing' way, Jameson writes, I believe convincingly:

> when one is immersed in the immediate – the year by year experience of cultural and informational messages, of successive events, of urgent priorities – the abrupt distance afforded by an abstract concept, a more global characterization of the secret affinities between those apparently autonomous and unrelated domains, and

of the rhythms and hidden sequences of things we normally remember only in isolation and one by one, is a unique resource, particularly since the history of the preceding few years is always what is least accessible to us. Historical reconstruction, then, the positing of global characterizations and hypotheses, the abstraction from the 'blooming, buzzing confusion' of immediacy, was always a radical intervention in the here-and-now and the promise of resistance to its blind fatalities. (Jameson, 1989: 33)

It is within the dominant discourses on the economy, the characterizations of current fiscal crises and their relevance to the future of the welfare state, that we are most likely to succumb to 'blind fatalities' rather than resist, first at the level of counter-theorization, the taken-for-granted 'certainties' which attempt to cover over the undertying imperatives and the resulting uncertainties. We see the value of a distancing abstraction in the attempts that have been made to identify the general characteristics of contemporary capitalist economies, variously labelled as Post-Fordist, Flexible, Disorganized or Post-scarcity forms of capitalism, compared with their immediate historical predecessors which flourished in the post-war Keynesian world (Giddens, 1994; Harvey, 1990; Lash and Urry, 1987). A comparison of Fordist and post-Fordist models of economies and their respective sets of social relations are presented by Rustin (1989) in a way which suggests that each is an abstraction, using a sociological ideal type which points to contrasts in discourses and practices. Rustin is critical of using the models as homogeneous, monolithic entities, not allowing for their continued *co-existence*. His is an important cautionary reservation, but the models have significant heuristic value for our discussion because they enable us to speculate on the interconnection between economics and social relations. Rustin's two models, in other words, are constructed in an attempt to provide a Marxist account of change, but in a form which avoids the rigid economic and technological determinism which would have characterized a more orthodox Marxist analysis. Nevertheless, the two models suggest a relationship between changes in the means of production and their consequences for class relations and ideologies. The summary of the two models presented in Table 5.1 is based on Rustin's presentation (1989: 56–7).

Although these models were originally constructed in order to theorize the relationship between changes in the economy and Thatcherism in Britain, they remain useful for wider discussion. Items 2, 3 and 4 in the two models have already received attention in Chapter 4, Items 5, 6, 7 and 9 will be discussed in the next chapter, while Item 8 will be considered primarily in our final chapter. In this chapter we will next look in greater detail at Rustin's Item 1, the new methods of manufacture, in particular, 'lean production', an innovation which characterizes post-Fordism, and then move to an examination of the consequences of the new economy for labour processes, employment and unemployment. The significance of these consequences for the provision of welfare will be considered in the conclusion of the chapter.

Table 5.1   *Fordist and Post-Fordist Modes of Production and Regulation*

	Fordism	Post-Fordism
1	Low technological innovation Fixed product lines Long runs Mass marketing	Accelerated innovation High variety of product Shorter runs Market diversification and nicheing
2	Steep hierarchy Vertical chains of command Mechanism organization	Flat hierarchy More lateral communication Organismic organization
3	Vertical and horizontal integration Central planning	Autonomous profit centres Network systems Internal markets within firm Outsourcing
4	Bureaucracy	Professionalism Entrepreneurialism
5	Mass unions Centralized wage bargaining	Localized bargaining Core and periphery Workforce divided No corporatism
6	Unified class formations Dualistic political systems	Pluralist class formations Multi-party systems
7	Institutionalized class compromises	Fragmented political markets
8	Standardized forms of welfare Prescribed 'courses' in education	Consumer choice in welfare Credit transfer Modularity and self-guided instruction 'Independent' study
9	Class parties Nationwide	Social movements Multi parties Regional diversification

Source: Rustin, 1989: 56–7

Lean Production and Re-engineering

We have already discussed, in general terms, the effect of new computer technologies on the globalization of capitalism. In particular, we have noted the communication resources it provides which enable rapid marketing and investment decisions to be made with relative ease, despite the negative economic and social consequences which might follow such decisions. But we need, now, to examine in greater detail the impact of such technology on production itself, both in manufacturing and service sectors, because recent developments in this field have direct consequences on levels of employment and wages and therefore have substantial relevance to welfare provision whether we are speaking of taxable income, unemployment insurance, the need for social security benefits, or the social and psychological strains produced by the continuous restructuring of labour processes.

In examining the application of technology to the production methods of the new economy, specifically 'lean production' in manufacturing and 're-engineering' in service industries, I am drawing heavily on the review of these developments undertaken by Head (1996). The lean production methods which originated in Japan and have subsequently been diffused throughout advanced capitalist countries, have certain basic characteristics in common: 'products must be easy to assemble ("manufacturability"); workers must be less specialized in their skills ("flexibility of labour"); and stocks of inventory must be less costly to maintain (components arrive at the assembly plant "just in time", and so save on both warehousing and financing costs)' (1996: 7). These characteristics are especially important to productivity in industries such as automobiles, electronics and machine tools, industries in which the application of lean production has made major strides. 'Manufacturability', for example, includes an incentive to reduce the numbers of parts and tools required in making a car or a machine tool, and as a consequence reducing an industry's reliance on highly skilled craft workers. Instead, the new forms of production require, as we saw in a previous chapter, the organizing of workers into teams. These groups of 'integrated workers' have few skills beyond the capacity and commitment to fit into the work team. Whereas the craft labour which was the cornerstone of post-war Fordist production, for example, in the German car industry, was compartmentalized within the rigid boundaries defined by the craft, in the new lean production era, flexibility, fluidity and deskilling are the norm. It is not surprising that such new methods are popular in the large corporations because it 'dramatically lowers the amount of high wage effort needed to produce a product of a given description, and it keeps reducing it through continuous incremental improvement' (Womack et al., 1990).

In the drive to increase profitability and maintain a competitive edge, lean production methods enable productivity to rise, but in the United States, for example, where industrial restructuring has had a major impact, this increase in productivity has not been accompanied by a rise in real wages, but instead by a fall. 'The average weekly earnings of ... rank and file [American] workers, again adjusted for inflation, fell by 18 per cent between 1973 and 1995. By contrast, between 1979 and 1989 the real annual pay of corporate chief executives increased by 19 per cent, and by 66 per cent after taxes' (Head, 1996: 47). This is not, of course, a surprising consequence of a rise in productivity which is accompanied by the removal of skilled workers and their replacement by the less skilled. Where trade unions are relatively weak and as a result bargaining power declines, the exploitation of labour goes up a few notches. It is the owners of capital, including shareholding senior executives, who reap the rewards of greater productivity. And it is because, in most Western countries, the trade unions are weakest in the sector of the smaller companies and paternalistic sweatshops that supply components for the large manufacturers, that wage levels are further depressed. The dramatic increase in the practice of contracting out, or 'outsourcing' in post-Fordist industrial development has been noted by numerous commentators (Harvey, 1990; Rustin, 1989; Swyngedouw, 1986). Contracting out the manufacture of components to non-unionized smaller concerns enables the large corporations, such as car manufacturers, to close plants and reduce their own more unionized workforce. Falling wage levels attest to the effectiveness of outsourcing as a technique of lean production: small component companies are often prepared to operate on minimal profit margins in order to secure orders from the large corporations who thus make profits greater than they would if they manufactured the components themselves.

While the restructuring which is driven by the idea of lean production proceeds to work its way through manufacturing industry, a similar process is taking place in the service industries, especially in banking, insurance and communications. Here the process is called 're-engineering' (Champy, 1995; Hammer and Champy, 1993). 'Just as Henry Ford once found a substitute for skilled craftsmen in rows of machines arranged along an assembly line, so the experts called "re-engineers" have combined the skills of specialist clerks and middle managers into software packages that are attached to desktop computers' (Head, 1996: 47). The purpose of re-engineering is to use information technology to speed up and simplify the routine activities in businesses such as banking and insurance. Computer software is able to undertake the tasks and often replace large numbers of relatively skilled workers. One employee using a software program can displace, indeed not only a large number of clerical workers, but even some 'middle management' staff (Hammer and Champy, 1993: 39). As in the case of lean production, re-engineering reduces rather than increases the level of skill required of the workers who remain or replace those who have been displaced. The workers who use desktop computers are often not only less skilled than those they have replaced but also have a lower level of education. The highly skilled employees that remain at work in a re-engineered company are likely to be either the technological experts who are in charge of a continuous process of re-engineering or contract workers, employed temporarily to meet a particular technical need and the least likely to be unionized.

The implications of lean production and re-engineering developments are profound: they have already made their impact on both large corporations and on the smaller subsidiary companies and sweatshops that supply them. The process of cost reduction, soaring profits in many sectors, deskilling and workforce reduction is still probably at a relatively early stage and 'rationalization' is likely to accelerate with technological innovations which lead to continuous incremental improvement in the interests of capital accumulation. If we take these developments in the technology of production alongside the increasing globalization of capital, the geographical mobility of investment and a world consumer market, we begin to build up a picture of what post-Fordist economies look like. It is an abstract, ideal type picture within which we must be aware of contradictions, counter trends and uneven development, but it is a representation which is of use to us. If we want to explore a *political economy* of post-Fordism, then we will need to return to the paradigm of the regulation school referred to earlier, namely one which links the *regime of accumulation* with a *mode of social and political regulation* (Aglietta, 1979; Lipietz, 1987). It is a paradigm which attempts to understand how changes in the capitalist global economy and its associated transformations in technology might create, influence or, less deterministically, be linked to change in social relations including ideologies, political strategies, class formations and cultural production. A political economy approach, however tentative in its explanations of the possible connections which may exist between post-Fordist economies and post-modern social conditions, 'the cultural logic of late capitalism', is a necessary discourse of resistance, in my view. It is a discursive intervention into a dominant narrative which attempts to separate the economic from the socio-political through attributing to economic decisions an autonomy that denies the embeddedness of a mode of production in sets of social and cultural relations which construct the subjectivities and practices of both capitalists and workers. Thus, abstracted 'economic realities' are said to determine 'what kind of welfare we can afford'. By examining the implications of these realities (technology, globalization, flexible accumulation and organization) for the social relations that generate discourses on welfare, we can, perhaps, challenge the economic determinism which characterizes contemporary debate about the welfare state.

New Economies and New Social Discourses

'Post-Fordism', 'flexible accumulation', 'globalization' are the terms we have used to signify changes in both economic practices and discourses. The organization of production, as we have seen, is not only the organization of inert material resources such as computers, stocks of components or assembly lines, but crucially involves the organization of human resources, of the living labour upon which production ultimately depends. In the previous chapter I argued that the organization of subjects might be usefully seen as a discursive process aimed at maximizing rationality and order and eliminating or, more realistically, reducing the threat of unpredictability, of the eruption of uncontrolled desire, or, in a word – disorganization. We have also noted that the organization of production requires the organization of consumption, the commodification of culture and the manufacture, management and, as far as possible, the control of desire. Thus, both the manufacture and marketing of products demand the organization of subjects, a process characterized, as ever, by an interaction between power and resistance.

The constitution of the subject positions required by the organization of post-Fordist production takes place within an entrepreneurial economic discourse which places central emphasis on the brutal necessity for the worker to change his or her participation in the labour process or else be displaced. Continuation in employment may be accompanied by wage reductions, with the alternative being unemployment. The new subjectivities required of most workers in a 're-engineered' enterprise are not those associated with the skills of a craft, but subordination to a software package. A certain pride in the attainment and utilization of a high level of skill is replaced by the routinization and powerlessness associated with dependence on a piece of technology. This process of deskilling human labour is not a new element in the capitalist organization of production, as Marx pointed out in 1844; the worker is tied to the machine and experiences the labour process as standing in opposition to the needs and desires of the individual subject:

> labour is exterior to the worker, that is, it does not belong to his essence. Therefore, he does not confirm himself in his work, he denies himself, feels miserable instead of happy, deploys no free physical and intellectual energy, but mortifies his body and ruins his mind. Thus the worker only feels at home outside his work and in his work he feels a stranger. (Marx, 1844/1971: 137)

Through re-engineering, this experience of estrangement or alienation is amplified because skills and aptitudes previously practised by workers – the mental aspects of labour – are appropriated for capital by senior managers and technological experts and encapsulated in a computer software package. This appropriation of intellectual labour is only the most recent example of a process whereby

> capital, as soon as it disposes of a mass of labour in any speciality – a mass adequate in size to repay the application of its principles of the technical division of labour and hierarchical control over execution by means of a firm grasp on the links of conception – subjects that speciality to some of the forms of 'rationalization' characteristic of the capitalist mode of production. (Braverman, 1974: 408)

The economic logic of the organization of subjects to the requirements of the new forms of production and labour process is proclaimed, within dominant discourses, as not only necessary but also desirable. One of the foremost exponents and implementers of re-engineering in the United States, Hammer, presents his utilization of technological innovations within a discourse which addresses those who are to be acted upon in the unmistakable language of power and domination, a language upon which the owners and managers of capital can act (Hammer and Stanton, 1995). Head (1996) summarizes this machismo discourse of toughness by quoting from Hammer and Stanton's book, *The Reengineering Revolution*:

> According to [Hammer] 'slapping people's wrists instead of breaking their legs' is 'another sign of weakness'; and again, 'making it clear that termination is the consequence of their behaviour is a very valid technique'. Hammer also writes with considerable frankness about the climate of fear that re-engineering can create. He mentions the 'trepidation and anxiety' of the work force, and the 'abject terror' and 'total inner panic' of those who are told that they are 'going to have to change what they do'. (Head, 1996: 50)

A discourse which maintains that 'change' in labour processes is necessary and that 'resistance to change' has to be overcome by whatever means are at hand, defuses and depoliticizes the nature of the change which is being experienced: the appropriation of skills, a possible reduction in income, the threat of termination and unemployment, and the longer-term uncertainty and insecurity produced by the prospect of 'continuous incremental improvement' in productivity through endless technological replacements of human labour.

Although it speaks of the joys of entrepreneurial innovation, the discursive tone of the dominant discourse of the new economy of lean production and re-engineering is often one of necessity rather than contingency, of the force of technology rather than the acts of will which produce the changes that workers experience. Technology is *used* in the pursuit of ever-higher levels of profitability, but technology does not *determine* the process of change. Technological determinism is a significant ideological strand in the legitimation of the pain, disruption and dislocation produced by the transition to a new economy: it masks the decisions that are made in the furtherance of particular class, gender and ethnic interests. The need for a non-reductionist political economy approach in order to decipher the discourses which justify the transformations of late capitalism in the language of economic and technological necessity is made clear in Rustin's analysis:

> One needs to see Fordism and post-Fordism as specific, willed resolutions of conflicts at the level of social relations, not as the automatic outcomes of the technological imperatives of 'mass production' or its information based successor. The key to understanding these forms are the relations between the *strategies* of capital and labour, and the material conditions in which they are conducted. These are, after all, relations of power. (Rustin, 1989: 63)

In the next chapter we will examine the *politics* of these relations between capital and labour; in this chapter I want to pursue the closely related theme of the process of power/resistance between the owners and senior managers of capital, on the one hand, and the workers on the other. We have seen already that the prospect of industrial restructuring, according to the 're-engineers', produces in workers feelings of panic and terror. But what is available to them as resources with which to resist the juggernauts of industrial transformation with their accompaniment of downsizing, deskilling, displacement and unemployment? Subjected to the dominant discourse of the economic necessity of individual adjustment, both blue collar workers and the now redundant middle managers face what is presented to them as a fact of life in the new economy. We cannot, after all, resist market forces and so we should embrace them, become small-scale entrepreneurs, learn new (computer) skills, accept lower paid temporary or part-time jobs or else join the ranks of the long-term unemployed, thereby adding to the 50 per cent of the unemployed population of European countries, for example, who have been out of work for more than twelve months (Kroeger, 1993: 26). Identification with the narrative of global market necessity is difficult to avoid given the massive media reproduction of this message. It is not surprising that being coerced and induced into the subject position of one whose previous skills and company loyalty are no longer needed is likely to produce intense feelings of inadequacy, guilt and depression. In a culture where the ethic of 'productive work' is traditionally so powerful, the individual subject's relationship to production is critical to a sense of coherent identity. To have no relationship to production, or to have one characterized by the insecurity which comes from belonging to a 'contingent workforce' of temporary contract labour, is to experience the most negative personal consequences of the restructuring of the new economy. While at the individual level the power of re-engineering and lean production may sometimes be met with the traditional defensive weapons of industrial sabotage, with avoidance, minor disruption, complaints and verbal confrontations, fear stalks the corridors and assembly lines of organizations going through a process of restructuring, a process often characterized by both brutality and brevity. The fear experienced by workers threatened with restructuring and unemployment is based upon a realistic assessment of the growing disparities of power between owners and senior executives who make the central investment and organizational decisions and the middle and lower level workers whose collective strength appears to be weakening daily. The lowering levels of unionization in the United States, for example, collapsing even in the major automobile corporations, virtually non-existent in the service industries, tells a story of a decline of collective resistance. Even in Britain, trade union membership, previously maintained at a very high level, is experiencing major decline.

Is the fact that union membership is declining the *result* of the application of the new technology to industry, a situation in which economic conditions have changed so radically that unions are no longer viable? Those who control the investment and technological power which drives economic restructuring would answer in the affirmative: unions are the antiquated relics of an earlier Fordist and Keynesian age where overall economic strategies were decided through bargaining and compromise between capital, labour and the state. This social democratic hegemony in the management of the economy, it would be argued, has given way to a freer, entrepreneurial individualism based upon a necessary respect for market forces and techno-logical innovation, a decline in state regulation and interference and a consequent collapse in the need for unions.

We might see this argument that the decline of union power is a *function* of economic change, a contemporary consequence of the historic capitalist dynamic of technological imperatives, as another determinist account which suggests that resistance is futile and that only adaptation is 'realistic'. Although in such an account human agency appears in the form of 'belief in market forces', it soon disappears again under the pressure to mask, in the language of necessity, the intention to maximize dividends. Even if we use the language of the regulation school, however, we may still ask ourselves whether the changed social relations which have resulted in a decline in union power were the *consequence* of changes in the economy, or whether an opposite flow of influences can be detected: that the new economy is a form of class struggle against the power of unions and the working class. The unions then become the target of change rather than merely a consequence of change. Let us pursue the dialectic of this relationship between capital and labour organization.

In a study called *The End of Organized Capitalism*, Lash and Urry (1987) see the new economies as characterizing a 'disorganized' capitalism, one of disintegration compared with the Fordist economies and strong unions which formed the basis of the post-Second World War accommodation between capital and labour in Western countries. Lash (1989) points to the fact that between the two world wars, 70 per cent of Britain's 'economically active' population comprised employed manual workers in manufacturing, mining or construction, providing the numerical basis for a strong and pervasive working class culture and institutions unmatched elsewhere. In other Western countries, this working class core was less than 50 per cent and in the United States less than 40 per cent. The decomposition and fragmentation of the working class in Britain, together with the 'embourgeoisement' of some of its population have led to a strange reversal: Britain has now a smaller working class than many other capitalist countries, including Sweden, Germany, France and Japan (Lash, 1989: 27). In attempting to explore the economic, cultural and political roots of the collapse of Fordism, Keynesianism and the organized working class, Lash and Urry (1987) point to a set of linkages between the new economy and its accompanying social relations which may be taken as a tentative explanation of the decline of collective resistance to the power of capital, though to describe the present capitalism as 'disorganized' is hardly a convincing label; in fairness, however, one might say that the ten years that have passed since Lash and Urry's work have demonstrated exactly how 'organized' post-Fordist capitalism is.

The links between the economy and labour organization, Lash and Urry argue, begin with recognition of a process of the deconcentration of rapidly increasing corporate power away from national markets and into a global market and the separation, in some cases, of industrial from bank capital. In terms of social stratification, there is a continued expansion of a managerial stratum of people who articulate their own individual and political agendas, quite distinct from traditional class politics. This development is accompanied by a relative or absolute decline in the traditional blue collar working class, contributing to a decline in the effectiveness of national collective bargaining, reinforced by the challenge to national boundaries presented by international corporations increasingly free from state regulation. Diverse class interests are no longer incorporated in a social democratic way within a national economic agenda negotiated between capital, workers and state bureaucracy: the interests of capital become, instead, freed from impediments to the imperative of maximizing profitability. The defence of working class interests collapses (Harvey, 1990: 175; Lash and Urry, 1987).

This is now a familiar account of a part of the transition from Fordism to post-Fordism. It places economic change in the centre of the picture and shows its possible relation to the decline of working class resistance, including the argument that changes in the nature and distribution of production processes may have been instigated specifically to avoid having to bargain with organized labour. There can be little doubt that 'outsourcing' and the use of a 'contingent workforce' of contract labour was designed by American automobile manufacturers to cripple the United Auto Workers. This latter argument is made more strongly by Rustin (1989), who sees the new post-Fordist economic strategies not simply as a profit-seeking response of capital to the potential of the new technologies, but more importantly as a strategic class response to the threat of labour collectivism. So far as capital was concerned, the later years of Fordism were a period in which the balance of class forces appeared increasingly weighted in favour of orga- nized labour, social democratic governments and forms of state intervention which increased the decommodified public sector and led, in some Western countries, to severe political and economic crises (O'Connor, 1973, 1986; Offe, 1984). So post-Fordism was, in part, a countermove by capital and its allied ruling classes, Rustin argues, against the social gains made by the subordinate classes, and provided the energy and commitment necessary for the emergence of a politics which encapsulated this strategy – Reaganism, Thatcherism and their successors.

> The underlying purpose of this [strategy] was to remove collectivist threats to capital accumulation and authority, and to give private capital access to potential markets (in health, insurance, pensions, education and training, transport, energy, prison building and management) from which it had been previously excluded. Capital as a whole sought to gain by recommodifying sectors recently excluded from the market, and by the disorganization of resistance to capital which followed from the restoration of market disciplines. (Rustin, 1989: 62)

The process of turning the tables on organized labour and interventionist Keynesian governments was most dramatically evidenced in the case of Britain under Thatcherism, but similar, if not always such abrupt, changes took place in other Western countries. New Zealand governments from the mid-1980s, for example, have pursued a policy of restructuring which has involved the privatization of state-owned corporations, the radical reduction of welfare state programmes, contracting out government services and the deregulation of many corporate activities (Kelsey, 1995). Thus the country which can claim to have given birth to the welfare state in the early 1940s, has undergone radical transformation in the interests of capital. Trade union membership has fallen from 41 per cent to 24 per cent of the labour force and real wages have also dropped, as they have in the USA. The number of New Zealand citizens who are considered to be below the poverty line increased by 35 per cent between 1989 and 1992. Whereas British and New Zealand governments began their countermoves against labour in the 1980s, in other countries the most severe ideologically driven assault on working populations in the interests of capital are gaining further strength in the late 1990s. The growth of an ultra-Right Republicanism in the USA is com- mitted to giving maximum support to most of the interests of entrepreneurial capital, although populist counter-trends within the same right-wing dis- course emphasize the plight of white male workers adversely affected by the investment strategies of international corporations searching for low wage labour markets. In Canada, the provincial governments of Ontario and Alberta are committed to a radical Right policy of massive cuts in public expenditure, reduction of the 'tax burden' on private enterprise, deregulation, and other measures designed to further change the balance of class forces in the interests, the victorious Ontario conservatives proclaimed, of a 'common sense revolution'.

Economy and Welfare

I have attempted, in the foregoing pages, to build a picture of the characteristics of the new economies which intersect and compete with each other within a global capitalist market. The move from old to new forms, signified by the terms 'Fordist' and 'post-Fordist' economies, have had dramatic effects on the subject positions of individuals, on the cultural discourses to which populations of workers/consumers are exposed, on the forms of work organization emerging in private and state sectors and on the balance of political and social forces in capitalist countries. The role of new technologies has been crucial in the economic transitions that have been experienced world-wide, but I have cautioned against assuming a technologically determinist position. In the dialectic of the technological means of production in relation to the social forces in which they are embedded, I have suggested that the transition was fuelled not only by technology but also by the willed intention of capitalist classes and their governments to roll back the social advances made by working populations in combination with Keynesian interventionist state programmes and regulations.

One important consequence of the transition to post-Fordism has been in the decomposition and restructuring of class positions and their intersection with the social divisions of gender, race, ethnicity and other socio-economic categories and sources of identity, subordination and resistance. We have noted already that the new restructured economies produce an increase in the populations existing under conditions of poverty. It is a population which now consists not only of what might be called the traditional poor – such as low wage earners (now increasing), single mothers living on welfare payments and disadvantaged racial and ethnic minorities – but also of other class fragments. As reinvestment, lean production and re-engineering work their way through capitalist economies, new segments of the population are displaced and many find their way into the ranks of the poor for the first time in their lives. These newly poor have never previously experienced long-term unemployment or the daily struggle for existence which characterizes life on a very low income, and the process of adaptation and resistance to a new subject position has its profound effects. Another segment of the working population is existing on outsourcing, temporary and part-time contract labour interspersed with bouts of unemployment, and experiences the intense insecurity which comes from being aware that other people's decisions could quickly place them in the ranks of the poor. The existence of this pool of contingent and reserve labour, precariously divided from the socio-economic segment below it, serves for the whole working and middle class population as a powerful source of labour discipline. Poverty, unemployment and insecure employment always play a crucial role in the social regulation of labour in capitalist economies: under post-Fordist conditions a wider population is subjected to this particular element of regulation which secures for capital a widening gap between increasing profits and reducing real wage levels.

One further class segment needs to be noted here. The new economy of late capitalism is one, as we have already argued in previous chapters, which depends to a major degree on *cultural production*. The manufacture of desire through television, film and advertising, the production of knowledge in the service of the corporate institutions that finance it through universities and the invention and utilization of new technologies all require a professional cadre equipped with the skills and motivations to serve (with whatever accompanying protestations of ambivalence and regret) the interests of capital. This segment of the population, infused by a spirit of cultural entrepreneurialism and a commitment to the acquisition, application and transmission of knowledge, is a moving force in the new economy. Although it provides for capital the specialized and irreplaceable knowledge required for innovative production and insatiable consumption, this intellectual stratum includes an element which is politically centrist or left-wing – feminist, social democratic or socialist, anti-racist, environmentally sensitive and committed to respect for social, cultural and sexual diversity. It might be called a 'critical yuppie' intelligentsia. It is a segment of an intellectual élite which has been largely formed by the new economy and has benefited substantially from it.

In writing about Britain in the late 1980s, Rustin (1989) points to this intelligentsia and the way in which its embracing of some elements of post-Fordist (and postmodern) political agendas concerned with issues of individual identity, decentralization, community control and consumer choice are all issues directed not to the poor but 'the active enfranchised participants in consumer and cultural markets' (p. 64). Rustin remarks on the fact that this élite group of professionals possess what might be called 'cultural capital' but little material capital and so its political critique of the new brutal economy reflects its relative cultural advantage and relative material disadvantage compared to the senior managers and owners of multinational capital.

> A field of battle is thus mapped out between 'material' and 'cultural' capital – roughly, business versus quality of life and the environment, commercial taste versus discriminating minority tastes and lifestyles – whilst the large part of the population who possess few capital resources at all, material or cultural, are allowed to disappear almost out of political sight. (p. 64)

These are interesting observations. We might say of Rustin's comments, however, that they referred specifically to Britain and that in the years since he wrote this, the position of this élite in Western countries has also changed in the direction of greater insecurity. As university tenure becomes more difficult to achieve, as 'soft funding' provides an increasing proportion of research salaries and as media competition intensifies, permanent, long-term professional employment becomes, for many, a thing of the past. An increase of insecurity in this group may have its effect in directing more political attention to issues of poverty, employment, trade union resistance and welfare provision.

In identifying some of the changes in class composition which appear to have been a consequence of the transition to a post-Fordist economy, my intention has been to highlight increasingly widespread experiences of poverty, unemployment, deskilling and temporary employment and the insecurity (material and emotional) which is produced in the individual subject as a result. The material conditions under which a growing population of not only working class but also some middle class people live, produce massive pressure on social welfare services and benefits, broadly defined. The contradiction encountered by the welfare state during a period of economic transition and personal and social disorganization is that the demand for welfare increases at the same time as dominant social forces insist on curbing social expenditures or, increasingly at the present time, reducing the real level of these expenditures. Unemployment, low wages and general insecurity lead to increased demand not only for state payments and benefits, but also for services which are intended to ameliorate the negative impact of economic change on the well-being of individuals and families. The social and material crisis produced by a change in the balance of class forces results in increased stress and illness which lead to more patient and client demand on health services. Poor nutrition over extended periods of time leads to numerous physical health problems, including the re-emergence of tuberculosis, and the emotional stress of poverty, insecurity, losses of identity and similar pressures are closely associated with depression, anxiety states and drug and alcohol abuse. Poverty, unemployment and insecurity present substantial obstacles to effective parenting, especially for women struggling alone as parents, often unable to nurture their children in the way they wish to. The impact on personal social services, especially in the area of child protection, of the filtering through to individual subjects (adults and children) of the dynamics of the new economy presents itself as further pressure on the human and material resources of the welfare state. Even in the field of higher education, for example, the effects of economic change are evident. Here, not only is government funding, in a number of countries, being reduced and student fees increased, but the demand for places often expands. This increase in demand is fuelled by increased competition for a declining number of high skill jobs for which extensive training is required, and by the perception that given the levels of unemployment delaying entry to the labour market might prove beneficial. The subject position of student, whatever the employment prospects, is to be preferred to that of unemployed person living on state benefits: the level of material subsistence may be identical but the respective social identities may be experienced as dramatically different.

When we speak of the impact of economic change on welfare, we must give attention not only to the populations defined primarily by their class positions, but also to the diversity represented within those populations. Racial and disadvantaged ethnic minority status without doubt increases the weight of the burden of changes in the balance of social forces. Within the context of an institutional racism which affects life chances in terms of education, health status and employment, we can expect minority Others to suffer more severely from the changed social relations which accompany post-Fordist production. Gender subordination simply compounds and exacerbates the position of these racial and ethnic minority subjects in relation to the economy and the welfare state.

Changes in the economy and their interconnection with changes in welfare are addressed, justified or challenged within political/theoretical discourses. In this chapter I have relied primarily on a Marxist analysis in order to attempt to describe, and more tentatively explain, the economic transitions we are experiencing. This is because I believe that no other perspective supplies at present the conceptual categories necessary to advance our understanding. In particular, a critical discourse of political economy, especially in its analysis of the dialectic of accumulation and regulation, provides us with a means of enhancing our perception of the dominant neo-conservative discourse on the economy and welfare, whether the discursive language is that of the Right or the Centre.

It is appropriate in discussing this dominant discourse to focus on the issue of *employment*. This is because high levels of unemployment are widely spoken of as problematic for both the economy (fewer productive workers and decreased domestic consumer demand) and for welfare (increased payments and a reduced tax base to fund them). Also, the policy aim of Fordist social democratic welfare states was *full employment* through a range of economic and social interventions which happily coincided with the long international economic boom of 1947–73. What is clear today is that there is a strong connection between full or high levels of employment and the prospects for the welfare state. Who is responsible for full employment, government or the investors of capital? Governments pursue policies of the retraining of workers, often on the assumption that achieving full employment depends upon having a highly skilled workforce. But this widely held assumption of Western governments is open to considerable doubt if we take account of our previous discussion of re-engineering and lean production methods. Increased productivity and therefore profitability are being achieved through the appropriation via technology of workers' high level skills and their replacement by less skilled workers: more can be produced, more cheaply, by fewer and less skilled workers. But despite the doubts we may harbour about the need for highly skilled workers, we can acknowledge that the dominant discourse sees full employment being no longer a responsibility of government but the consequence of capital investment decisions made in the light of market forces. Writing specifically on the Canadian economy, but in terms which have widespread application, Kerans (1994) addresses the assumption that the question of full employment is entirely in the hands of investors, an assumption that has underpinned political discussion and has informed

> the discourse of many socially minded economists who, using human capital theory, argue that the tool of social policy is to provide healthy, well motivated and skilled workers in order that our economy be 'competitive'. The implications of this assumption, however, are deadly for the welfare state ... [because] the ability of trans-national corporations to move their productive facilities to almost any place on the globe has enabled them to demand more and more tax breaks to the point where Canada has a fiscal crisis. (Kerans, 1994: 125)

The dominant discourse on the beneficial relationship between capital investment and high levels of employment fails to admit, Kerans points out, that investment is not undertaken in order to create jobs but to increase dividends, a pursuit of greater profits through control of the productive process which involves, as we have seen, either the elimination of jobs or rendering them less skilled and lower waged: 'Little wonder that the collective belief that we must rely on investors and tax policies that reflect that reliance has produced a fiscal and a welfare crisis' (1994: 125).

In the new post-Fordist economy then, a return to high levels of employment fuelled by capital investment appears to be an unlikely outcome of present trends in lean production, re-engineering and the further application of computer technology generally. The pursuit of maximizing profit and the organization of social relations in such a way as will enable this objective to be achieved are the cornerstones of the capitalist mode of production. It is when that process of capitalist growth, innovation and control over labour is perceived as under serious challenge, as it was in the 1970s, that the interests of capital, connected as they are to the institutions and practices of patriarchy and institutional racism, are impelled to mount a counter-attack. Thus social struggles take a new turn, the balance of forces changes, and we enter an era of transition during which, Gramsci (1971: 276) famously remarks, 'the old is dying and the new cannot be born'. In the transition, capital has, at present, the upper hand, and so we cannot expect it to be favourable to the twin social guarantees which were the foundation of the challenge they have, for now, repelled – full employment and the Keynesian welfare state. High levels of unemployment are, after all, a central tool for the regulation of labour – unemployment reduces resistance to increases in the rate of exploitation of labour power through wage reduction and submission to increased control. At the same time, the welfare state, because it reflects the class compromises previously arrived at between capital and labour, performs its own role in the disciplining of labour and social regulation in general. It controls the incidence and level of poverty through its benefit systems, monitors the unemployed and engages in the surveillance, discipline and punishment of those at the bottom of the social order who are most oppressed by the new economy. It is for this reason that the more 'enlightened' members of the capitalist class tend to remain committed to retaining the regulatory and controlling functions of the diminishing welfare state, while seeking to abandon its more caring and empowering aspects, even though such aspects may be seen as more potential than actual.

Although capitalism is without doubt a revolutionary force in world history, transforming whole societies and bringing a form of modernity to countries across the globe, it remains prone to crises. We might see these crises in part as the result of the difficulty of matching the imperative of accumulation to the necessary forms of regulation. As a means of social regulation the welfare state may not always perform satisfactorily in functioning as a mechanism of control and a manager and diffuser of social crises. Its unreliability is always a source of concern, and at times it may need itself to be brought more directly under the control (discursive and institutional) of those whose primary interests the economy is intended to satisfy. But alongside the crisis which may come from a failure to coordinate the goal of the maximization of profit with the requisite social relations, come the crises which are the product of the triumphal discourse of modernity – the drive for growth and dynamic innovation as the indelible mark of 'progress'.

Like the necessity for the regulation of labour, commitment to growth, despite social and ecological consequences and technological innovation regardless of social disruption, has not been an optional element in capitalist economies. The pursuit of profitability is the central dynamic of the whole economic system – it is what has produced both its successes and its failures (the judgement of which, of course, depends upon your standpoint). What is especially difficult to achieve in capitalist economies over long periods of time is a degree of harmony between a steady rate of growth, the necessary level of productivity through the exploitation of labour and technological innovation in order to remain competitive. That these three requirements are often out of kilter with each other may be seen as an explanation of the crisis tendencies which are endemic to capitalist economies.

How do these crisis tendencies manifest themselves? Marx's answer, upon which Harvey (1990) builds, is that the three conditions necessary to a capitalist economy – growth, labour exploitation and technological innovation – are contradictory and cannot produce steady and unproblematic growth. The result of these crisis tendencies is that economies experience periods of over-accumulation, characterized by idle plants, a glut of commodities, surplus finance capital and high levels of unemployment. This is a fundamental tendency in capitalism, one which can never be eliminated, the only question therefore is 'how the over-accumulation tendency can be expressed, contained, absorbed or managed in ways that do not threaten the capitalist social order. We here encounter the heroic side of bourgeois life and politics, in which real choices have to be made if the social order is not to dissolve into chaos' (Harvey, 1990: 181).

Every choice that is made is a difficult one because responses to problems of accumulation have their effect on the social relations which sustain the capitalist economy. Each alternative in terms of the policies of corporations and governments can never, therefore, be made as simply *economic* decisions, but are complex strategies made up of many strands of tactical response and longer-term planning which must consider the balance of social forces and the means by which these forces can be managed. This is where social welfare institutions and practices enter in as one of the available means of the social management of crises. This is also where, at another level, dominant discursive formations play their critical role in attempting to legitimate and naturalize decisions about capital and labour so that they become, as far as possible, sedimented into a new 'common sense'.

One set of economic practices revolve around decisions to *devalue* commodities, productive capacities and the value of currency in order to reduce surpluses of capital. This will involve writing off the value of capital equipment, disposing of surplus stocks at reduced prices, inflationary erosion of consumer purchasing power, falling incomes and high levels of unemployment. The consequences of general devaluation as a response to over-accumulation are problematic for capital: the negative impact is felt by segments of all classes (bankruptcy, falling dividends, incomes and wages) if devaluation gets out of hand as it did in the 1930s, producing both Right and Left challenges to the capitalist order, including demands that the state intervenes in order to exercise control over the economy. The impact on the population of devaluation strategies, even relatively controlled ones, is severe: increases in poverty, falling incomes and a general climate of social disorganization may produce a dangerous level of demoralization in which the casualties of devaluation are left to the mercies of market forces and both capital and the state face a 'legitimation crisis'.

Although small-scale and controlled devaluation has played its part in meeting over-accumulation problems in the past twenty years, generally, since the Second World War until the mid-1970s, the strategy of choice has been Keynesian state intervention and regulation which kept over-accumulation under control and enabled a period of economic growth to take place before crisis erupted again. The management of the economy by the state and capital depended on the involvement of organized labour in many macro socio-economic decisions. The welfare state was one of the major gains achieved by labour in the bargaining process which was at the centre of economic management. The welfare state employed large numbers of the population, thus making its own contribution to a full employment policy, while at the same time both providing a healthier and better educated labour force and managing the substantial numbers of social casualties omnipresent in capitalist economies.

In the present post-Fordist period of transition, Keynesian intervention is no longer favoured, though the state continues to play an economic role, primarily to clear a path for the market decisions which capital must make in order to control its crisis tendencies. As we have seen, dramatic reductions in corporate tax levels is a policy understandably favoured by capital as a means of increasing dividends, but its consequences can also be problematic. The greatly reduced tax base leads ultimately to cuts in public expenditure which, in turn, have negative consequences for the health, well-being and ideological consent of the labour force on which capital depends. Such a process may, once again, eventually lead to a legitimation crisis. Another post-Fordist response to the problem of over-accumulation is to absorb excess capital and labour by developing new regions of the world where capitalist economies can flourish. Political changes such as the collapse of state socialist regimes can signal the opening up of new opportunities for production, consumption and relatively lower labour costs. Long-term capital investment across the globe absorbs surpluses and so avoids, at least for the short to middle term, the problems of over-accumulation. Following the Free Trade Agreement between the USA, Mexico and Canada, in 1995 the International Monetary Fund granted a loan of $17.8 billion to the Mexican economy; in 1996 it decided to provide credit to Russia of $10.1 billion provided it pursued the aim of developing a full capitalist market economy.

None of the means of managing the crisis tendencies of capitalist economies can, Marxist analysis suggests, provide a permanent solution.

> If continuous geographical expansion of capitalism were a real possibility, there could be a relatively permanent solution to the over-accumulation problem. But to the degree that the progressive implantation across the face of the earth extends the space within which the over-accumulation problem can arise, so geographical expansion can at least be a short-term solution to the over-accumulation problem. The long-run outcome will almost certainly be heightened international and inter-regional competition, with the least advantaged countries and regions suffering the severest consequences. (Harvey, 1990: 183)

The discussion of the emerging features of post-Fordist economies in their global market context has shown that it is not possible to consider these developments solely with an abstracted concept of 'economics'. The dynamic interplay of transformations in the economy with forms of organiz-ation, ways of life, cultural production and changes of subjectivity is difficult to grasp and interconnections can only be identified with consider-able tentativeness. The connection between the economy and the politics of labour regulation, however, appears more discernible. Certainly, major capitalist economic decisions carry with them profound implications for social and political relations which have to be taken into account in the calculation of advantage, disadvantage and risk. Alongside a politics of capitalist economic decisions, and posing always a problem for it, is the other politics, that of resistance. It is to this politics that we turn in the next chapter.

6

Politics

There is, perhaps, something bizarre about writing a chapter entitled 'politics' in a book that attempts to approach the crisis of the welfare state using a perspective that draws heavily on postmodernism, feminism and Marxism. For feminism and Marxism, the debates we have examined concerning the constitution of the subject, relationships between cultures, forms of organization or the imperatives of accumulation are all able to be reduced, to a substantial degree, to issues concerning the dynamics of patriarchy and capitalism and their ideological internalization: political struggle, in other words. From postmodernism, the politicization of the issues we have discussed operates at an even more profound level, because its epistemological challenge to the knowledge claims of modernity argues that once we have torn away the mask of rationality and objectivity legitimated in the name of progress, we are able to see that the exercise of power is as crucial a mechanism in the production of knowledge as it is in capital accumulation, the gender division of labour, or the commodification of culture. When we speak of power, we speak, then, of a politics of domination, struggle and resistance. In our analysis of the aims and organization of welfare, we have noted how the politics of the state's interest in the health and well-being of its populations has taken the form of the construction of appropriate subject positions in which the body is a site for the dynamic play of power and resistance. Furthermore, I have argued that the exercise of political power takes place increasingly in the context of cross-cultural contestation of the neo-colonial domination of populations of the Other. This confrontation of the negative elements of modernity by the Other, both internal and external to the nation state, ultimately develops itself in the international setting of the dynamics of the economic and political project of a global market.

If everything we have discussed so far is essentially political, then what is the focus of this chapter? The answer lies in what we have so far omitted: the possibility of *organized collective political resistance*. We have already acknowledged the omnipresence of a micro-politics of resistance to the exercise of discursive and institutional power, a form of individual resistance which feminism, above all, has enabled us to acknowledge as both political as well as personal. But if we go further and explore how a collective form of resistance is, or might be, mounted against dominant discourses and practices, are we going to collide, almost immediately, with the ghost of a politics already pronounced dead: the mass politics of the Left? Certainly, the idea of a postmodern mass politics of welfare reads as an oxymoron, because it seems to imply a return to phenomena already deconstructed by postmodernism: metanarratives of revolutionary progress, the establishment of bureaucratic party structures and the further reproduction of institutions of gender, ethnic, sexual or other forms of domination in the name of a universal welfare subject. But is this an unavoidable outcome of attempting to *organize* a politics of welfare on a broad front? Postmodern sceptics would certainly say so, and thus reveal themselves as able to establish a critique of the supposed monolith of late capitalism, but unable to offer us any way of counteracting, through the building of alternative, common discourses and practices, the prodigious powers of international corporations and governments. Marxist cultural critics of late capitalism such as Jameson (1984) and Eagleton (1986) have complained about the lack of a notion of revolutionary political action in much of postmodern writing, but have themselves often succumbed to near despair at the difficulty of confronting politically the cultural and economic monolith of the global market. Both the critique of the more world-weary and distancing elements of postmodernism and the sense of being overwhelmed by the idea of mounting a serious challenge to dominant discourses on the economy, cultural production or the welfare state, are entirely understandable, the optimism of the will, to use Gramsci's famous phrase, being almost obliterated by the pessimism of the intellect.

So, we have a difficult agenda for this chapter, one in which we may find that the serious political limitations of postmodernism will need to be balanced by a new application of a Marxist perspective on political intervention filtered through a postmodern reading of gender, cultural diversity and the organization of power/resistance. In what follows, I shall first explore what remains of a Marxist theory of political struggle after it has attempted to move in a 'linguistic' direction. This will lead to a discussion of the problems besetting the 'political' under postmodern conditions: the eruption of cynicism, pessimism and disgust, the collapse of transcendental guarantees for the 'correct' pathways to emancipation, and the emergence of a postmodern politics of the 'cool' as a trivial pursuit. We will then examine what, in the context of current politics, postmodernism might offer in terms of an *ethics* which could guide us in thinking about a politics which was affirmative in terms of emancipation, rather than cynical. This will enable us to evaluate the emergence of the new social movements as the political form of resistance favoured under postmodern conditions, and explore how such movements are articulated, at the local level, with a welfare politics of community action and what might be the limitations of such forms of struggle. Finally, we will return to the idea of *interdependency* and discuss the extent to which such an idea could help us develop a strategy of welfare politics which combined diversity with broad-based solidarity to form a foundation upon which claims about human need could be mounted.

Critical Marxism and Political Action

We have seen already, in an earlier chapter, how Marxist critics such as Althusser, Jameson and Eagleton became increasingly concerned with the language of cultural domination, with the mechanisms by which, through identification with dominant discursive formations, the individual subject of capitalism is rendered largely submissive to the social order. This 'linguistic version of Marxism', a conservative critic hostile to both Marxism and postmodernism (Himmelfarb, 1994: 157–8) maintains, places its protagonists in a 'popular front' with postmodernists, 'marching separately to a common goal'. Whilst such a view may be generated by the anxiety produced within the traditional academic establishment as a result of the successive assaults of Marxism, feminism and postmodernism on its authority, it indicates that a political common cause between postmodernism and a significant torch bearer of one version of modernity seems possible, at least to those who view such an alliance with distaste. But if we are to discuss such an alliance in terms of political action, then we must first backtrack a little and examine an attempt, from within the Marxist tradition, to rectify those problems in Marxist theory and politics which were made manifest in the historical changes which have taken place in capitalism in the twentieth century. I refer to the critical theory of the Frankfurt School and especially its major post-war philosopher, Habermas. We previously discussed Habermas's theory of communicative action when we explored its possible contribution to cross-cultural dialogue about human needs. Now, I must turn to the wider canvas of Marxist political theorization in order to identify the major elements of an attempt to reconstruct critical theory. This reconstruction enabled it to take the linguistic turn exemplified in the emphasis Habermas gives to the development of rational communication.

In his critique of the work of Habermas, Roderick (1986) leads into a discussion of the problems of critical theory by quoting a passage from Habermas which so sharply defines the problem he perceives in traditional Marxism that it deserves presenting here.

> What today separates us from Marx are evident historical truths, for example, that in the developed capitalist societies there is no identifiable class, no clearly circumscribed social group which could be singled out as the representative of a general interest that has been violated . . . Both revolutionary self-confidence and theoretical self-certainty are gone. (Habermas, cited by Roderick, 1986: 22)

In this passage, Habermas is pointing to uncertainty, to a series of doubts about the efficacy of Marxism not only as a revolutionary philosophy, but also as a political practice. Gone is the redemptive figure of the proletariat as the bearer of the forces of emancipation. Gone is the epistemological certainty upon which Marxist politics was once based. In the quarter century since Habermas wrote these words, pointing, he argued, to a profound crisis in Marxism and one to which critical theory should address itself, uncertainty has become even more deeply felt. Under the postmodern conditions of late capitalism, the decomposition and reconstitution of classes and the political struggles of women, racial and ethnic minorities, and other representatives of the excluded, all mark the transformation in the political terrain which Habermas already recognizes and which the contemporary linguistic and postmodern Marxists continue the attempt to understand. Without the guarantees of a scientific philosophy of historical materialism, Marxists turn elsewhere in the search for a foundation from which a politics can emerge. They still draw upon the insights which historical materialism provides as of a method of analysis, but see it now as a historically and culturally contingent discourse amongst other discourses.

But if uncertainty has replaced the self-confidence (perhaps arrogance would be a better word) of Western Marxists, then upon what new basis could a socialist politics of emancipation be established? Ultimately, as we saw in Chapter 3, Habermas answers by arguing that the traditional Marxist paradigm of production must be replaced by a paradigm of communication. Rational democratic communication in which the 'better argument' wins the day, provides, as we have seen, Habermas's means by which dominant ideologies are unmasked and an emancipatory consensus is established. In the earlier discussion, I questioned whether in the context of cross-cultural dialogue such communication required the guarantee of a notion of universal rationality and I need not repeat the argument here. Instead, I want to suggest that within the critical theory tradition and critical (as opposed to 'scientific') Marxism generally (Gouldner, 1980) there resides an element which provides a connection with postmodern critique. I am referring to the *process of self-reflection.*

Within critical theory, the process of self-reflection refers not only to the individual subject attempting to struggle against the internalizations of dominant ideology, but is also seen as a collective enterprise. Just as the individual might draw upon psychoanalytic insights in order to understand the formation of her or his own subjectivity, so a class or other social grouping can develop *reflexive knowledge* of the dominant ideologies which constrain them and limit their freedom. The point of developing a self-reflective knowledge is that, given the massive legitimating power of dominant ideology in late capitalism, the project of emancipation might be seen as securing freedom from *self-imposed* constraints. Emancipation on the basis of self-reflection (at individual and collective levels) is the central purpose of the critical theory of Habermas and it is this purpose which leads to an interest in language – the discourses within which ideology is embedded. For Habermas, as we have seen, emancipatory self-reflection is rooted in the search for at least one transcendental guarantee – a form of rationality which can provide the level of certainty needed to distinguish the truth of the oppressed from the ideology of the oppressors. It is this search for an objective rationality, of course, which divided Habermas from his postmodern critics.

But we do not have to retain Habermas's categorical distinction between emancipatory forms of rational communication and dominant ideology in order to make use of the process of self-reflection as a political practice. The knowledge which is developed as part of an emancipatory political struggle, such as the Marxist analysis of the economy used in the previous chapter, is itself grounded in specific historical situations from which there can be no escape. Self-reflection is a political process which enables a social movement to recognize that its ideas, even though expressing resistance, are still reflections of the social order from which they spring. We can search by self-reflection for the traces of dominant discourses embedded in our narratives of subordination and struggle, but we cannot eliminate them. And some discourses we may not even want to eliminate if we assume that dominant discourses contain contradictions (for example in the theory and practice of bourgeois democracy) reflecting the emancipatory potential still residing in them. On the other hand, those dominant discourses which we choose, in the name of emancipation, to oppose root-and-branch – such as those which legitimate various forms of racism – we may still find, if we are part of a white majority, embedded in our consciousness and from time to time revealing themselves to us, painfully. This is why those who are part of a population that has benefited and continues to benefit from institutional racism can never claim to be non-racist. We can still assume the sign of *anti-racist*, however, a word which signifies a commitment not only to fight the external forms of racism but also to struggle, through self-reflection, against the racism which is internalized. Those discourses which we would wish to appropriate for our own political objectives, such as the idea of democracy, we may also use as part of a method of 'internal criticism'. This practice of critiquing the dominant social order by identifying the conflict, internal to capitalism and produced by its own contradictions, between certain social ideals (such as democratic participation) required for the legitimation of the system, and the social practices necessary for the continuation of the system (centralized hierarchical decision making) demands a substantial degree of collective self-reflection. The ideal and limited practice of democracy may be seen, historically, as that which was extracted from previous ruling élites by a triumphal bourgeoisie in pursuit of its class and gender interests and extended as a result of further political struggle. Rethinking the idea of democracy as an element of further emancipation requires reflection on how deeply embedded within the discourse on democracy are the bourgeois and patriarchal assumptions about representation, leadership, majority rule, dissent and diversity.

If the practice of self-reflection aims to help us struggle against 'self-imposed' constraints, then it also provides us with a possible defence against dogma. If our own political beliefs and commitments are to be seen not as absolute Truth, but as insurgent critical discourses, bearing the indelible traces of their particular historical and cultural origins, then we may be more open to communication with significant political others, including the excluded Other. Perhaps a high level of self-reflection, individual and collective, is a necessary precondition for the development of solidarity on the foundations of diversity. Whether some degree of ontological self-doubt, a product of postmodern critique, is a source of political strength in the struggle for emancipatory advances or whether it is a handicap which results in mindless relativism and a blunting of political purpose remains subject to debate. We will turn to this debate in the next, and final, chapter.

To conclude a discussion of issues arising from the Marxist account of political struggle, we can identify a number of salient points. Let us turn to the debate about how a struggle against the ideologies which legitimate the capitalist exploitative productive process can be mounted. In the Fordist period of the Keynesian welfare state it was mainly argued (by Habermas) that capitalism no longer has to legitimate itself by reference to social ideals, but that legitimacy can be secured primarily by a technology-driven meeting of an apparently insatiable need to consume. The rise of capitalist legitimacy strategies based on consumption marks the final demise, it is suggested, of any possibility of a revolutionary class struggle against the process of production. This is a powerful argument made more cogent by the post-Fordist emphasis on the cultural manufacture of desire, the process of the decomposition of the traditional working class and the rise of neo-conservatism. But a Marxist analysis of the crisis tendencies of capitalism and the political consequences of the various choices available to capitalist decision makers when faced with over-accumulation (discussed in the previous chapter) indicates that the situation is more complex and perhaps more unstable than might first appear. Capitalism has not solved its crisis tendencies and cannot, we have argued, do so. The consequences of changes in the technological forces of production are not only to be seen in the expansion of consumption, but also in the disruption, deskilling and impoverishment of a wide section of the population of many Western societies. As the gap widens between those who are benefiting most from the re-engineering of production (shareholders and senior company executives) and those who are suffering most (unemployed or low waged workers) a class analysis re-enters into political discourse. A political intervention at this point might emphasize the exploitative nature of class relations, an analysis which would possibly resonate with the experiences of a substantial segment of workers, those forced to rely on state benefits, and displaced members of the lower end of the middle class.

In practice, the possibility of reinventing a politics of class struggle on a mass scale seems extremely difficult. It is, after all, one thing to identify, theoretically, a set of common class interests (of those impoverished, displaced and rendered redundant by the 'new economy') and it is another to assume a *consciousness* of these common interests. From a socialist or Left feminist standpoint, the economy of late capitalism is unjust because it is exploitative and objectifying, but from within the foundational assumptions of the capitalist mode of production no such critique can be mounted. Dependency on the labour market, 'freedom' to sell one's labour and to consume without constraint are the rights and responsibilities embedded in the dominant cultural discourses of capitalism. A critical distance is there-fore required in order to be able to hear and respond to a socialist, feminist or anti-racist discourse on 'justice' or 'exploitation': the postmodern culture of late capitalism, it is argued, makes such a distance especially difficult to achieve. Marxist ideas about political resistance and struggle, in taking a linguistic turn whereby the explanatory paradigm of production is joined by a paradigm of communication, meet the uncertainty generated by postmodern conditions.

Politics Under Postmodern Conditions

At various points in earlier chapters of this book I have indicated the difficulties that prominent cultural critics have encountered in envisaging a form of emancipatory politics appropriate to postmodern conditions. One explanation of these difficulties lies in their perception of late capitalism as an economic and cultural *monolith* which renders its subjects powerless in the face of dominant discursive formations. They tend to return, in other words, to Foucault's early formulation of 'inert bodies' – that which he formulated before he developed his more politically optimistic idea that power always meets with resistance. It must be admitted, however, that the sense of powerlessness which accompanies present social and economic uncertainties is widespread amongst critics, perhaps because in seeing how difficult it is to achieve 'critical distance' from the dominant culture they reflect a pervasive uncertainty about, if not rejection of, the 'political' in terms of the efficacy of organized resistance. It is the detachment of the theoretician, perhaps, who indeed views the social world 'at a distance', looks into the abyss and draws back, horrified. In a critique of postmodern writers which includes the work of Foucault, Derrida, Jameson, Eagleton and Rorty, McGowan (1991) pinpoints the political limitations of their approaches as follows:

> postmodern theory aims to discover some alternative principle of action to that offered by contemporary Western society, but . . . this aim is vitiated by the habitual association of opposition with distance and exteriority. Internal strategies of disruption and of generating pluralism are only fitfully employed by the writers I discuss. On the whole, these writers remain wedded to modernist notions of distance and disengagement as enabling radical critique, notions that their own attack on autonomous models of selfhood renders inoperable. (1991: 211)

What is argued here is that the postmodern theorist's desire to attain 'cultural distance' contradicts a view of subjectivity as so culturally conditioned and linguistically imprisoned that the required distance cannot be achieved. It is this problem which lies at the root of a certain political impotence characteristic of most postmodern perspectives: what to *do* with critique appears overwhelmingly difficult. The defence of difference, for example, is seen as essentially unachievable at a macro level, and can only be struggled with at individual and local community levels.

The problem of trying to square critical distance with cultural conditioning is situated in the difficulties arising from the disappearance of the unified, humanistic subject. From an orthodox humanist Marxist perspective, it is difficult to conceive of the individual subject as *alienated*, because the concept of alienation seems to suggest a unified, coherent sense of self from which the individual becomes alienated as a result of the process of the exploitation of labour. It is the struggle against alienation which is at the core of a Marxist conception of political struggle, one in which people's sense of their own identity enables them to pursue emancipatory projects over time and plan futures for themselves. If a sense of self as a unified subject with a fixed identity ('working class male', 'disaffected female bourgeois intellectual') is essential to the central political idea of radical agents creating their own history, then we are, indeed, in deep trouble if we cling to a form of determinist postmodernism which has no room for the voluntaristic agent. The political problems which such cultural determinism presents us with arise because, Harvey maintains, if 'as Marx insisted, it takes the alienated individual to pursue the Enlightenment project with a tenacity and coherence sufficient to bring us to some better future, then loss of the alienated subject would seem to preclude the conscious construction of alternative social futures' (1990: 54). For some postmodernists, notably Lyotard, and perhaps for many others disillusioned with the mass Leftist politics of the past, the 'loss' is easily borne because the 'construction of alternative social futures' is doomed to result in new oppressions under the banner of new metanarratives of liberation.

Some elements of postmodernism – the near impossibility of critical distance, the inescapable cultural and linguistic moulding of the individual, the death of the subject as agent – even when they are nervously embraced by socialist and feminist critics, appear to mark the political demise of widespread collective resistance and the notion of 'overcoming' the present social structures. What appears to emerge from the 'linguistic turn' of Marxism, together with feminism, is that while postmodern critique is a powerful tool for unmasking the domain assumptions of Western culture and deconstructing the pursuit of knowledge/power embedded in these assumptions, its deconstruction of the individual subject as agent is the kiss of political death. In order to envisage a possible politics of collective resistance it is necessary, in McGowan's words, to have 'an account of the self's inevitable immersion in the social that also explains how selves can experience themselves as integral agents capable of dissenting from or choosing alternative paths among the options social situations present' (1991: 211).

On what basis might such an account of the subject as an agent of collective emancipatory political change be established so that socialist, feminist, anti-racist and postmodern linkages can be forged of sufficient strength to allow for the possibility of some degree of solidarity? I will attempt a fuller answer to this question, especially as it addresses the politics of welfare, in the final chapter. At this stage, however, it is possible to point out some of the preconditions of a conception of the subject as agent: a recognition of the contradictions and recurrent crises which continuously confront capitalist economies and political institutions; the relative autonomy of economic, political and cultural discourses and practices rendering the smooth coordination of them in order to meet dominant interests always problematic and charged with conflict; the omnipresent meeting of power with resistance. It is in the conception of a contradictory, crisis-laden, porous and contingent society, rather than an overwhelming monolith, that the re-entry of the subject as agent becomes possible. Dominant cultures and economies are always subject to resistance because it is in their contra-dictions that individual and collective agents insert themselves. The subject, although multiple in her or his identities and, like the social order itself, containing contradictions, is ultimately based upon resistance to power, a resistance which struggles for some level of autonomy and the creation of new identities in a world over-determined, one might say, by the cultural and the economic. Such a conception of the subject is obviously necessary to assure the collective resistance required by contemporary social move-ments.

Although I have noted the problems associated with the attempt to link the notion of collective political resistance to a postmodern concern with critical distance, the cultural formation of the subject and the issue of the voluntar-istic agent, more needs to be said about the political *milieu* of postmodernity. There is little doubt that the milieu of uncertainty and cynicism is of benefit to the Right because it suggests that as the freedom of the market is preferable to totalitarian state planning, then we must choose the former because there is no other choice. As Agger (1990) points out, postmodern-ism is experienced as post-rationalist in the sense that it stands against the over-confident sweep of Enlightenment reason and thus often reflects the despair and disgust which come with the perceived failure of the attempt 'to impose reason's order on the recalcitrant, bitter world' (1990: 13). Post-modernism as a cultural phenomenon might also be seen as reflecting the interests, lifestyles and *angst* of a professional middle class, a yuppie, often academic, world where 'hip endures as the quintessential postmodern sensibility, expressing a combination of self-satisfaction and aversion to the passions and polemics of the political' (p. 9). The idea that postmodernism resonates with a certain segment of bourgeois intellectuals is difficult to dispute because its continual flourishing within the academy and the obscure language with which it engages in its debates indicates, perhaps, the political price which is being paid for the insights that postmodern critique provides. The argument that might be made here, then, is that the cool distancing, class origins and linguistic élitism of postmodern discourse make it an unlikely *cultural* vehicle for a radical mass politics of the Left, setting aside any theoretical objections postmodernists might have to the very idea of an emancipatory project.

There are, of course, different versions of the postmodern perspective which deeply affect the kinds of politics that might emerge from them. In this book, I have focused on what might be termed a Left postmodernism, one which has ties with feminism and, more problematically, with Marxism and the struggle against racism and neo-colonialism. In attempting to draw together, in an admittedly schematic and simplifying way, the various philosophical and political strands in postmodernism, Rosenau (1992) distinguishes between *sceptical* and *affirmative* postmodernism. Sceptical postmodernism, she argues, is inspired by Heidegger and Nietzsche and is about 'fragmentation, disintegration, malaise, meaninglessness, a vagueness or even absence of moral parameters and social chaos' (1992: 15). It is a perspective which tells us that no social or political project is worthy of consideration, because where there is no truth 'then all that is left is play, the play of words and meaning' (p. 15).

If sceptical postmodernism appears unlikely to provide much sustenance for the Long March of an emancipatory project, the other major strand that Rosenau identifies, although more congenial and obviously populated by some of the feminists, neo-Marxists and cultural critics we have already encountered, is nevertheless problematic in its own way. Affirmative postmodernists, Rosenau contends, take a more optimistic view of postmodern conditions, a view which reflects, perhaps, North American and British culture, in contrast to Continental Europe, where the sceptics reign. Affirmative postmodernists are 'either open to positive political action (struggle and resistance) or content with the recognition of visionary, celebratory personal nondogmatic projects that range from New Age religion to New Wave lifestyles and include a whole spectrum of postmodern social movements . . . and issue-specific political coalitions' (p. 16). Although we might object that a binary classification imposed upon an inchoate and confused terrain of discourses and practices is a typical strategy of modernity operating on a principle of non-contradiction, none the less the characteristics ascribed to affirmative postmodernists point to the predominantly white middle class lifestyles and chic political choices which appear to be associated with certain postmodern perspectives sometimes thought of as critical or radical (Agger, 1990; Foster, 1983).

The impact of postmodern ideas on Left politics may be of considerable benefit in terms of cultural critique, sensitivity to difference and an awareness of the ever-present dangers of domination which reside in meta-narratives of emancipation, but they often carry with them a particular baggage of political ideas. 'Designer socialist' is the term used by Rustin (1989) to refer to those who are well situated to benefit from and contribute to the flexible economy and cultural production of postmodern times. This segment of intellectuals is strongly influenced by postmodern ideas that lead them, in pursuit of the ideals of locality, community, consumer choice, flexibility and the deconstruction of professional expertise, to pursue characteristic welfare goals. These goals include decentralization, greater consumer choice in welfare, a larger informal or voluntary sector, and local community organization as an appropriate, if modest, form of political struggle. But to what extent are these ideas mainly subtle adaptations to a neo-conservative political agenda of fitting welfare into the mould of the private market culture, along with the specifically conservative ideas of user fees and outright privatization? Rustin points out that 'there are great dangers in turning commodity markets into a normative model for other social relations. For good reasons, socialists have historically subordinated rights and powers of individual choice in the sphere of health, welfare and education to the claims of relative and absolute need' (1989: 59).

The point I am making here is that postmodern ideas or at least the political conclusions that are frequently drawn from them, appear to have little to do with an emancipation project which is recognizably socialist or feminist. This is not to say that a Left feminist and Marxist form of postmodern critique and action are not possible, but that the appropriate politics will be likely to be especially difficult to establish in the field of welfare as elsewhere. Postmodernism, even of the most 'affirmative' kind, does not yet appear to have developed a politics which would enable it to provide some basis for reconstructing welfare as an emancipatory project. I am suggesting that only Marxism and feminism are likely, at the present time, to be able to connect to postmodern critique and so provide political strategies for reconstruction.

Ethical Judgements Without Rules?

The reason why a postmodern politics directed towards 'emancipation' or 'social justice' is problematic, is due to the fact that any impulse to *act* immediately meets a contradiction: how can we act ethically (according to some notion of the Good) in any collective way if we have already abandoned a belief in universal moral rules? How can we arrive at the ethical judgements necessary to engage in a politics of solidarity in the first place? Bauman (1992) refers to this as 'the ethical paradox of postmodernity' produced by the collapse of the guarantees provided by modernity:

> ethical choice and moral responsibility assume under the postmodern condition a totally new and long forgotten significance, an importance of which modernity tried hard, and with considerable success, to divest them, moving as it did toward the replacement of ethical discourse with the discourse of objective, translocal and impersonal truth. (1992: xxii)

Bauman here appears to assume that this transition to an individualized ethics has already occurred, as if the state's interest in maintaining a dominant discourse of rules has already withered away, arguably an over-optimistic (or pessimistic, depending upon your view) perception of what is happening. But the grip and attributed legitimacy of universal moral rules (of religion, of the state, of political ideology) do appear to be weakening and, from a postmodern perspective, we are encouraged to welcome these signs of the gradual attrition of hegemonic power. The paradox lies in the fact that, on the one hand, the postmodernity of late capitalism is apparently restoring to individual subjects an increased ethical autonomy while at the same time depriving them, Bauman suggests, of the comfort of universal guidance that modern self-confidence once promised. 'Ethical tasks of individuals grow while the socially produced resources to fulfil them shrink. Moral responsibility comes together with the loneliness of moral choice' (p. xii). If we read Bauman's argument as a commentary on the present, then there are some reservations to be made. One is that the state does not appear as yet to have given up an interest in common forms of morality. Rather, under the influence of a new resurgence of an ethics of capitalist development, it has shifted from a morality that included some social obligations to others, to one that rests overwhelmingly upon the ethical imperative of labour market dependency and continuously expanding consumption. It is a shift in ethical discourse which marks the disintegration of the idea of the welfare state. At the same time, the perceived opening up of wider moral choices results, as we have already noted, in the attractiveness of the fundamentalisms of religion and politics, with their assertions of their own brand of moral rules concerning the family, sexuality, ethnic identity and other manifestations of inclusion/exclusion.

In spite of reservations about how far a process of retreat from universalistic moral claims has gone, we can accept that for most people in Western countries a greater number of moral choices appear to be available, and that at the same time world-wide media communication emphasizes the existence (and to some degree, legitimacy) of cultural and moral relativity. Postmodernism welcomes this expansion of choices and even the chaos and chronic uncertainty which accompany the collapse of many of the self-confident ethical *authorities* of the past. The fact that one of these ethical authorities was once called Socialism, a moral idea which had the power to mobilize people to a single cause, might be seen as a necessary price to pay for surrendering the dreams of those who claim to exercise power over people 'in their own interests'. The fact that the same price must be paid by feminism and those who fight racism and other forms of oppression, namely the relinquishing of universal moral claims, may make us pause before we cheer too loudly the collapse of moral certainty. When considering the individual subject's lonely moral choices, shot through with uncertainty and ambivalence, we have to ask on what basis such choices should be made: we ask a prescriptive question. But the *context* of the 'should' question is that cultural discourses (multiple as they may be) influence or even determine the answer we give. The cultural discourses of late capitalism may tell us, in effect, that there is so much choice available to us as individuals, that our only guide left is to consider our own personal self-interest or that of those closest to us, adopting a strategy of *moral isolationism*. This entry of extreme ethical individualism, speaking with the voice of sceptical postmodernism, performs a certain function for late capitalism, giving moral priority to the individual over all social entities more inclusive than the family or immediate communities of interest. This individualistic moral priority serves, by a remarkable sleight of hand, to exclude from ethical discourse those social entities represented by the discursive formation and practices of corporate capitalism, thus rendering them almost invisible.

Fortunately, postmodern approaches to ethics also include ideas which have the potential of moving beyond simple individualism toward providing criteria on which to base a notion of well-being. The central idea of a postmodern ethics is constructed on the basis of its critique of modernity's obsession with *sameness*, with supposed essential unities, and its exclusion of the Other. Against this, a postmodern ethics is concerned with the recognition of difference, in ourselves and others, with the diversity of culture, ethnicity, gender, sexuality and similar differences that have been polarized and excluded by the classificatory schema of modernity. Post-modern ethics might be described, then, as concerned with *responsibility to otherness* (Fox, 1994; White, 1991), thereby challenging the ethics of modernity which established a morality that, while claiming universality, was in fact partial and reflected the political interests of those with a will to mastery. The ethics of modernity is an

> obligation to acquire reliable knowledge and act to achieve practical ends in some defensible manner. This responsibility derives from the character of being in the world both physically and politically . . . What the postmodern thinker wants to assert here is that meeting this responsibility always requires one, at some point, to fix and close down parameters of thought and ignore or homogenize at least some dimensions of specificity or difference among actors. (White, 1991: 20–1)

So, in place of the will to control and homogenize, postmodern ethics asserts a responsibility to otherness. How might this ethics work in practice? One answer is to focus on the Other, on the excluded, those on the margins, people who have no control over their lives and who have never known what it is to be the *author* of a project, text, discourse (Rosenau, 1992). Perhaps a postmodern ethics implies the attempt to clear a space for the voices of those who have been reduced to objects, have never spoken as active subjects, but have always been acted upon by 'those with knowledge'. It might even imply (though this is more difficult and dangerous) speaking, initially, on behalf of those who have been silenced, but without trying to control or discipline them. This ethics of responsibility to otherness might be seen as underlying the political spirit of the new social movements, especially in the field of welfare, and we will turn to these movements later in the chapter. But how can an ethics of responsibility to otherness avoid being also an ethics of responsibility to *act* and, in so doing, to practise the power of surveillance, control and discipline? Does the urge to emancipate others (and the otherness inside ourselves) always imply the urge to take over, to lead, to impose order on disorder?

This is where we arrive at the crux of the ethical problem of acting in the interests (as we see them) of the well-being of others, specifically of patients, clients, claimants, service users, 'targets of intervention' and other subjects of welfare. Perhaps we must see the ethical practice of caring as composed of two parts: first is the response to others and otherness, secondly is the resistance to the urge to assimilation and control. This resistance can be seen, in effect, as a resistance to the power of that internalized modern cultural imperative to *mastery* which has dominated the history of welfare in the broadest sense. If we are to develop a new ethics of caring, one which celebrates difference and resists the temptation to obliterate it, then, White (1991) suggests, we have to approach otherness in a spirit of what he calls 'grieving delight' – grieving at the injustice of needless suffering at the same time as delighting in the existence of difference.

> The delight with the appearance of the other brings with it the urge to draw it closer. But that urge must realize its limits, beyond which the drawing nearer becomes a gesture of grasping. And that realization will be palpable only when we are sensitive to the appearance of the particular other as testimony of finitude. Then delight will be paired with a sense of grief or mourning at the fragility and momentary quality of the appearance of the other. (White, 1991: 90, cited in Fox, 1994)

We might say that all caring relationships contain within them this urge to enfold the other in an embrace which can soon turn into control or possession: parent and child, lovers, friends, and especially therapist and patient, social worker and client, because professional caring involves a particular knowledge/power imbalance between carer and cared for. In relationships less close to us than caring relationships, the urge to control the other, to encompass difference to make it one with us, may be weaker, easier to resist. Perhaps, however, an ethics of responsibility to difference faces another issue, that of distinguishing between tolerance and indifference. We need to tolerate difference, but we need to do more, because tolerance might mean that we *do not care about* the other; diversity might be put up with, on sufferance, rather than be celebrated. Celebrating or delighting in difference demands something morally stronger than tolerance, necessary as this is; it requires a solidarity based upon the assumption of a degree of equivalence between the differences that exist on various dimensions, even though we may argue about them from our own particular perceptions of the true and the good. Bauman argues that

> tolerance as such is possible *only* in the form of solidarity: that is, what is needed is not just refraining from converting ambitions (an abstention that may well result in a breakdown of communication, in the declaration of indifference and the practice of separation), but a practical recognition of the *relevance* and *validity* of the other's difference, expressed in the willing engagement in the dialogue. (1992: xxi; emphasis in original)

In practice, the ethic of being responsible to otherness does not require us to abstain from acting, to sit on the sidelines, only observing. To establish solidarity in defence of difference requires a will to act collectively rather than retreat into atomistic individualism. But before we act, we pause, we listen. Even when we might be carrying the guilt of association with historic oppression, and feel impelled to act in order, perhaps, to ease our con- sciences, we might reflect before acting. When we face the enormity of the cultural losses experienced by many Aboriginal peoples at the hands of state health, welfare and education services, we may feel compelled to act, to put things right again, in their interests. But we are told to listen first, to glimpse the overwhelming pain which cultural loss brings and to remember that it was the modern responsibility to act which led to the cultural losses in the first place. We may act if the Other wishes us to, and on their terms, but only after reflection, trying to relax the imperative to organize and classify with our plans and projects, aiming 'to create slack and space within which the mood of delight can flourish' (Fox, 1994; White, 1991: 129).

Although the postmodern perspective leads us to relinquish universal guarantees for our ethical judgements, it none the less can avoid extreme moral individualism through its principle of responsibility to otherness, a principle which requires us to reflect before acting, and celebrate difference on a foundation of solidarity. There appears, however, to be one further step to take in this discussion. The postmodern ethics we have discussed are rooted in the assumption that the individual subject has the capacity to act as a moral agent, the capacity to make choices between different means and different ends: to be an agent able to engage in ethical discourse. I think this assumption of moral agency, culturally produced as it is, implies a *right* to be treated by others as a moral agent. This right is also historically and culturally contingent, but not less important, because it lacks a transcendental universal foundation. The subject of postmodern ethics is only relatively autonomous but is still assumed to be able to make moral choices and to have *the human right to act as a moral agent*.

This right to be a moral agent, while still a product of culture, nevertheless appears to carry with it certain political implications. It leads to the question of what are the conditions required for a subject to lead the life of a moral agent. We might at this point say simply that we could not expect a person to act as a moral agent whose conditions of life appear to preclude the possibility of any substantial agency *in practice*: those living at such a level of material existence, for example, that life is reduced to a daily struggle for survival, or those who occupy subject positions which deny them the right of agency and in its place demand only obedience. The absence of the possibility of acting as a relatively autonomous moral agent, for economic, social or political reasons, provides us with one focus for the reconstruction of an emancipatory project to which postmodern ethics makes a necessary contribution.

Social Movements and Social Identity

We are now in a position to focus more directly on the politics of collective resistance and of solidarity in the pursuit of welfare objectives. Social solidarity was once seen as essential to furthering the idea of welfare: the evening up of the life chances of individuals and groups through the provision of state services and state intervention in the economy. This solidarity was expressed in a social movement which was founded on a particular set of identities, cultural assumptions and shared historical experiences, namely, the labour and trade union movement and the various socialist, social democratic and communist parties associated with it. The primary social identity of those who belonged to this movement, and who engaged in a politics directed towards the expansion of state welfare as an instrument of socialist advance, was a class identity. The mass of this movement, especially in European countries, were self-defined as belonging to the working class, an identity formed primarily in the workplace out of the necessary engagement in direct struggle with capital. In countries such as Britain, where, as we have noted earlier, working class culture was a powerful social force, working class identity was strongly reinforced by class-based cultural traditions and institutions centred on the family and various educational and recreational activities. The other main element in labour movements consisted of those who identified with, supported and, in many cases, provided the leadership of the movement, those who might be briefly described as disaffected bourgeois intellectuals.

This political mass played a crucial role in the establishment of the Keynesian welfare state in all Western countries, including the United States, where working class consciousness had taken a different, weaker and more transient form than that to be found in European social democracies. It was a social movement intent on gaining state power in the interests of subordinate populations, but it saw those populations and its interests through a white patriarchal lens, unable to accommodate a range of social identities which could not simply be subsumed under the sign of class. More generally, we can say that with the ideological collapse of the organizing metanarrative of class struggle, together with the decomposition and restructuring of classes in the post-Fordist era, social movements based upon the identities of class, union membership and the ideals of socialism appear to have lost the will and resources to mount an effective resistance to the radical Right discourse on welfare.

If the old social movements, based on class and workplace, appear unable, in the name of socialism, to mount a collective resistance to developments in late capitalism which adversely affect the well-being of large populations, where can we turn? We have only one place to look at present: to the new social movements concerned with gender, ethnicity, sexuality, human rights, ecology. Could these new movements be seen as pursuing socialist aims by different means and with a wider agenda, so that socialism becomes redefined as the struggle for equality and human welfare amongst the differences of culture, gender, class, race, sexuality, age and other social divisions? Apart from appearing at first sight like the appropriation of the diverse critical politics of postmodernity by the old (van)guard of proletarian struggle, the degree of fit between the old and the new is not close, as Giddens points out:

> While the aspirations of some such movements stand close to socialist ideals, their objectives are disparate and sometimes actively opposed to one another. With the possible exception of some sections of the green movement, the new social movements are not 'totalizing' in the way socialism is (or was), promising a new 'stage' of social development beyond the existing order. Some versions of feminist thought, for example, are as radical as anything that went under the name of socialism. Yet they don't envisage seizing control of the future in a way the more ambitious versions of socialism have done. (Giddens, 1994: 3)

What has changed between the old and the new social movements might be characterized as a collapse in the self-confidence (or arrogance) of a critical form of modernity intent on reshaping the world in accordance with a plan which claimed to be in the interests of *all* subordinate populations. In its place, the diverse movements of postmodernity no longer claim universality but particularity, a focus on the different, the local, the specific human need, which arguably in turn leads to their own political limitations. Can they be directed towards rectifying some of the large-scale social injustices which have traditionally concerned those who saw the furtherance of welfare as demanding attention to total social systems of labour exploitation, dehumanizing production, and the grossly unequal distribution of economic, social and cultural resources? This is a question to which we will return, but first we must discuss the forms of identity and interest which characterize the new social movements.

The first distinguishing characteristic of the new social movements is their identification with the discourse of *community*. Although the state often uses the term to legitimate its decentralization policies (control mechanisms nearer to the populations being monitored) or its strategies to increase volunteer resources (transfer of care costs to unpaid women) the idea of community resonates throughout the new social movements. Community as that to which one affiliates may be spoken of as one of interest, of subject identity, or of geographical location, but it is also an *imagined community* (Anderson, 1983; Bauman, 1992). It is the discourse of community, its practices of identity formation and its production of a sense of belonging which, under postmodern conditions, is sought as a replacement to that belief in universal reason and progress which no longer seems convincing. Communities are imagined insofar as 'belief in their presence is their only brick and mortar, and imputation of importance their only source of authority' (Bauman, 1992: xix). Social movements as communities are not part of the state apparatus, nor do they have strong institutional supports, and as a consequence may be unstable and transient (especially when they are formed to pursue a single policy issue). But they have, on the other hand, a strength which is sometimes lacking in that other kind of community in which membership is automatic or taken for granted, a community of proximity and common culture as a way of life, where the subject experiences effortless belonging. The imagined communities of social movements consist of those who *apply* for the rights and responsibilities of belonging, whose subject positions include a certain commitment to a set of ideas, even though some of them may be internally contested. Furthermore, because social movements tend to be community-based and because the workplace can rarely be thought of as a community, the traditional labour movement conflict with capital, its owners and senior managers, tends to be lacking. Among the exceptions to this tendency, although still not workplace-based, are the struggles by the various ecology organizations against capitalist corporations engaged in the exploitation of natural resources considered harmful to the environment and to human welfare.

The fact that the new social movements do not organize around production is a major reason for the absence in these movements of a specific class identity: the relation between workers and owners is a relation between labour and capital, the most central of class relations. In place of the priority of class identity are other identities – gender, culture, race, sexuality – in which class has not ceased to exist but no longer acts as the organizing principle of political struggle. Distinct populations within the large fragmenting cities become the ground upon which community consciousness is based, so that culture and gender carry the leading role once assumed by class. 'Identity, community and culture become the contexts through which people come to construct and understand political life' (Fisher and Kling, 1994: 9).

The new social movements are, in postmodern conditions, a major means by which people articulate their needs and make welfare claims intended to meet them. In this, they are the successors of the old labour movements whose political struggle secured the concessions necessary to establish the welfare state. In defining needs and making claims on the state's resources, the new social movements exercise a significant pressure on social policies and the distribution of scarce government resources. Most importantly, they give voice to those who previously had no voice, those who were excluded and marginalized, and in so doing create new identities, empowered by participation in forms of resistance that produce new knowledge about political systems. The profoundly significant learning experiences gained through the process of campaigning for resources are an important element of identity formation within social movements concerned with welfare. The unmasking of the ideologies and interests of dominant political structures is a necessary step in securing support for a collective demand directed to the state and requires the development of considerable expertise. This is an expertise which does not necessarily depend upon the knowledge of professionals, sometimes regarded with considerable suspicion, but arises directly from engaging in the action itself, as Drover and Kerans point out:

> participants in a group process to articulate their needs will also have to recognize those hegemonic relations which result in their subordination and strategize to overcome them. Thus, when finally articulated by claimants, needs will be expressed inevitably as a criticism of the institutional order to which members of the group have been uncritically and submissively subjected and which has hitherto not recognized or deprived them of their needs. (1995: 23)

If the production of knowledge about institutional systems and the instigation of public debate about the justice of the existing distribution of resources are characteristics of the politics of social movements which might be seen as contributing to a wider solidarity in the pursuit of human welfare, other characteristics are seen as more problematic. Insofar as the new social movements can be characterized as representing a politics of *identity* – gender, culture, sexuality, age, disability, race – they can be seen paradoxically both as a characteristic expression of postmodernism, and as its contradiction.

In general, postmodernism and identity politics conflict in ways not easily resolved. The assertion of identity necessarily involves the drawing of boundaries around that identity, while postmodernism is dedicated to the transgressing of boundaries. The self-ironizing component of postmodernism runs directly counter to the self-righteousness that often accompanies the assertion of suppressed identities. If, on the other hand, we accept the postmodern claim that identity is constructed from social representations – diverse, heterogeneous, contradictory and even incoherent – and that each individual is, in effect, a coalition of multiple identities, how can people organize to act in common? (Rosenthal, 1992: 96)

We need not answer this question in terms of abstract theorization: the relation between postmodernism and identity politics may be philosophically as problematic as that between feminism and Marxism – the immediate question is surely whether these problems prevent certain political alliances taking place or whether engagement between them is possible. I would suggest, in fact, that the problem with identity politics is that while it is a necessary part of a new emancipatory politics, it is by no means sufficient. We have already discussed (in Chapter 2) the opposition which postmodern critique erects to the singular, fixed identity of the modern subject. In its opposition, postmodernism demands space for a multitude of subjectivities, those previously excluded and rendered invisible. But identity politics runs into the danger of letting in fixed identities by the back door and so reproducing again ideas of essential identities and the exclusion of those who do not reside within the boundary of a particular identity. Fuss (1989) maintains that certain kinds of identity politics – she is referring to feminist practice here – tend to so emphasize shared identity, shared experiences of domination and the guilt of others outside of the group, that oppression is psychologized and rendered as an issue almost exclusively of subjectivity. What is needed to fill out this necessary first emphasis on identity and the subject is, Fuss argues, a materialist analysis of the structures of exploitation. Following a similar path, Hennessy (1993) argues that a postmodern analysis of the subject, of identity, while on its own does not guarantee an oppositional politics, none the less opens up political discourse to issues of language and of difference. 'Materialist feminists have seen in postmodernism a powerful critical force for exposing the relationship between language, the subject, and the unequal distribution of social resources,' Hennessy (1993: 6) writes, in pointing to the need for an engagement between postmodernism and Marxism in the pursuit of an emancipatory politics.

The need to place a politics of identity within an analysis of material exploitation (including the economic exploitation manifested in class relations) requires a focus on the similarity of different forms of oppression as well as their particularity. The dangers of an identity politics which emphasizes only *difference*, a binary opposition between 'we' and 'others', is that it fails to explore the grounds for solidarity.

Focusing only on the other as different is as problematic as only focusing on sameness. Should we not go beyond simply producing the mirror image or precise opposite of that which we critique – itself a dualism or oppositional category? False unification or a focus on sameness obviously excludes, while a focus on difference tends to construct 'aliens' or 'others' (Bordo, 1990: 140). Moreover, differences between groups are too frequently essentialized, and differences within groups are negated. (Brown, 1994: 42)

The limitations of those social movements that are based exclusively on a politics of identity then, is that their exclusivity may blind them to the possibilities of wider solidarities. At the same time, exclusivity may lead to a demand for conformity within the identity group, thus reproducing the very mechanism of singular and stereotypical identity formation which social movements are, at another level, committed to opposing. The consequence of an identity politics which fails to acknowledge the wider discourses and structures of oppression and their impact on large populations is a fragmentation of opposition. Although emphasis on the local community and the diverse claims to welfare of different groups is a strength in terms of its recognition of diversity and the importance of democratic control of welfare initiatives at the base, its limitations are also clear. Emphasis on difference may be utilized by the state as a relatively safe, money-saving rationale for concentrating small-scale adjustments among competing social groups (micro redistributions of resources) resulting in the fragmentation of populations into ever-smaller communities of interest. Collective resistance may thereby be dispersed and weakened and the possibilities of constructing solidarities diminished. A politics of diversity and identity *on its own* may find itself, so far as the wider structural inequalities resulting in poverty and exploitation are concerned, to be a form of opposition readily managed by governments acting upon a neo-conservative agenda. The dispersal and fragmentation of opposition serves many of their interests. An opposition of alliances based on both difference and solidarity could be an opposition to be feared and it is, of course, for this reason that such a form of opposition should be mounted.

Interdependence and Collective Action

At various points in this book I have attempted to deconstruct the discourse on 'welfare dependency', that is, dependency on the state, and compared it to the discourse on 'independence', showing it to be simply another, more acceptable form of dependency, that of dependence on the labour market. A politics of welfare, of the articulation of needs and of claims for resources, if it is to be emancipatory, demands a rejection of discourses on dependence and independence and in their place argues for a discourse on *interdependence*. Independence is both an abstraction and an ideological device. Our reading of Foucault leads us to understand how dependency is a relationship of power and resistance and constitutes our subjectivity as humans. But these dependencies are not one-way phenomena; they are mutual: 'where there is power, there is resistance'. Human needs might be seen as an expression of the mutual interdependency of human subjects, an interdependence which dominant discourses attempt to mask in their opposition to a politics of collectivity which ultimately rests on the mutual dependency of subjects upon each other. It is, perhaps, a recognition of this mutual interdependence which would be at the root of a reinvented idea of welfare, an idea which is alien to the ideological commitments of those who would diminish it in the interests of a Hobbesian and neo-Darwinist conception of welfare as, at most, a grudging, residual function of the state.

A concept of mutually interdependent subjects, then, is crucial to a politics of collective resistance and, in particular, community action. The point is to extend the actual experience and realization of interdependence beyond the boundaries of a politics of particular identities, 'imagined communities' or single-issue social movements. Only by such an extension to include, at least potentially, all the communities and social identities that experience the present social order as domination, is postmodern particularist politics likely to have any possibility of rectifying its present weakness – its inability to challenge the politics, economic priorities and mass culture of late capitalism. Is it possible to advance a discourse on welfare which is based, in other words, upon the interdependence of various social struggles as well as the mutual dependence of individual subjects? If we take the plight of the poor, the long-term unemployed, and single parent families, all in the context of relations of class, gender and racial domination manifested in the large urban concentrations, then we must acknowledge interdependence.

> Single community-based efforts are not large enough to challenge the enormous power of corporate capital or centralized government. Because community problems almost always originate beyond local borders, the ability to effect change depends to a great extent upon building coalitions, alliances, networks and progressive political parties. The success of such efforts, however, ultimately will be based upon whether specific ways can be found to break down the racial and cultural barriers that are so prevalent and threatening in the United States, Europe and throughout the world. (Fisher and Kling, 1994: 17)

This is an observation on social movements and community action which is part of a broader argument in favour of *even using political parties*, provided they are 'progressive' (Foucault turns in his grave), as a necessary part of a struggle for emancipation. This is a bold proposal for a critical political practice under postmodern conditions of disillusionment and failed ideals. It is based on the assumption that whereas the new social movements until now have been content to influence state power as well as contest it, to resist but not to wish to gain major power, they should now move in a different direction. This is not the direction of earlier revolutionary socialism, exhorted by Lenin to 'seize' state power, but is an injunction to win state power democratically and try to hold on to it. Given the massive hegemony of corporate capitalism, only the state might provide a terrain for some forms of resistance to the prodigious economic and political power of a capitalist global market. Certainly, without the state, even given its weakened ability to defend its populations from the consequences of economic growth, innovation and the recurrent crises of the system as a whole, effective collective resistance is impossible.

This is an attractive and even partially convincing argument, namely that solidarity amongst the differences must eventuate in the winning of state power. Would winning state power be a step towards emancipation? In the past twenty years, left political parties gaining power have not noticeably advanced welfare as an emancipatory project, but have often followed a predominantly neo-conservative political path accompanied by expressions of regret, reluctance and the need to bow to necessity. Such parties also invariably reflected in their culture and organization the forms of domination and exclusion which existed in the oppressive structures of the wider society that they were ostensibly opposing. So what kind of political parties do we require to advance the claims of human need and social justice, if they are required at all? Or must we be content to influence, pressure and agitate, furthering the diverse interests of many different struggles in the belief that emphasis on particularity and locality is the most effective means of contributing to human welfare? These questions will be among those considered in the final chapter.

7

Reconstruction

These are hard times for those who are searching for new ways of advancing human well-being. We may call them 'postmodern times', a period in which we experience the impact of massive and disruptive economic and social changes, but there is a sense in which these times are not new, but rooted in tendencies which have existed since the beginning of capitalism and certainly before the modern post Second World War welfare state was established. It was in the 1940s that Adorno and Horkheimer undertook their critique of 'consumer capitalism' in *The Dialectic of the Enlightenment*, published in German in 1947, and only available in English in the 1970s (Adorno and Horkheimer, 1972). Theirs is an unremitting gloomy picture of the type of society which they saw as emerging, and which many might see as confirmed in the experiences of the late 1990s. Although Fascism was defeated in the Second World War, the reconstructed capitalism which was now immensely strengthened would carry with it forms of oppression and control, Adorno and Horkheimer argued, which assured us of a future in which human welfare would be continuously subordinated to new kinds of domination. In his sympathetic but critical discussion of Adorno and Horkheimer's predictions, Inglis (1993) describes their depressing vision of the future (now, arguably the present) as follows:

> It would be relentlessly exploitive of nature and of human nature. It would stifle dissent, and do so not with the use of policemen but by incorporating the forms of thought within . . . technicism: the magicking of dialectics into problem solving, of political argument into the management of assent. It would deny solidarity, and affirm individuality. It would celebrate risk as the justification of profit. The future was perfectly bleak and blank, even while it glistened with the promised illusions of consumerism. The wintry prophets would commend no programme of action, because no historical agency capable of a progressive rescue remained alive. Class and party had been dissolved by commercial culture. Only the duty to dissent remained. (Inglis, 1993: 70)

Sounds familiar? If we see ourselves as trapped within a monolith, then it is a picture which may resonate with feelings of powerlessness and near despair because it is painted with the tones which dominate our current experiences: consumerism, the resurgence of individualism, economic uncertainty, the virtual collapse of Left politics and the advance of the Right. Insofar as it is a widely shared view of the possibilities of an emancipatory project, it is one which must be contested strongly because it fails to take account of the resurgence of social critique in the newer forms of political movements which challenge the dominant order in the name of equality and diversity. They present us with the possibility of future forms of resistant solidarity. The struggle for human welfare as an emancipatory project requires an analysis which leads not to paralysis but to a politics of hope. Hope generates the commitment to emancipation, a commitment dependent not only on theoretical analysis – the necessary abstractions of intellectual work – but on a certain kind of feeling which is not a 'cool' distancing stance, separated from the heat of political struggle, but one which touches us in a more profound way. I speak here of *anger*, of rage at the degrading conditions of existence – material, social, cultural – which are experienced by millions of people in the Third World and in 'advanced' capitalist countries. These conditions, and our understanding of them as economically and socially produced – the result of human action – are the basis of critical discourses and practices which are fuelled by a sense of moral outrage at the structures of domination and injustice which are manufactured, reproduced and disseminated under late capitalism. Not intellectual *detachment* but anger is the human attribute which has the most possibility of generating the kind of individual and collective resistance which is a necessary precondition of emancipation.

'Anger is a gift,' Lim (1996) writes in his study of responses to racism; anger can be mobilized from internalization as anxiety and depression into its externalization as collective resistance. Collectively, anger emerges as a moral protest at injustice. The ethics which are counterpoised to domination are culturally produced out of the material experience of oppression and injustice, a discourse of resistance which explicitly or implicitly assumes the possibility of the relative autonomy necessary to make moral choices.

If a new, emancipatory project of welfare is to be developed it must be based upon a moral critique of modernity *from within*. This internal criticism directs its attention to the side of the Enlightenment implicated in domination and contrasts this with the emancipatory potential remaining in those critical discourses of modernity expressed in the revolutionary ideals of liberty, justice and equality. Internal criticism acknowledges that the project of modernity continues – no other appears available to us – but draws upon the interrogation of Marxism and feminism by postmodernism as its major source of critique. For human welfare to flourish, modernity must take a different path, a form already prefigured in a multiplicity of oppositional (and identity) types of politics. It must be the basis for the kind of welfare which no longer excludes the Other, nor includes it as a dominated part of itself, but which respects the diversity of the Other because it understands that its knowledge as an agent of welfare is not absolute or universal but based upon cultural discourses and practices which are always open to critique. It is a form of welfare in which the subject is seen not as potentially homogeneous but as reflecting diversity and constituted by resistance. A conception of the subject as a *resistant moral agent* provides one means by which a welfare project can be reconstructed. Such a project does not accept that a description of the present can be reduced to one of monolithic domination, but emphasizes its contradictions, evidenced in part by the multiplicity of challenges to moral, political and cultural authority character-istic of present times.

An emancipatory project of welfare under the conditions of late capitalism must turn its face against the kind of totalizing programme which was the ideal of many of the protagonists who established the old welfare state. It cannot be based upon some overall grand *plan*, some new, complete *re-organization* of welfare, because the over-ambitious planning, programming and organization of welfare institutions, its professionals and subjects, produced the paradox that a commitment to welfare resulted, to a large degree, in a system of domination in the interests of exclusion, homogeniz-ation and the defence of expert power. All social change is rooted in history, the product of the historical preconditions necessary for human actors to make choices. Reconstructing the project of welfare will be rooted in the possibilities emerging under present conditions. It will, in other words, emphasize *process* rather than plan, a process based upon certain culturally produced assumptions which act as discursive signposts to assist us in the pursuit of welfare as an emancipatory idea. It is a process, furthermore, which stimulates us to imagine diverse ways of meeting human needs and to explore the possibilities open to people in furthering their own welfare, moving on from resistance to the creation of change.

In what follows in this final chapter, I attempt to draw together the prescriptive, reconstructive elements embedded in the previous discussions of the critique of modernity and its characteristic forms of welfare. The kinds of critical questioning about welfare currently emerging, and the forms of political practice with which they are often associated, provide, I suggest, the beginnings of reconstruction. New forms of welfare discourse, in other words, will emerge as extensions of the present – its crises, its contra-dictions, its critiques – rather than being founded on a completely fresh beginning, a clearing away of the debris of the past and a starting again from scratch. The postmodern condition may be described, writes Bauman (1992: 188) as 'modernity emancipated from false consciousness', but if we are to seek the enhancement of human welfare we must also, I believe, build upon what is worthwhile in the radical traditions of feminism, of socialism and of anti-colonial and anti-racist struggles. It is from the present challenges to the idea of welfare in its previously triumphant modern form – the Keynesian welfare state – that we can detect the emerging principles and practices upon which new forms of welfare begin to sediment themselves into political consciousness as *possibilities*. In trying to identify the emergent forms arising from current critique and practice, I shall focus on three questions. What might be the ethical discourses of means and ends which would drive an emancipatory form of welfare? What types of practice might be built upon such moral foundations? Would the winning of state power be necessary to furthering critical conceptions of welfare and, if it were, what preconditions would be required to attain this political objective?

The Ethics of Reconstruction

If we are to pursue the idea that welfare has an emancipatory potential as yet only half-revealed in the modern welfare state, then we must consider how we are to navigate our way through the turbulent waters produced by two moral obligations which in practice have often stood in conflict with each other: to *difference* and to *solidarity*. I have expressed the former as a responsibility to otherness, to the diversity of subjects, communities and cultures, and to a recognition of the validity of the Other, even though such recognition does not absolve us from making, where necessary, moral judgements and acting upon them in the light of our perceptions of risk or harm. The obligation to acknowledge and, whenever possible, to celebrate difference is a fundamental ethical assumption of a reconstructed welfare project. The implications of this obligation are evident in many elements of the contemporary struggle for welfare. It assumes that the individual subject resists in diverse ways cultural inscription by experts, whilst at the same time being constituted through such resistance. Patients, clients and welfare claimants are all subject to the professional gaze of those who are assumed to have superior knowledge, and it is through resistance that difference is articulated, and new approaches to welfare practice begin to appear which focus on supporting this resistance. These newer practices may be expressed, for example, in de-pathologizing the experiences of subjects and renaming them as the effects of racism or other discourses and practices of social domination. A moral responsibility to otherness also takes the form of drawing back from the tendency to express caring in terms of an homogenizing expert narrative which so fills up the discourse on illness, or distress, or material and emotional need, that space for the expression of difference – of the varieties of experience and meaning resulting from the diversities of culture, gender, class, sexuality, ability, age – becomes so confined that the subject's narrative is effectively excluded. The emerging practice which attempts to counteract this homogenizing impulse embedded in professional expertise emphasizes co-authorship of a joint narrative about problems, needs and claims. Because every narrative (of the professional as well as the client) is open to interpretation, we are speaking here of efforts to establish a dialogue of the interpretations of narratives where recognition of the diversity of subjects is established as a priority.

If the recognition of diversity is to be central to the practice of 'experts' and their claims to exclusive and invariably superior knowledge reduced to the status of a narrative alongside other narratives, then the organization of welfare must equally provide spaces for the expression of difference. The cultural relevance and accessibility of services become a major objective of social policy and because exclusion of the Other is historically rooted in institutional racism, it is an objective which requires a commitment to combat the usually unreflecting racism embedded in the discourses, practices and policies of modern welfare. Responsibility to otherness implies, furthermore, that any common, widespread political struggle towards new emancipatory forms of welfare will be subject to debate and argument often expressed in terms of differences of class, gender, race, ethnicity, sexuality or other sources of social identity and experiences of domination. The result of this diversity is that any broad social movement directed towards new conceptions of welfare can be assumed to take the form of an arena where intense struggle between differences (of identity and interest) takes place and where arrival at consensus is always a provisional state of affairs.

It is when we begin to speak of an organized critical politics of welfare that the tension between the ethics of diversity and those of solidarity, of mutual interdependence, becomes sharply evident. It is not, I believe, a tension that can be overcome, finally transcended in the name of welfare as an emancipatory project. This is a necessary tension, an unresolvable contradiction between moral imperatives which must, with whatever difficulty, be continually balanced against each other. The ethical practice which results from this tension is one which observes continuous vigilance to avoid either imperative obliterating the other. The danger of an unrestrained emphasis on difference is that it will lead to cultural exclusiveness, restricted identities or intense individualism. The comparable danger of a triumphant and unreflecting solidarity is that domination and homogenization become a practice legitimated by a discourse on mutual interdependence.

The moral responsibility to acknowledge and act upon the mutual interdependence of human subjects should not, however, be seen mainly as a *problem*, a principle which we see primarily in terms of its tension with a responsibility to otherness. Recognition that mutual interdependence is at the core of our subjectivity and that it therefore constitutes a foundation for any reconstructed welfare project is a precondition for any effective ideological counter-move to the dominant, narcissistic individualism of the culture of late capitalism. The collapse of the forms of solidarity and community which characterized the social struggles for the old Keynesian welfare state has been accompanied by the rise of a neo-conservative discourse on welfare which aims at securing widespread allegiance to an ethics of individual interest and independence founded upon market dependency, competitiveness and survival of the fittest. A strengthening of the discourse of human interdependence is necessary not only in the broad ideological struggle against the radical Right and other unsavoury features of late capitalism, but in the way in which welfare practice itself is conducted. We have seen that the negative side of the *individuation* of welfare subjects – patients, clients, claimants, service users – is that exclusive emphasis on individual biography fragments resistance and leads to a focus on an assertion of individual pathology which is innocent of the structural forces which constitute the determining context of people's health and well-being. An alternative practice is one which, while recognizing individual difference and cultural diversity, engages in a discourse on the similarities between subjects confronting problems of health, personal identity or material survival, similarities which may be embedded in common experiences of class, gender and race. Such a practice, in other words, emphasizes a *potential*

solidarity between the individual subjects of welfare. Emphasis on common-
ality, solidarity and interdependence serves not only to counteract self-
invalidating and destructive internalizing of shame and guilt, but also
enables subjects to express individual resistance to domination and the
possibility of participating in collective resistance in the pursuit of claims for
welfare. Feminist practice in psychiatry, psychology, social work, counselling and therapy stands, at present, as the exemplar of the possibilities of an
approach to solidarity in the context of diversity which could be further
widely developed within the welfare field.

Having identified the two ethical discourses – on difference and interdependence – which may be seen as driving an increasing awareness of a
need to reconstruct welfare in new directions, we can now turn more
specifically to the primary objectives and means which characterize this
commitment to an emancipatory welfare project. We will identify the
objectives as consisting of the increasingly effective meeting of *common and
particular human needs*, and the *promoting of moral agency*. Amongst the
means by which such objectives might be pursued, I select two practices for
attention: the encouragement and support of *collective resistance*, and a
process of *welfare building*.

The Objectives of Welfare as Emancipation

How can we speak of the *objectives* of a new kind of welfare without falling
into the traps lying in wait for us, traps labelled 'dogma', 'certainty', 'central
planning', even 'objectivity'? Talk about objectives resonates with mem-
ories of 'management by objectives' and other devices by which forms of
bourgeois rationality attempt to bring order to a recalcitrant world. Objectives, in other words, might be taken to imply hierarchy, control and an
exclusive emphasis on an instrumentality directed to the monitoring and
surveillance of the subjects of welfare, always, of course, 'in their own
interests'.

There is, however, another way of looking at objectives, one which is not
immediately directed to organization or practices, although organizational
and practice implications flow from these objectives. The objectives I am
concerned with here are those which are contained within a disputable and
culturally embedded moral and political discourse on needs and autonomy.

Discourses which argue for the political idea of common human needs,
and by direct implication, common human rights to have these needs met,
usually claim universal guarantees for such needs and rights. Through
sensitivity to historical and cultural contingency, we may not wish to make
claims to universality and objectivity: the idea of common needs, however,
is an invaluable moral premise on which to build solidarity amongst
diversity. Although the welfare objective of meeting the assumed common
needs of human subjects – economic, physical and social – is based upon a
culturally generated set of values, it none the less provides a foundation on
which debates about justice and equality can be mounted. The objective of

meeting common human needs brings to the forefront the issue of the poverty of the mass populations of the Third World, and those in Western societies, especially women, children and racial minorities, whose lives are a continuous battle for material and social survival. The idea of common needs implies an optimal level of protection against serious harm and suffering, a protection which requires not only the curative elements of health and social care, but also measures to prevent avoidable harm and suffering – an environment and way of life which is conducive to health and well-being.

Alongside a commitment to common human needs – the needs which must be met if we are to have the opportunity to *act* in the world as well as be acted upon – are needs which may be considered to be more culturally specific and concretely related to diverse identities. These specific needs are necessarily articulated by those who lay claim to them. They are the needs expressed through resistance to homogenization and the demand for the recognition of difference. All of these needs, common and specific, are established, at least provisionally, through debate, dialogue and a listening to others which eventually may lead to a sufficient consensus upon which to build social policies and struggle to achieve them. Clearly, the state has a major role in ensuring the meeting of the common needs of human subjects, not least because despite its relative weakening in the face of international capital, it remains the only holder of resources and arbiter of claims of sufficient weight to be able to undertake the task. It is because of this political and economic reality that we shall need, towards the end of this chapter, to address the issue of state power.

The state will also be concerned to ensure that because common needs are mediated through cultural difference, attention is given to the interaction of commonality/diversity, and that the ethics of responsibility for otherness are pursued even in the provision, for example, of common health care services. But in response to specific, culture-bound needs, the state's role may be less central, because health and welfare practice in the area of culturally specific needs suggests that they are best met directly by those who articulate them, although drawing upon the resources of the state in their provision. Here, the state may still be required to act as a final arbiter of the degree to which cultural difference is morally acceptable. Many cultures, Western included, are likely to generate practices which are deemed seriously harmful, especially to the least powerful in most societies – women, children, minorities. In these circumstances, we are obliged to make moral judge-ments which limit the degree of cultural variation in the interests, as we see it, of the needs of subordinate populations within a wider culture.

But to speak of ourselves, we who are writing, reading and interpreting this book, as being obliged to make moral judgements, is to assume that we have the practical possibility of acting as agents, of making choices, of being at least relatively autonomous human subjects. Is the opportunity to act as a moral agent something which all subjects should have? I think it would be difficult to answer this except in the affirmative, and in saying 'yes', we acknowledge a particular element of common human needs, namely the preconditions necessary to exercise this agency, as Doyal and Gough (1991) argue.

This second objective of welfare as emancipation, although it might be considered to be an element of common human needs, deserves separate attention. This is because the other needs we have identified – economic, physical and social – are the preconditions of maximizing the opportunity to act as agent. The daily struggle for material survival, for the very means of sustaining a bare existence, is not an experience of life conducive to the exercise of autonomy, and neither is a life lived under rules which demand only obedience to power and where the consequent space for resistance is minimal. And so with this objective we mount a major challenge to that role of welfare which, within the discourse of modernity, subordinated its subjects to the rules of rational, scientific knowledge and engaged in the development of apparatuses of surveillance, control and treatment within which the individual submitted to professional and bureaucratic power. To encourage and support the opportunities for agency involves particular attention to the power exercised by professional experts, and the resistance it encounters, because resistance is a foundational element in the striving for autonomy. Those who are employed as practitioners of health care, social service, education or income maintenance are now being encouraged increasingly to reflect anew, or for the first time, on their exercise of power and its consequences for the autonomy of the subject of welfare. It is a reflection which goes beyond the often rhetorical flourish associated with the notions of 'patient rights' or 'client self-determination' and explores in depth the dynamics of that relationship between dominant discourse and subject to which Foucault devoted his studies. It is an unstable dynamic, that which exists between power and resistance, and its very instability, the ever-present threat of disorder and disorganization, provides the opportunity for an individual to act as a moral agent.

But not all power is malignant nor every resistance benign when we evaluate power and resistance against the moral and political values of a reconstructed welfare project. After all, in the tired and somewhat debased language of 'empowerment', power is something which subordinate populations need to acquire, or at least to share, against the resistance of those who can hardly imagine a greater calamity than that of losing any of *their* power. The building of an emancipatory project of welfare requires that the relatively powerless gain power, but how will that power be exercised once it is achieved? The major problem here is that the exercise of power in late capitalist societies is deeply implicated in the project of modernity with its prodigious drive to hierarchical authority, the exclusion of the dissenting voice of the Other, and the search for order. As power is gained in collective organizations, communities, social movements and also in the state apparatus itself, a danger point will be reached by those who strive to develop an emancipatory form of welfare: will the commitment to promoting moral agency remain an ethical priority? The danger, of course, is that the modern discourse on knowledge, power and order will prove to have been so deeply internalized that once again authority will be exercised in order to limit agency and resistance in the supposed interests of emancipation. No social order can exist which does not limit autonomy, because interdependence requires it. However, we must develop reflexive abilities with which to question continuously the extent to which we reproduce features of the power/resistance process that limits others' agency to a degree which is in excess of that required to maintain the mutual interdependence of subjects. Marcuse (1969) referred to this as *surplus repression*.

These observations on the ethical problematics of gaining political power at any level in the social structure are not made in order to cast gloom on the prospects of emancipation, but to enter a note of caution perhaps hardly necessary to those who have witnessed the authoritarian features of modern social movements and parties of the Left. The tendency to abuse power and unnecessarily limit the agency of others is an outcome of history and culture; it is the result, in short, of human action. In the pursuit of welfare as an emancipatory project human action can, instead, create the historical and cultural conditions which give a priority to providing the social, economic and subjective preconditions for maximizing the opportunities for people to live their lives as moral agents.

Strategies of Resistance and Welfare Building

There are many different types of social practice which, existing already, prefigure the kinds of activity which would characterize a reconstructed welfare project. Some of these practices have been referred to briefly in the previous chapters – joint narratives in counselling, social work and therapy, the processes of collective self-care, the practice of cross-cultural pluralism, subversive interpretations of cultural commodities, the development of alternative forms of collectivist organization, internal criticism of the social order in the context of recurrent economic crises. From the range of existing and possible kinds of practice, I select two strategies which represent a logical though not necessarily temporal progression from an emphasis on confronting the structures of domination in welfare, economy and culture, to an emphasis on overcoming the oppressive elements of modernity through a gradual process of reconstructing health care and social policies and pro-grammes and the discourses within which they are located. These two types of strategy – collective resistance and welfare building – are, of course, dynamically intertwined, because collective resistance often implies a demand for a system change, and constructing and implementing new policies goes hand in hand with continued resistance to manifestations of a power which denies responsibility to human well-being, diversity and interdependence.

I begin with the strategy of *collective resistance* because not only is that where we must logically start – with a negation – but because such resistance is already manifested in some of the new social movements

organized primarily on the basis of social identity and having the potential to
be active at every level in the social structure. Collective resistance has both
a form and an object. Its form is usually characterized as the attempt to
develop a collective organization of subjects which, in contrast to the
hierarchical and bureaucratic structures of the state, emphasizes wide
participation in decision making and the de-differentiation of roles. Because
its object is to confront and negate dominant discursive formations, the
continuous effort to ensure that form is congruent with object necessarily
assumes a high priority. If the object of collective resistance is to challenge
dominant discourse, against what targets might such resistance be mounted
in the struggle for a reconstituted idea and practice of welfare? I select three
targets for discussion: the disciplinary power of professionals, the commodification of culture and the manufacture of desire, and the economic discourse
of global market necessity.

   The first target of collective resistance is that which is closest to home: it
is generated by the interactions which subjects experience when they receive
a service from a professional expert. These interactions, at their most benign,
show us that they are none the less an experience of disciplinary power and
individual resistance, a resistance often hardly articulated as such, but
perceived more as discomfort, uncertainty, the wish to suggest issues for
attention other than those given priority by the professional. In other
circumstances, the expert/subject interaction will be experienced more
negatively as one of monitoring, surveillance and control legitimated by
reference to the subject's 'best interests' or those interests of others at risk of
being adversely affected. Whether professional expertise is experienced as
predominantly positive (as in many areas of health care) or mostly negative
(for example, in child welfare, mental health or social security benefits
programmes), the exercise of disciplinary power is of such salience in the
construction of subject positions that it demands major attention. Individual
resistance to professional power, although omnipresent, is insufficient to
ensure, to the maximum, the subject's right to agency and the respect of
difference. It is because the exercise of individual resistance, embedded in
the micro-processes of everyday interaction with the welfare system, is
necessary but insufficient, that we turn to collective forms of resistance.
These collective forms aim to counteract, through intervention in the media,
the organization of continuing education and the support of patients, clients,
service users and other subjects of welfare, the exclusive knowledge claims
of experts. Collective resistance points to the authenticity of the subject's
narrative which requires consideration alongside that of the expert. It
proposes that subject/professional interactions take, as far as possible, a
dialogical rather than an authoritarian form and, on the assumption that
knowledge is socially produced, that the *interpretation* of complementary or
divergent narratives is seen as a legitimate arena of contestation, compromise and, where possible, agreement. Submission to the will of the
professional, to the disciplinary power of those who are assigned the tasks of
expert carer, makes way for a more balanced relationship built into the

organization of caring services themselves. Thus collective resistance manifests itself in arguing against the depersonalization often experienced by service users, the experience of being acted upon as objects rather than responded to as subjects-as-agents. It uses the method of 'internal critique' to point to the contradiction between an ethical commitment to caring and the process of objectification, or to the rhetoric of multi-culturalism in a context of a drive to homogenization and its resultant suppression of the voices of the Other.

The well-being of the subjects of late capitalism is increasingly recognized as being crucially affected by cultural production, by the impact of image, text, discourse on the meanings we assign to ourselves, our social identities and our perceptions of the social world. Although individual resistance to mass commodified culture is obviously present, its apparent weakness when confronting culture as an instrument of social control and a mechanism for the production of desire, contributes to the pessimism of cultural critics. The strengthening of collective resistance to the power of dominant cultural discourses is, therefore, a necessary element in the struggle towards an emancipatory idea and practice of human welfare. The aim of this resistance is to disseminate the means by which some level of critical distance can be attained from cultural messages that exploit subjects, homogenize differences and induce profound dependencies on the market. One of the most telling examples of the power of a commodified culture to constitute and reconstitute, on a daily basis, the subjectivities of significant segments of the population is to be found in the process of the inscription of women's bodies. Although individual resistance to this inscription concerning body weight, shape and style certainly occurs, the existence of populations especially vulnerable to such inscription, for example, teenage girls, indicates the need for strengthening collective resistance. The consequences of the cultural inscription of women's bodies – eating disorders, issues of female identity, the health consequences of media-manufactured dieting regimes – all indicate that resistance must become more collective in the interests of women's welfare. As exposure to cultural messages about identity, the presentation of self and the expansion of commodity consumption reaches directly into the previously privatized arena of the family, so children become as vulnerable as adults to the manufacture of desire, and the earlier boundaries between childhood and adulthood decompose in typical postmodern fashion. The organization of collective resistance to dominant cultural discourses centres on the need to develop a powerful critique that can enter more fully into public debates about needs, desires, differences, risks and harm. Such a critique points to the connection between the media recognition and promotion of diversity as a means of identifying market 'niches', and homogenizing messages about the moral superiority of individualism (in choice, in competitive struggle, in deference to 'market forces') over all concern for solidarity, collectivity, wider communities and the well-being of others. The fact that a mass culture serves predominantly to reproduce the ethics of capitalist exploitation, to induce submission through the internalization of dominant discourses in the constitution of subjectivities, is the central thrust of that counter-discourse upon which collective resistance rests. The aim of this cultural resistance is to disrupt the taken-for-granted assumptions which even under postmodern conditions are sedimented into 'common sense', and attempt to replace them by new uncertainties about how benign, inevitable, unopposable and rational domi- nant culture/politics/economy actually *is*, and to induce a more reflexive response to that social force which constitutes our subjectivities.

Although cultural production becomes, under postmodern conditions, a central focus for critique and social struggle, this critique and struggle, as an expression of collective resistance, is forced ultimately to turn its attention to that wider economy which culture largely legitimates through its various discursive texts. This third target of collective resistance can be understood as a complex of discourses which speak of the commercial operations of national and international organizations of capital in the abstract and increasingly determinist language of 'world market conditions'. These globalizing conditions – the rapid movement of capital, the continuous search for higher productivity and lower labour costs, the need for 'down- sizing', the demand for individual resilience and flexibility – are presented predominantly as impersonal economic relations, the result of new technol- ogies and means of communication.

In the imperative to search continuously for higher profits in order to survive, capitalists themselves are often portrayed as subject to these impersonal market forces, as being ultimately acted upon in a way not dissimilar to the lowly redundant worker: both have to submit to forces outside their control. The implications of these interconnected determinist economic discourses – the dominant metanarratives of late capitalism – are profound for all aspects of living under present conditions; for welfare they are disastrous. The effective evacuation from dominant discussion about the relation between the economy and welfare of reference to *willed action*, to capitalists, shareholders or senior executives as moral agents, indicates the almost unthinking ideological substratum upon which contemporary discus- sion rests. The policies which emerge from this discussion – cuts in health and social services, lowering personal and corporate taxes, increased harass- ment of welfare claimants, the abandonment of state strategies to maintain full employment – are buoyed up by taken-for-granted assumptions about 'necessity', economic survival and the determining effects of global market forces over which *no one has any control*. Collective resistance must take the form of a fully articulated ideological critique of this discourse on the economy, one which consistently argues, through media and education, that economics are the results of acts of will. Given the present balance of social forces (compared with the period of the Keynesian welfare state) it is the will of capitalists which predominates. Collective resistance aims to move the dominant social discourse from one which speaks of the blind forces of the market to one which at least gives substantial space to the effects of human intentions and the consequent need for moral judgements on these intentions. Opening discourses on the economy and welfare to alternative explanations is a necessary (though not sufficient) precondition for any resistant political mobilization of both the 'old' and the 'new' poor in the name of the implications of an ethics of mutual interdependence. Ultimately, the aim of organizing such resistance and dissent amongst those most negatively affected by continuous economic restructuring in the interests of profitability is to generate a legitimation crisis with which to confront governments and corporations faced with having to manage the crisis tendencies of the economic system as a whole.

The coinciding of economic with legitimation crises is a potent historical moment in a social order: it may permit shifts to take place in assumptions, meanings and whole discourses in ways which enable change to take place because human consciousness itself may shift to accommodate new emancipatory possibilities. Under such dramatic circumstances, or equally when critical agitation and the impetus for change moves more gradually, collective resistance will have been accompanied by efforts to establish some prefigurative policies, organization and practices – a process which enables the *possibility* of change to be grasped hold of, firmly. In the context of my attempt to envisage emancipatory possibilities already existing in current critiques and political activities in the field of welfare, I am referring to this prefigurative process as *welfare building*.

Because in the provision of state welfare the ethic of organized caring represents the positive side of the contradiction of modernity, an expression of emancipation still residing there in spite of its accompaniment by surveillance and control, we can envisage welfare building as aimed at introducing elements, tendencies and experiments in caring-without-surplus repression. The building of new forms of welfare would not be based on a Master Plan in which policy proposals are promulgated from the top down: what is built develops, rather, as extensions of the groundwork of many activities emerging from the collectivities which already exist in the new social movements. They would include the dissemination of examples of programmes provided by community groups and alternative organizations and the encouragement to experiment with and improve upon such services. The experience of collective resistance, and the critique which is developed through the process of resistance, becomes crucial to the building of new policies and practices. Resistance to the disciplinary power of the professional expert, for example, is transmuted into a practice which attempts to develop prefigurative relationships between professional 'helper' and 'client' in which the interaction is characterized as 'subject to subject' and where distancing and objectification are expected to wither away. Feminist counselling and therapy leads the way in these attempts to deconstruct and then reconstruct the knowledge/power relations of welfare encounters. Control by the users of services is a crucial feature of welfare building, an exercise of power which we can envisage as founded on the ethical principles of responsibility to otherness and the acknowledgement of mutual interdependence. Maximizing the opportunities for the subjects of prefigurative emancipatory forms of welfare to act as moral agents involves respecting the otherness within their subjectivities, their changing social identities, and so being continuously watchful of the dangers of assuming fixed patient or client identities.

So far, welfare building seems an impermanent, ramshackle, parochial, ever-experimental and provisional kind of enterprise. And so it is, because it attempts, in the name of difference and of the narrative of the local, to set its face against the arrogance and terrifying certainty of the side of modernity which has resulted in the experience of welfare as a system implicated in domination. In building a reconstructed practice of welfare, risks will need to be taken in order to relax the grip of control and allow, as far as possible, the eruption of disorganization and dissent. The model of this relaxation of the suffocating and authoritarian embrace of certainty will be found in Paulo Freire's work on liberating dialogical education (McLaren and Leonard, 1993), a model upon which we can draw in envisioning an educational process for professionals within a new welfare project.

But is the building of a reconstructed welfare from the ground floor upwards a sufficiently sturdy structure, capable of protecting its inhabitants from risk and harm, and able to withstand the storms which rage as economies lurch from one crisis to another? Many of the rooms within the building are small-scale and self-made, the product of the practices of community groups, of organizations centred on particular social identities, of innovations undertaken in the pursuit of cultural diversity. But the building cannot exist simply as a proliferation of rooms, of spaces where individuals and collectivities engage in resistance as a step in the construction of their own models of well-being: it must have walls and a roof. There must, in other words, be some overall structure which provides resources and protection for the diversity of programmes and practices which are attempting to pursue the emancipatory project. A reconstructed welfare concerns itself, we have argued, with common human needs, the needs which must be met if subjects are to lead lives as moral agents. The structure, resources and protection necessary to ensure that these common, basic objectives are met can only, at the present point in history, be provided by the state. The Western democratic state, however, is the progenitor of the whole enterprise of modernity, the founding vehicle of the project of Emancipation which we now see as deeply flawed. The modern nation state was established as the collective expression of those ideals of universal reason and order which, on their obverse side, underpinned the structures of domination: control, exclusion, homogenization, discipline and worse.

And so we come to the most difficult of issues. In reconstructing welfare in an emancipatory form we need the power and resources of the state to provide a framework of services through which common needs can be met, risk and harm reduced and diversity and interdependence flourish, with health care, education, social care and income maintenance being the primary elements. But how can the state, locked into the contradictory legacy of modernity and implicated in the political economy of late capitalism possibly serve such an emancipatory purpose? Can the state be trusted? Should state power be contested and, if possible, won? How might this be achieved in the dismal political terrain that currently confronts any critical, oppositional force which might be established to contest and win state power? It is to these questions that I now turn in the remainder of this final chapter.

State, Party, Difference

Writing in anticipation of a mass meeting and demonstration which was held in Washington, DC in 1996 called 'Stand for Children', the American feminist Betty Friedan (1996) argues that a new political paradigm is emerging in the United States, one which aims to develop solidarity, initially around the needs of children. 'The old paradigm of "identity politics" – a rights-based focus on narrowly defined grievances and goals – has increasingly shown its limitations. A future of separate and warring races, genders and generations is in no one's interest' (1996: 6). She suggests strongly that by joining a movement concerned with children's rights and their material and social needs, feminists are not surrendering their gains but are recognizing that 'increasingly, women are realizing that they cannot afford an exclusive fixation on even so fundamental an issue as abortion rights at a time of wider threats to their well-being'. In the American context, these threats come in the familiar form of economic 'restructuring' (loss of jobs and job security) and a hard Right commitment to dismantling what remains of the welfare state: a scenario which, with cultural variations, is being acted out in most Western countries. Friedan sketches the outline of a political agenda which is certainly wider than gender issues, narrowly defined, and encompasses issues of racism, class and the economy:

> The list begins with confronting the politics of hate, the momentum of extreme income inequality, and the concentrations of wealth in the top 0.5 per cent. And it includes alternatives to downsizing, among them job sharing and a shorter work week, to meet the needs of parents of both sexes in the child-rearing years, people who combine school and work throughout life and older people who want to keep working; and, given the reality that most mothers at every level of society now work, a national commitment to professional child care, such as exists in France and Germany. (1996: 6)

This is an interesting agenda, one which, in the American context, would certainly enhance, if it were implemented, the welfare of a substantial population and penalize some of those who are benefiting most from the economic dynamic of late capitalism. How would it become a viable political programme rooted in common material interests and organized to challenge the growing hegemony of the Right in American politics? Here, Friedan becomes vague: the voluntary organizations and social movements do not have the political power nor the economic resources to provide alternatives if public sector services are demolished, but organizing in defence of children 'is a new kind of power' which, 'with luck' could result in 'a renewed spirit of community'.

These sentiments, the search for solidarity on basic economic and social issues while retaining a commitment to responding to diversity, are of considerable political importance in most Western countries. The problem lies in where they lead us. In the context of the overwhelming power of the Right either in government or through setting the economic and welfare agenda for a wide political spectrum, the practice of social movements, voluntary agencies and community organizations attempting to form tactical alliances in order to put pressure on the state in relation to specific issues seems an inadequate response. In the context of the economic power of capital, combined with established political parties organized precisely to gain state power, the ability of the new social movements to make a decisive and far-reaching impact on the welfare agenda appears to be declining in its effectiveness.

As reflection on the limitations of identity politics, local community action and single-issue alliances becomes more urgent, we turn to the question of whether these diverse expressions of interest could form the basis of a firmer kind of solidarity. This would be an *organized* solidarity founded on a common interest in the development of policies which benefited all of the identities (class, gender, race, age etc.) while retaining a commitment to diversity and forms of organization which enabled that diversity to be continuously expressed. But in order to overcome the limitations of identity politics, an organized solidarity would need to aim for the winning of state power through the electoral process: it would need, in short, to take the form of a political party committed to an emancipatory project of welfare expressed in concrete policies and underpinned by an ethics of diversity and mutual interdependence. Organized solidarity might or might not require the formation of a new political party, depending on specific circumstances. In some instances, an existing political party might prove amenable to the radical reconstruction necessary to enable it to encompass the dialectic of diversity/solidarity. In other circumstances, the Centre-to-Left spectrum of parties may have so capitulated to the social and economic discourse of neo-conservatism, so internalized the structures of domination in their gender, class and ethnic relations, so entrenched themselves in uncritical modernity, that they have become disqualified as vehicles of an emancipatory impulse to change. In such a situation the difficult task of constructing a new kind of political party becomes a priority for debate amongst the various social movements; they might find themselves increasingly drawn together, initially in mutual defence, as the consequences of economic restructuring and radical Right social policies lead to mounting social distress and the early signs of a legitimation crisis.

The new kind of party, whether or not based on a pre-existing one, could be described as *a confederation of diversities* in which member organizations join together not to obliterate their separate identities, but to express them, in part, through solidarity. But such a party could not maintain itself exclusively on a political coalition forged by the leadership of the component organizations. It would be based on the establishment of dialogue at every level between those who experience different forms of domination and exploitation. Furthermore, the party would need to commit itself to an internal political culture which prefigured the relationships between subjects seen as crucial to an emancipatory project. It would be a culture which resisted the urge to homogenization even while it continued to build solidarities; which encouraged discourses of difference and sought to reclaim and articulate previously hidden narratives of subordination and exclusion.

I use the phrase 'confederation of diversities' in order to suggest a political formation more solidly built on perceived common interests than is usually denoted by the term coalition, as in the idea of a 'rainbow coalition'. To me, the term coalition implies a political organization too unstable and transitory to serve the purpose of winning state power in the interests of emancipatory forms of welfare. A confederation of diversities suggests a long-term commitment of participant organizations and individuals to a federation which is envisaged as representing their diversities as well as furthering their common interests. As such a political formation cannot be spontaneously constituted but must emerge from already existing conditions, we must ask what these conditions are. I have already suggested, at various points throughout the book but especially in this and the previous two chapters, what these conditions – economic and political – might be. Here I can summarize them briefly, making the generalizations necessary to encompass the differences that exist between capitalist countries.

One condition is to be found in shifts in the economic circumstances most likely to impinge upon the political consciousness of substantial populations: the dramatically increased disparities between rich and poor; the impact of mass unemployement and the increased exploitation of labour, including that of middle income sectors; growing insecurity and a general sense of disillusionment, the result, in part, of shifts in the composition of classes and their perceived material opportunities. Another condition might be identified as the often belated realization within Left politics that state power cannot be won, alone, on the basis of a traditional combination of the 'organized' working class (decomposing and being reconstituted) and disaffected middle class intellectuals. A third condition is the complementary recognition amongst political movements outside the often discredited Left parties that identity politics, although necessary, is not sufficient to meet the demands of human welfare. Betty Friedan's call, cited previously, is a typical feminist example of a growing political shift in consciousness which has a direct bearing on the possibilities of establishing a confederation of diversities committed to a struggle for welfare.

I am suggesting that signs of discontent and critique are mounting; that pressure is increasing to explore new forms of politics as the existing ones become discredited and show signs of no longer representing that sector of the political spectrum which is most critical of the existing social order. Whether this present critical situation will lead to the eventual formation of new kinds of mass political parties dedicated to solidarity in defence of diversity remains to be seen. We have at our disposal no comforting metanarrative of historical inevitability, no determinist story of the effects of impersonal forces. The future is determined by acts of human will within concrete cultural and historical conditions: human subjects act, 'but not in the circumstances of their own choosing'. Is the current political situation in many Western countries one which is ripe with the possibilities of challenge? I believe it is. Will that challenge be mounted? The question cannot be answered at this point.

Whether the state can play a decisive role in the promotion of welfare as an emancipatory project depends, I believe, on the extent to which its personnel, institutions and practices can be induced to change in the direction of a more critical view of modernity. This would involve an abandonment of the urge to control and homogenize populations 'in their own interests' and instead return to those values which form the critical, emancipatory side of modernity: a belief in equality and justice. It is because such a shift in the discourse which drives the state apparatus is a precondition of welfare as emancipation that achieving power over that apparatus is necessary. The establishment of a party as a confederation of diversities would be a difficult task but one which would be, after all, a particular discursive and material expression of present discontents and of a growing realization that establishing solidarity between particular interests is the only way to mount resistance to the depredations of a globalizing late capitalism and to establish the possibility of alternative forms of modernity. There are four major social movements whose interests in the effective meeting of common needs appear to be converging: the feminist movement, trade union organizations, anti-racist rights movements and the ecology movement. Many tensions exist between these various interests as to the priority (and even validity) of their political claims, but all give attention to the detrimental effects of the economy and the dominant culture on the welfare of large populations. All might, as a result of dialogue, be able to agree, as a beginning, to endorse those 'universals by cross-cultural consensus' which were referred to at the end of the first chapter. Then, we described those culturally produced universals as respect for diversity and a commitment to fight poverty and exploitation. Now we can go further and suggest agreement on a programme designed to meet common needs more effectively (health, education, material conditions of life) as the grounding of particular, different and culturally specific needs, and as the preconditions necessary to enable people to act as diverse moral agents. The establishment of organized solidarity in the form of a party based on the meeting of diversities demands also that it recognizes the interdependence of national economies and explores the possibilities of cross-national resistance to the detrimental effects of the globalization of production and markets. Priority might be given to the effects on North–South relations and global poverty, on 'development and modernization', on the increased rate of labour exploitation, on the threats to vulnerable cultures and on environmental hazards and the exploitation of nature – all crucial to human welfare.

None of the issues I have addressed in outlining the possibilities of a reconstructed discourse on welfare is *new*. I have attempted to identify forms of politics and practice *which already exist* and which appear to constitute some elements of an emancipatory project. Extrapolation and speculation have played their part, but within a discourse of critical postmodern sensibility where nothing is fixed and certain, and where there are no transcendental guarantees, moral agency plays a central role. Because nothing is historically inevitable and because the dominant features of modernity in its capitalist form are the result of willed human action under particular structural conditions, we are able to envisage alternatives. These alternatives draw, in part, on the critical, liberating side of modernity itself and in part on the resistance to modernity mounted in the name of the Other. Postmodern reflection enables us to understand more fully the contradictions of modernity and identify the sites of resistance and struggle available to us in the renewal of welfare as an emancipatory project.

References

Abercrombie, N., Hill, S. and Turner, B. (1986) *Sovereign Individuals of Capitalism*. London: Allen and Unwin.

Adorno, T. and Horkheimer, M. (1972) *The Dialectic of the Enlightenment*. London: New Left Books.

Agger, B. (1990) *The Decline of Discourse: Reading, Writing and Resistance in Postmodern Capitalism*. Basingstoke: Falmer Press.

Aglietta, M. (1979) *A Theory of Capitalist Regulation: The U.S. Experience*. London: Verso.

Althusser, L. (1971) *Lenin and Philosophy and Other Essays*. London: New Left Books.

Anderson, B. (1983) *Imagined Communities: Reflections on the Origins and Spread of Nationalism*. London: Verso.

Baudrillard, J. (1983) *Simulations*. New York: Semiotext(e).

Bauman, Z. (1992) *Intimations of Postmodernity*. London: Routledge.

Benhabib, S. (1992) *Situating the Self: Gender, Community and Postmodernism*. Cambridge: Polity Press.

Bennett, T. (1989) 'Texts in History: The Determination of Readings and Their Texts', in D. Attridge, G. Bennington and R. Young (eds), *Post-Structuralism and the Question of History*. Cambridge: Cambridge University Press.

Bennington, G. (1989) 'Demanding History', in D. Attridge, G. Bennington and R. Young (eds), *Post-Structuralism and the Question of History*. Cambridge: Cambridge University Press.

Berman, M. (1982) *All That is Solid Melts into Air*. New York: Simon and Schuster.

Bhabha, H. (1983) 'The Other Question . . .', *Screen*, 24 (6): 18–36.

Bordo, S. (1990) 'Feminism, Postmodernism and Gender Scepticism', in L. Nicholson (ed.), *Feminism/Postmodernism*. New York: Routledge.

Braverman, H. (1974) *Labour and Monopoly Capital: The Degradation of Work in the Twentieth Century*. New York: Monthly Review Press.

Brown, C. (1994) 'Feminist Postmodernism and the Challenge of Diversity', in A. Chambon and A. Irving (eds), *Essays on Postmodernism and Social Work*. Toronto: Canadian Scholars' Press.

Butler, J. (1991) 'Imitation and Gender Insubordination', in D. Fuss (ed.), *Inside/Out: Lesbian Theories, Gay Theories*. New York: Routledge.

Chambon, A. (1994) 'Postmodernity and Social Work Discourse(s): Notes on the Changing Language of a Profession', in A. Chambon and A. Irving (eds), *Essays on Postmodernism and Social Work*. Toronto: Canadian Scholars' Press.

Champy, J. (1995) *Reengineering Management: The Mandate for New Leadership*. New York: Harper Business.

Clegg, S. (1990) *Modern Organizations: Organization Studies in a Postmodern World*. London: Sage.

Crosland, C.A.R. (1967) *The Future of Socialism*. London: Cape.

Daenzer, P. (1994) 'Black Women and Social Welfare'. Participatory Action Research Report, Canada.

Daly, M. (1979) *Gyn/Ecology*. London: The Women's Press.

David, S. (1995) 'Burnout in Human Service Organizations'. Unpublished research paper, McGill University, Montreal.

Dayan, D. and Katz, E. (1987) 'Performing Media Events', in J. Curan, A. Smith and P. Wingate (eds), *Impacts and Influence: Essays in Media Power in the Twentieth Century*. London: Methuen.

Dean, H. and Taylor-Gooby, P. (1992) *Dependency Culture: The Explosion of a Myth*. London: Harvester Wheatsheaf.

Deleuze, G. and Guattari, F. (1984) *Anti-Oedipus: Capitalism and Schizophrenia*. Minneapolis, MN: University of Minnesota Press.

Derrida, J. (1978) *Writing and Difference*. Chicago: University of Chicago Press.

Deveaux, M. (1994) 'Feminism and Empowerment: A Critical Reading of Foucault', *Feminist Studies*, 20 (2): 223–47.

Dirlik, A. (1987) 'Culturalism as Hegemonic Ideology and Liberating Practice', *Cultural Critique*, (6): 13–50.

Donaldson, L. (1985) *In Defence of Organisation Theory: A Response to the Critics*. Cambridge: Cambridge University Press.

Donnison, D. (1970) 'Liberty, Equality and Fraternity', *The Three Banks Review*, December.

Doyal, L. and Gough, I. (1991) *A Theory of Human Need*. London: Macmillan.

Drover, G. and Kerans, P. (1992) 'Toward a Theory of Social Welfare', *Canadian Review of Social Policy*, (29/30): 66–91.

Drover, G. and Kerans, P. (1995) 'New Approaches to Welfare Theory: Foundations', in G. Drover and P. Kerans (eds), *New Approaches to Welfare Theory: Making and Sorting Claims*. London: Edward Elgar.

Eagleton, T. (1984) *The Function of Criticism*. London: Verso.

Eagleton, T. (1986) *Against the Grain*. London: Verso.

Eco, U. (1983) *Postscript to the Name of the Rose*. Orlando, FL: Harcourt, Brace, Jovanovich.

Ekins, P. (1992) *A New World Order*. London: Routledge.

Fisher, R. and Kling, J. (1994) 'Community Organization and New Social Movement Theory', *Journal of Progressive Human Services*, 5 (2): 5–23.

Fleming, M. (1995) 'A Critical View of Cultural Essentialism'. Unpublished research paper, McGill University, Montreal.

Foster, H. (1983) 'Postmodernism: A Preface', in H. Foster (ed.), *The Anti-Aesthetic: Essays on Postmodern Culture*. Port Townsend, WA: Bay Press.

Foucault, M. (1965) *Madness and Civilization* (trans. Richard Howard). New York: Pantheon Books.

Foucault, M. (1973) *Birth of the Clinic*. London: Tavistock Press.

Foucault, M. (1975) *Discipline and Punish*. London: Allen Lane.

Foucault, M. (1980) *The History of Sexuality*, vol. 1. New York: Vintage.

Foucault, M. (1983) 'The Subject and Power', in H. Dreyfus and P. Rainbow (eds), *Michel Foucault: Beyond Structuralism and Hermeneutics*. Chicago: University of Chicago Press.

Foucault, M. (1984) *The Foucault Reader*. New York: Pautheon.

Foucault, M. (1988) *Politics, Philosophy, Culture* (ed. L. Kritzman). New York: Routledge.

Foucault, M. (1991) 'Order of Discourse', in S. Lash (ed.), *Post-structuralist and Postmodernist Sociology*. Aldershot: Edward Elgar.

Fox, N.J. (1994) *Postmodernism, Sociology and Health*. Toronto: University of Toronto Press.

Friedan, B. (1996) 'Children's Crusade', *New Yorker*, 3 June.

Friedman, M. and Friedman, R. (1980) *Free to Choose*. London: Secker and Warburg.

Fuss, D. (1989) *Essentially Speaking: Feminism, Nature and Difference*. New York: Routledge.

Geertz, C. (1973) *The Interpretation of Cultures*. New York: Basic Books.

Geertz, C. (1986) 'The Uses of Diversity', *Michigan Quarterly Review*, 25(1): 105–23.

Geras, N. (1987) 'Post-Marxism?', *New Left Review*, (167): 40–82.

Giddens, A. (1984) *The Constitution of Society*. Cambridge: Cambridge University Press.

Giddens, A. (1990). *Consequences of Modernity*. Stanford, CA: Stanford University Press.

Giddens, A. (1994) *Beyond Left and Right*. Stanford, CA: Stanford University Press.

Giroux, H. (1992) 'Language, Difference and Cultural Theory: Beyond the Politics of Clarity', *Theory Into Practice*, XXXI: 1–9.

Gough, I. (1979) *Political Economy of the Welfare State*. London: Macmillan.

Gouldner, A. (1980) *The Two Marxisms*. New York: Basic Books.

Glassner, B. (1989) 'Fitness and the Postmodern Self', *Journal of Health and Social Behaviour*, 30, 180–91.

Gramsci, A. (1971) *Selections from the Prison Notebooks*. London: Lawrence and Wishart.

Habermas, J. (1981) 'Modernity versus Postmodernity', *New German Critique*, 22 (Winter): 49–55.

Habermas, J. (1985) 'Questions and Counter-Questions', in R. Bernstein (ed.), *Habermas and Modernity*. Cambridge: Polity Press.

Habermas, J. (1987) *The Philosophical Discourse of Modernity*. Cambridge, MA: MIT Press.

Halberstram, J. (1993) 'Imagined Violence/Queer Violence: Representation, Rage and Resistance', *Social Text*, 37 (Winter): 187–201.

Hall, S. (1991) 'Brave New World', *Socialist Review*, 21: 57–64.

Hammer, M. and Champy, J. (1993) *Reengineering the Corporation: A Manifesto for Business Revolution*. New York: Harper Business.

Hammer, M. and Stanton, S. (1995) *The Reengineering Revolution: A Handbook*. New York: Harper Business.

Handler, J. and Hasenfeld, Y. (1991) *The Moral Construction of Poverty*. Newbury Park, CA: Sage.

Hanson, A. (1989) 'The Making of the Maori: Culture Invention and its Logic', *American Anthropologist*, 91 (2): 890–902.

Harvey, D. (1990) *The Condition of Postmodernity: An Enquiry into the Origins of Cultural Change*. Oxford: Blackwell.

Haskell, T. (ed.) (1984) *The Authority of Experts: Studies in History and Theory*. Bloomington, IN: Indiana University Press.

Hayek, F. (1973) *Rules and Order*. London: Routledge.

Head, S. (1996) 'The New, Ruthless Economy', *The New York Review*, XLIII (4), 29 February.

Hennessy, R. (1993) *Materialist Feminism and the Politics of Discourse*. New York: Routledge.

Henriques, J., Hollway, W., Urwin, C., Venn, C. and Walkerdine, V. (1984) *Changing the Subject*. London: Methuen.

Heydebrand, W. (1989) 'New Organisational Forms', *Work and Occupations*, 16 (3): 323–57.

Himmelfarb, G. (1994) *On Looking into the Abyss*. New York: Knopf.

Hobsbaum, E. and Ranger, T. (eds) (1983) *The Invention of Tradition*. Cambridge: Cambridge University Press.

Holloway, J. and Picciotti, S. (eds) (1978) *State and Capital*. London: Edward Arnold.

hooks, bell (G. Watkins) (1991) *Yearning: Race, Gender and Cultural Politics*. London: Turnaround.

Huyssen, A. (1986) *After the Great Divide: Modernism, Mass Culture, Postmodernism*. Bloomington, IN: Indianna University Press.

Inglis, F. (1993) *Cultural Studies*. Oxford: Blackwell.

Jacobs, S. (1985) 'Race, Empire and the Welfare State', *Critical Social Policy*, 13: 6–28.

Jameson, F. (1984) 'Postmodernism, or the Cultural Logic of Late Capitalism', *New Left Review*, 146: 53–92.

Jameson, F. (1989) 'Marxism and Postmodernism', in D. Kellner (ed.), *Postmodernism/Jameson/Critique*. Washington, DC: Maisonneuve Press.

Jordan, G. and Weedon, C. (1995) *Cultural Politics: Class, Gender, Race and the Postmodern World*. Oxford: Blackwell.

Joshi, S. and Carter, B. (1985) 'The Role of Labour in Creating a Racist Britain', *Race and Class*, XXV (3): 53–70.

Kelsey, J. (1995) *The New Zealand Experiment*. Auckland: Auckland University Press.

Kerans, P. (1994) 'Universality, Full Employment and Well-Being: The Future of the Canadian Welfare State', *Canadian Review of Social Policy*, 34: 119–35.

Klaff, V. (1980) 'Pluralism as an Alternative Model for the Human Ecologist', *Ethnicity*, 7 (1): 102–18.

Kluckhohn, C. (1953) *Personality in Nature, Society and Culture*. New York: Knopf.

Kroeger, A. (1993) 'Globalization, the Labour Market and Social Welfare Spending'. Proceedings of the Sixth Biennial Social Welfare Policy Conference, St John's, Newfoundland.

Laclau, E. and Mouffe, D. (1985) *Hegemony and Socialist Strategy*. London: Verso.

Larson, M. (1984) 'Defining the Problem', in T. Haskell (ed.), *The Authority of Experts: Studies in History and Theory*. Bloomington, IN: Indiana University Press.

Lash, S. (1989) *Sociology of Postmodernism*. London: Routledge.

Lash, S. and Urry, J. (1987) *The End of Organized Capitalism*. Cambridge: Cambridge University Press.

Lemert, C. (1992) 'General Social Theory, Irony, Postmodernism', in S. Seidman and D. Wagner (eds), *Postmodernism and Social Theory*. Oxford: Blackwell.

Leonard, P. (1979) 'Restructuring the Welfare State', *Marxism Today*, 23 (12).

Leonard, P. (1984) *Personality and Ideology*. London: Macmillan.

Leonard, P. and Nichols, B. (1994) 'The Theory and Politics of Aging', in B. Nichols and P. Leonard (eds), *Gender, Aging and the State*. Montreal: Black Rose Books.

Lim, O. (1996) 'Anger is a Gift'. Unpublished research paper, McGill University, Montreal.

Lipietz, A. (1985) *The Enchanted World*. London: Verso.

Lipietz, A. (1987) *Miracles and Mirages: The Crises of Global Fordism*. London: Verso.

Lovibond, S. (1989) 'Feminism and Postmodernism', *New Left Review*, 17 (8): 5–28.

Lyotard, F. (1989) 'Defining the Postmodern', in L. Appignanesi (ed.), *Postmodernism: ICA Documents*. London: Free Association Books.

Mandel, D. (1975) *Late Capitalism*. London: Verso.

Marcuse, H. (1969) *Eros and Civilization*. London: Sphere.

Marx, K. (1844/1971) *Early Texts* (ed. D. McLellan). Oxford: Oxford University Press.

Marx, K. and Engels, F. (1848/1948) *The Communist Manifesto*. London: Allen and Unwin.

Marx, K. and Engels, F. (1970) *The German Ideology*, (ed. C.J. Arthur). London: Lawrence and Wishart.

McGowan, J. (1991) *Postmodernism and its Critics*. Ithaca, NY: Cornell University Press.

McLaren, P. and Leonard, P. (eds) (1993) *Paulo Freire: A Critical Encounter*. London: Routledge.

Mendelson, M. (1993) 'Social Policy in Real Time'. Proceedings of the Sixth Biennial Social Welfare Policy Conference, St John's, Newfoundland.

Mitchell, J. (1975) *Psychoanalysis and Feminism*. Harmondsworth: Penguin.

Morgan, G. (1986) *Images of Organization*. London: Sage.

Nettleton, S. (1991) 'Wisdom, Diligence and Teeth: Discursive Practices and the Creation of Mothers', *Sociology of Health and Illness*, 13: 98–111.

Nicholson, L. (1992) 'On the Postmodern Barricades: Feminism, Politics and Theory', in S. Seidman and D. Wagner (eds), *Postmodernism and Social Theory*. Oxford: Blackwell.

O'Connor, J. (1973) *The Fiscal Crisis of the State*. New York: St Martin's Press.

O'Connor, J. (1986) *Accumulation Crisis*. Oxford: University of Oxford Press.

Offe, C. (1984) *Contradictions of the Welfare State*. London: Verso.

Osborne, P. (1992) 'Modernity is a Qualitative, Not a Chronological, Category', in F. Barker, P. Hulme and M. Iverson (eds), *Postmodernism and the Re-reading of Modernity*. Manchester: Manchester University Press.

Pêcheux, M. (1982) *Language, Semantics and Ideology*. London: Macmillan.

Piddock, J. (1995) 'The 1990s Hollywood Fatal Femme: (Dis)Figuring Feminism, Family, Irony, Violence', *CineAction*, 38: 64–72.

Ramsay, H. and Haworth, N. (1984) 'Worker Capitalists? Profit Sharing and Juridical Forms of Socialism', *Economic and Industrial Democracy*, 5 (3): 295–324.

Roderick, R. (1986) *Habermas and the Foundations of Critical Theory*. London: Macmillan.

Rorty, R. (1985) 'Habermas and Lyotard on Postmodernity', in R. Bernstein (ed.), *Habermas and Modernity*. Cambridge, MA: MIT Press.

Rorty, R. (1986) 'On Ethnocentrism: A Reply to Clifford Geertz', *Michigan Quarterly Review*, 25 (3): 525–34.

Rorty, R. (1989) *Contingency, Irony and Solidarity*. Cambridge: Cambridge University Press.

Rosaldo, R. (1989) 'Imperialist Nostalgia', in *Culture and Truth: The Remaking of Social Analysis*. Boston, MA: Beacon Press.

Rose, N. (1989) *Governing the Soul*. London: Routledge.

Rosenau, P. (1992) *Postmodernism and the Social Sciences*. Princeton, NJ: Princeton University Press.

Rosenthal, M. (1992) 'What Was Postmodernism?', *Socialist Review*, 22 (3): 83–105.

Rothschild-Whitt, J. (1979) 'The Collectivist Organization: An Alternative to Rational-Bureaucratic Models', *American Sociological Review*, 44 (4): 509–27.

Rubin, G. (1993) 'Thinking Sex: Notes for a Radical Theory of the Politics of Sexuality', in A. Abelove, M. Basale and D. Halperin (eds), *The Lesbian and Gay Studies Reader*. London: Routledge.

Rustin, M. (1989) 'The Politics of Post-Fordism: Or, the trouble with "New Times"', *New Left Review*, 175: 54–78.

Ryan, M. (1982) *Marxism and Deconstruction: A Critical Articulation*. Baltimore, MD: Johns Hopkins University Press.

Scharpf, F. (1991) *Crisis and Choice in European Social Democracy*. Ithaca, NY: Cornell University Press.

Seidman, S. and D. Wagner (eds) (1992) *Postmodernism and Social Theory*. Oxford: Blackwell.

Sève, L. (1975) *Marxism and the Theory of Human Personality*. London: Lawrence and Wishart.

Smart, B. (1993) *Postmodernity*. London: Routledge.

Stedman-Jones, G. (1971) *Outcast London*. Oxford: Clarendon Press.

Swyngedouw, E. (1986) 'The Socio-spatial Implications of Innovations in Industrial Organization'. Working Paper No. 20, Johns Hopkins European Center for Regional Planning Research, Lille.

Titmuss, R. (1968) *Commitment to Welfare*. London: Allen and Unwin.

Titmuss, R. (1970) *The Gift Relationship*. London: Allen and Unwin.

Veblen, T. (1931) *Theory of the Leisure Class*. New York: Random House.

Venn, C. (1992) 'Subjectivity, Ideology and Difference', *New Formations*, 16: 40–61.

Weber, M. (1930) *The Protestant Ethic and the Spirit of Capitalism*. London: Unwin.

Weber, M. (1947) *The Theory of Economic and Social Organization* (eds A.M. Henderson and T. Parsons, trans. T. Parsons). New York: Oxford University Press.

West, C. (1988) 'Marxist Theory and the Specificity of Afro-American Oppression', in C. Nelson and L. Grossber (eds), *Marxism and the Interpretation of Culture*. Urbana, IL: University of Illinois Press.

White, S. (1991) *Political Theory and Postmodernism*. Cambridge: Cambridge University Press.

Williams, R. (1981) *Culture*. London: Fontana.

Womack, J., Jones, P. and Roos, D. (1990) *The Machine that Changed the World: The Story of Lean Production*. New York: HarperCollins.

Woodiwiss, A. (1990) *Social Theory after Postmodernism: Rethinking Production, Law and Class*. London: Pluto.

Index